Palgrave Studies in Global Citizenship Education and Democracy

Series Editor

Jason Laker
San José State University
California, USA

This series will engage with the theoretical and practical debates regarding citizenship, human rights education, social inclusion, and individual and group identities as they relate to the role of higher and adult education on an international scale. Books in the series will consider hopeful possibilities for the capacity of higher and adult education to enable citizenship, human rights, democracy and the common good, including emerging research and interesting and effective practices. It will also participate in and stimulate deliberation and debate about the constraints, barriers and sources and forms of resistance to realizing the promise of egalitarian Civil Societies. The series will facilitate continued conversation on policy and politics, curriculum and pedagogy, review and reform, and provide a comparative overview of the different conceptions and approaches to citizenship education and democracy around the world. If you have a proposal for the series you would like to discuss please contact: Jason Laker, jlaker.sjsu@gmail.com

More information about this series at
http://www.springer.com/series/14625

Krista M. Soria • Tania D. Mitchell
Editors

Civic Engagement and Community Service at Research Universities

Engaging Undergraduates for Social Justice,
Social Change and Responsible Citizenship

Editors
Krista M. Soria
Office of Institutional Research
University of Minnesota
Minneapolis
Minnesota
USA

Tania D. Mitchell
College of Education and Human
Development
University of Minnesota
Minneapolis
Minnesota
USA

Palgrave Studies in Global Citizenship Education and Democracy
ISBN 978-1-137-55311-9   ISBN 978-1-137-55312-6   (eBook)
DOI 10.1057/978-1-137-55312-6

Library of Congress Control Number: 2016941233

Printed on acid-free paper

Cover illustration: © jvphoto/Alamy Stock Photo

This Palgrave Macmillan imprint is published by Springer Nature
The registered company is Macmillan Publishers Ltd. London

NOTES ON THE CONTRIBUTORS

Cynthia M. Alcantar is a research associate with the Institute for Immigration, Globalization, and Education and a doctoral student in the Graduate School of Education and Information Studies at the University of California, Los Angeles. She earned a master's degree from Claremont Graduate University and a bachelor's from the University of California, Riverside. Her research centers on college access, transfer, and degree completion of underserved and underrepresented students, especially as it relates to higher education policy and practice.

Douglas Barrera is an assistant director with the UCLA Center for Community Learning. His teaching and research focus on critical civic practice and the development of a critical consciousness among undergraduates. He is coauthor of the Council of Europe publication *Advancing Democratic Practice: A Self-Assessment Guide for Higher Education*. Barrera holds a PhD in education from UCLA.

Rose Cole is a PhD student at the University of Virginia at the Center for the Study of Higher Education. She holds a master's degree in public administration from West Virginia University and worked for both the honors college and leadership studies program at that same institution before pursuing her doctoral studies. Her research interests include globalization, diversity and equity, and citizenship and civic engagement in higher education.

Claire Erickson is an undergraduate student in the Communication Studies Department at the University of Minnesota, Twin Cities. Her research interests include interpersonal communications and small group communications.

Marla A. Franco is the director of student affairs assessment and research at the University of Arizona and a doctoral student in the Department of Higher Education at Azusa Pacific University. Her research employs an anti-deficit perspective to examine the effects of college on the outcomes of diverse student populations.

Andrew Furco is an associate professor of higher education at the University of Minnesota, Twin Cities, where he also serves as an associate vice president for public engagement and the director of the International Center for Research on Community Engagement.

Laura Segrue Gorny is a doctoral candidate in educational psychology–quantitative methods at the University of Minnesota and holds an MS in higher education administration from Syracuse University. She held a research assistantship in the Office of Institutional Research at the University of Minnesota, Twin Cities.

Jacob Grohs is an assistant professor of engineering education at Virginia Tech. His research focuses on learning environments that cultivate reasoning capacity related to complex, ill-structured problems. A 2015 recipient of the K. Patricia Cross Future Leaders Award from AAC&U, Grohs holds a BS and an MS in engineering science and mechanics, an MA in educational psychology, and a PhD in educational psychology from Virginia Tech.

Ibby Han is a third-year undergraduate student at the University of Virginia. She is pursuing a degree in political and social thought. Her research interests include student activism and grassroots social movements.

Walter F. Heinecke is an associate professor of research, statistics, and evaluation at the Curry School of Education at the University of Virginia. He holds a doctorate from Arizona State University in educational policy studies. He teaches courses in research, evaluation, and educational policy studies. He is coauthor of *Political Spectacle and the Fate of American Schools* and *Educational Leadership in an Age of Accountability*. His research interests include policy implementation, diversity, and equity in education and citizenship, democracy, and policy.

Ronald Huesman Jr. is the director of institutional assessment at the University of Minnesota, Twin Cities, where he also serves as the managing director and principal researcher of the Student Experience in the Research University, Association of American Universities (SERU-AAU) Consortium.

Wayne Jacobson is the assessment director in the Office of the Provost at the University of Iowa. His office supports assessment of student learning and experience in academic programs and institutional student-success initiatives. He holds a PhD in adult education from the University of Wisconsin–Madison.

Matthew Johnson is an assistant professor in the Department of Educational Leadership at Central Michigan University. He holds a PhD in college student personnel from the University of Maryland, College Park. His research focuses on the intersections of civic engagement, leadership, and social justice.

Daniel Jones-White is a senior analyst in the Office of Institutional Research at the University of Minnesota, Twin Cities. He received a BA in history, politics, and law from Webster University, an MA in political science from the University of Missouri, Columbia, and a PhD in organizational leadership, policy, and development from the University of Minnesota, Twin Cities.

Young K. Kim is an associate professor of higher education at Azusa Pacific University. She holds a PhD in higher education from UCLA. Her research addresses student–faculty interaction, college impact, college student development, and diversity and equity in higher education.

Gary R. Kirk is the director of VT Engage at Virginia Tech. His interests are in the areas of nonprofit and public organizations, public service motivation, and university–community partnerships. He received a BA in ecology and evolution from New College of Florida, and an MA in public and international affairs and a PhD in environmental design and planning from Virginia Tech.

Brandon W. Kliewer is an assistant professor of civic leadership in the Mary Lynn and Warren Staley School of Leadership Studies at Kansas State University and an associate scholar with Points of Light. Kliewer specializes in deliberative civic engagement, community-engaged scholarship, collective impact, and crosssector collaboration and partnership. He is currently working on a series of manuscripts that report the results of civic leadership development programs, deliberative civic engagement forums, and community engagement practices. His scholarship often involves undergraduate and graduate students, community members, and working professionals in ways that create the conditions to mobilize new knowledge in order to make progress on tough challenges.

Keali'i Troy Kukahiko is a PhD student in UCLA's Department of Higher Education and Organizational Change. He focuses his research on programs in higher education that will improve the transition, persistence, and degree attainment of student-athletes of color. He founded the Pacific Islander Education and Retention (PIER) program at UCLA in 1998, and Prodigy Athletes in 2005.

Nqobile Mthethwa is a third-year undergraduate student at the University of Virginia. She is majoring in political science and minoring in global sustainability. Her research interests are privatization of higher education, energy, and water.

Tania D. Mitchell is an assistant professor of higher education at the University of Minnesota, Twin Cities. Her teaching and research focus on service-learning as a critical pedagogy to explore civic identity, social justice, student learning and development, race and racism, and community practice. Mitchell is a recipient of the Early Career Research Award from the International Association for Research in Service-Learning and Community Engagement (IARSLCE) and the American Fellowship from the American Association of University Women. With 15 years of higher education, administrative, and teaching experience, she has been published in numerous books and journals. Mitchell is also coeditor of *The Cambridge Handbook of Service Learning and Community Engagement*.

June Nobbe is an assistant vice provost for student life at the University of Minnesota, Twin Cities. She holds a PhD in educational policy and administration from the University of Minnesota, Twin Cities. Her research focuses on the civic mission of public higher education.

Kathy O'Byrne is the director of the UCLA Center for Community Learning. She has published numerous journal articles and book chapters on service-learning and civic engagement in higher education. In 2004, she received the California Campus Compact Richard E. Cone Award for Excellence and Leadership. O'Byrne earned a PhD in psychology from the University of Southern California.

Luis Ponjuan is an associate professor of higher education administration and the executive director of the Investing in Diversity, Equity, Access, and Learning (IDEAL) research project in the Department of Educational Administration and Human Resource Development in the College of Education and Human Development at Texas A&M University, College

Station, Texas. Ponjuan has developed a comprehensive research agenda focused on access and equity in higher education for underrepresented students and faculty members of color.

Victoria Porterfield is a research analyst in the Office of Institutional Research and Academic Planning at Rutgers University. She holds a master's degree in educational statistics and is currently pursuing a PhD in planning and public policy from Rutgers University. Prior to her employment at Rutgers, Porterfield spent several years employed as a statistical associate at Educational Testing Service (ETS).

Kerry L. Priest is an assistant professor in the Mary Lynn and Warren Staley School of Leadership Studies at Kansas State University, where she teaches undergraduate courses emphasizing civic leadership development and practice. Her scholarship explores the intersections of leadership and learning in the form of leadership pedagogy/high-impact practices for leadership education. She is also interested in the identity development of leaders and leadership educators.

Liz A. Rennick is a doctoral student and graduate research assistant in the Department of Higher Education at Azusa Pacific University. Her research addresses equity and opportunity in higher education, community college students, transfer students, and Latino college students.

Sarah SanGiovanni is the program coordinator for the Iowa Initiative for Sustainable Communities, an engaged learning organization in the University of Iowa's Office of Outreach and Engagement. She holds a master's degree in urban planning from the State University of New York at Buffalo.

Krista M. Soria works as an analyst with the Office of Institutional Research at the University of Minnesota, Twin Cities. She is interested in researching high-impact practices that promote undergraduates' development and success, the experiences of first-generation and working-class students in higher education, and programmatic efforts to enhance college students' leadership development, civic responsibility, and engagement in social change. Soria has worked for more than a decade in higher education, serving as an admission advisor, TRIO education advisor, academic advisor, and adjunct faculty for the University of Minnesota, Hamline University, St. Mary's University of Minnesota, St. Cloud State University, and the University of Alaska Anchorage.

Teniell L. Trolian is a doctoral candidate and graduate fellow at the University of Iowa. Her research interests include college student outcomes and connections between K–12 and postsecondary education.

Jeremy L. Williams is a doctoral student and graduate fellow at the University of Iowa. He holds a master's degree in leadership in student affairs from the University of St. Thomas. His research interests include student veterans, public engagement, and the history of higher education.

Lauren N. Willner is a PhD candidate in UCLA's Department of Social Welfare. She is a critical organizational scholar whose research focuses on nonprofit organizations. Willner holds a master's degree in social work from the University of Pennsylvania and a bachelor's degree in feminist studies and photojournalism from New York University.

CONTENTS

LIST OF FIGURES

LIST OF TABLES

Developing Undergraduates' Civic Capabilities: The Unique Contributions of American Public Research Universities

Krista M. Soria, Tania D. Mitchell, and June Nobbe

The world has become more interconnected and will require future leaders who are equipped for responsible participation in a diverse democratic society (Bernstein and Cock 1997; Checkoway 2001; Colby et al. 2003; Ehrlich 2000; Jacoby 2009; Levine 2007; Thomas 2010). In their critical roles as "agents of democracy," colleges and universities across the USA are charged with preparing their graduates to be active, effective citizens who can consciously contribute to the nation's dynamic democracy (Boyte and Hollander 1999, p. 8). The roots of this charge can be traced to the birth of the colonial nation, when Thomas Jefferson combined the principles of American democracy and education with objectives to produce public leaders of talent and virtue at the University of Virginia. Since that time, citizenship education has been recognized as a primary function of public higher education in the USA, with a particular accentuation placed upon research universities to educate future citizens, given their intersecting missions of innovation, knowledge generation, public engagement, and education. Given their prioritization on research, scholarship, entrepreneurship, technology, and medicine, among other areas, research universities encounter pressure to contribute back to their immediate communities or support state and federal development; thus, these

© The Editor(s) (if applicable) and The Author(s) 2016
K.M. Soria, T.D. Mitchell (eds.), *Civic Engagement
and Community Service at Research Universities,*
DOI 10.1057/978-1-137-55312-6_1

1

institutions are inherently driven to be public-oriented or civic-minded in their approaches.

Research universities are resource-rich in that they possess immense intellectual and human capital, structural support mechanisms, laboratories and academic support facilities, and the capacity to generate more resources with their prestige. As such, research institutions often exercise a "disproportionate influence over other colleges and universities" because of their emphasis on producing scholarship that influences all academic disciplines, spearheading initiatives sparking changes in other institutions, and educating the majority of faculty who work at other colleges and universities (Checkoway 2001, p. 126). American research universities embody their original missions—to serve a strong public purpose, build the nation, and develop future leaders; yet, as leaders with significant influence on other colleges and universities in the USA, scholars and policymakers have argued that research universities should work harder to renew their civic missions and serve as exemplars for citizenship education (Boyte and Hollander 1999). Public research universities, in particular, are closely connected with the states in terms of state regulations, funding structures, and governing boards, thus further enhancing the public nature of their work.

As research universities seek to respond to these calls to reinvigorate their civic missions—especially as they relate to educating undergraduates for participation in democracy—several practical concerns arise. First, there is a significant lack of research regarding the extent to which undergraduates at these institutions are engaging in community or civic efforts. Without such data, administrators and researchers are left with little understanding of whether they are achieving their citizenship education goals, how they might compare to peer institutions, and whether their undergraduates leave their institutions prepared to work with others from diverse backgrounds to effect social change. Research universities are also left with little awareness about whether their students receive equitable opportunities to engage in community-based efforts.

Second, while research associated with the benefits of undergraduates' civic and community engagement abounds, research focused specifically on the outcomes achieved by undergraduates at research universities is limited to date. Given the unique opportunities available at research universities—including the community contexts within which these institutions are situated, opportunities to work in collaborative research with faculty, ongoing community partnerships in research or medical centers, and much more—students' outcomes based upon their engagement work may differ from those of students at different types of institutions.

Finally, an absence of literature and scholarship specific to research universities may lead to assumptions that the "status quo" remains the best pathway to citizenship education when, in fact, radical alterations may be required given the significant changes to the constitution of our democracy in the last several decades. Without critical examinations of citizenship education, systems of power and privilege are reinforced, and students are not educated in a manner conducive to genuine social change.

The purpose of this volume is to respond to those three gaps in our current understanding of citizenship education in research universities. Below, we offer a deeper historical context of citizenship education in research universities, with a particular focus on public universities. Next, we describe the impetus for continued work to enhance undergraduates' citizenship education at research universities. Finally, we offer a preview of the contents of this volume.

EXAMINING THE HISTORICAL LEGACY OF CITIZENSHIP EDUCATION

Dewey (1916) believed the American democratic society required civic engagement to realize the potential of its citizens and communities—and that education was the key to fostering civic engagement. Nodding (2000) affirmed the deep connection between civic engagement and education in the nation by writing that "A liberal democracy depends on the continuing and voluntary affirmation of a critical citizenry ... thus the state has a compelling interest to enforce forms of education that will produce such a citizenry" (p. 291). Enlightened through education, the citizenry preserves the ideals of a democratic society, such as human rights and equality, and contributes to the overall social good.

Research universities—especially public research universities—were explicitly founded with the goals of educating citizens to contribute to the nation's pluralistic democracy. The public intersection with administration and control was written into the charter of the University of Virginia, which made it a public enterprise (Brubacher and Rudy 1997). The public university in America is an established social institution, one that was "created and shaped by public needs, public policy, and public investment to serve a growing nation" (Duderstadt and Womack 2003, p. 6). The public university, created by public policy and supported through public tax dollars, serves the function of a *public good*. In exchange for public support, the public university provides service to society through research, development of professional fields, preparing leaders for public service, educating citizens to serve democracy, and contributing to economic development (Duderstadt and Womack 2003; Kezar et al. 2005). Distinguished from elite private universities that have been historically important in "setting the standards determining the character of higher education in America," public universities "provided the capacity and diversity to meet the nation's vast needs for postsecondary education" (Duderstadt and Womack 2003, p. 204).

In 1862, the federal government entered the arena of higher education with the passage of the Morrill Land Grant Act, which provided land in exchange for serving the educational needs of society via mechanical, agricultural, and military sciences. The first Morrill Act and subsequent Acts were also implemented to expand access to higher education and to advance democracy (Benson et al. 2005; Brubacher and Rudy 1997; McDowell 2001). Kerr (2001) identified this development as significant in linking universities closely with the daily life of individuals in American society. McDowell wrote, "Both by virtue of their scholarly aims and who they would serve, the land-grant universities were established as people's universities. This was their *social contract*" (2001, p. 3, emphasis added). The extent to which the social contract or charter in public higher education has been upheld, neglected, or in need of renegotiation is a source of significant discussion among authors and in national higher education organizations such as Campus Compact, the American Council on Education, the National Forum on Higher Education for the Public Good, and the Association of American Colleges and Universities (AAC&U).

CALLS TO RENEW THE CIVIC MISSION OF PUBLIC HIGHER EDUCATION

Harry Truman was the first USA President to engage with a national higher education policy when he appointed the President's Commission on Higher Education. Among the recommendations in the 1947 Truman Commission report, one called for a curriculum that would promote a sense of common culture and citizenship (Smith and Bender 2008). Nearly four decades later, the Carnegie Foundation (Newman 1985) released a report that called upon colleges and universities to assume more responsibility in what was perceived as a need for economic, political, and social renewal in the USA. While the need to respond to a new world economy was identified as important, Newman (1985) argued that "the most critical demand is to restore higher education to its original purpose of preparing graduates for a life of involved and committed citizenship" (p. xiv). Newman called for a transformation of liberal education to go beyond the provision of a broad base of knowledge and intellectual skills to include a focus on the development of an entrepreneurial spirit and a sense of civic responsibility. One of the primary recommendations associated with civic responsibility was to provide more student aid for student involvement in community service.

In the *Wingspread Declaration on the Civic Responsibilities of Research Universities*, Boyte and Hollander (1999) called on research universities to renew the civic mission of American higher education. The authors critiqued research universities as drifting away from their civic missions and neglecting to prioritize citizenship education amid their other objectives. Ehrlich (2000) and Bok (2006) argued that higher education can play a role in reversing the declining trends in civic engagement and political participation and should revitalize citizenship education. Bok argued that the role of higher education in the civic engagement arena takes on special significance given the connection between the level of education and voting rates, and the likelihood that college graduates will assume leadership roles in the public sphere. Bok stated that "developing citizens is not only one of the oldest educational goals but a goal of great significance for educators themselves" (p. 193). He called upon faculty and college leaders to model the way and encourage students to participate in politics, public issues, student organizations, and service opportunities.

National organizations such as Campus Compact, the American Council on Education, the National Forum on Higher Education for the Public Good, and the AAC&U have become active in the arena of enhancing civic engagement by promoting research, experiential learning, and the review of institutional accreditation to highlight the moral and civic development of undergraduate students. For example, the AAC&U created a consortium of institutions committed to advancing ethical, civic, and moral development in order to respond to the nation's unprecedented ethical and civic challenges. The Research Universities Civic Engagement Network (TRUCEN) was established in 2005 by Campus Compact and Tufts University and includes over 30 universities interested in fostering the civic education of their students (Hollander 2011). The National Forum on Higher Education for the Public Good (formerly the Kellogg Forum on Higher Education for the Public Good) was established in 2000 at the University of Michigan. The forum evolved "out of concern for the shifting role that colleges and universities were playing in addressing important social issues and preparing their students for the civic, economic, and cultural demands of this and future generations" (Chambers 2005, p. 17).

Other efforts have led to reforms in the ways in which research universities have reprioritized their focus on citizenship education. For instance, in 2007, the Carnegie Foundation for the Advancement of Teaching added an elective classification of "Community Engagement," which requires that teaching, learning, and scholarship engage faculty, students, and community in mutually beneficial collaborations that address community-identified needs, deepen students' civic and academic learning, contribute to the well-being of the community, and enrich scholarship. As of January 2015, there are 361 institutions that have received the community engagement classification and, among the first-time recipients, 29 were classified as research universities (Carnegie Community Engagement 2015).

Citizenship Education: A Renewed Call to Action

A renewed call to action is warranted given the state of civic engagement in the nation. Evidence suggests undergraduates' civic engagement, interest in social justice, and interest in social change are lower than desired—and dwindling over time. Although rates of community service and volunteerism among undergraduate students have risen over the last few decades, experts report that many students lack a deep sense of personal and social responsibility necessary to advance the democratic nation (Hurtado et al. 2012). For instance, a recent survey of 153,015 first-year students enrolled at 227 USA colleges and universities indicated that approximately one in three students believed that helping to promote racial understanding was "very important" or "essential" to them personally, a number that has remained stagnant for more than two decades (Eagan et al. 2014). When asked about their knowledge of others from different racial or cultural backgrounds, 44.2 % of students indicated that they were "somewhat strong" or that this knowledge was one of their "major strengths" (Eagan et al. 2014). Only 50.3 % of first-year students believed there was a very good chance that they would vote in state, local, or national elections that year. Finally, 35.8 % indicated that becoming a community leader was "essential" or "very important" to them.

There are also differences between students' civic engagement between public and private universities that suggest public universities may not be fulfilling their civic missions. For instance, data suggest that first-year students attending private institutions are more likely than those attending public institutions to indicate that the ability to see the world from someone else's perspective, work cooperatively with diverse people, and discuss and negotiate controversial issues are major strengths or somewhat strong areas for them. Students at private institutions are more likely to believe that they would participate in volunteering or community service (46.3 %) compared to those at public institutions (34.4 %) (Eagan et al. 2014).

Other data paint a concerning picture of students' growth in citizenship abilities as a consequence of attending higher education. Comparisons of first-year students and undergraduate seniors show that there are few major areas of growth in civic outcomes; for instance, longitudinal studies suggest only 4.2 % more students were likely to indicate that becoming a community leader was essential or very important between their first year and senior year (38.3 % to 42.5 %) (Franke et al. 2010). The same data suggested seniors were only 3 % more likely to indicate that influencing the political structure was essential or very important (20.6 % to 23.5 %), 3.5 % were more likely to indicate promoting racial understanding was essential or very important, and 6.2 % more likely to indicate participating in a community-action program was important (29.8 % to 36 %). Furthermore, while 81.3 % of first-year undergraduate students reported volunteering in at least 30 minutes of community service per week, the number dropped to 56.2 % by students' senior year of study (Franke et al. 2010).

Similar studies, such as the longitudinal Wabash National Study of Liberal Arts Education, suggest that one-third of students experienced no growth or a decline in their commitment to socially responsible leadership and 58 % experienced no growth or a decline in their political and social involvement (Finley 2012). It is estimated that nearly two-thirds of students reported no growth or a decline in their openness to diversity and challenge (Finley 2012). Similar statistics suggest that approximately one-quarter of undergraduate seniors reported having much stronger knowledge about problems facing their communities, abilities to get along with people from different races and cultures, leadership abilities, and knowledge of people from different races or cultures (Franke et al. 2010). While 69.3 % of undergraduate first-year students reported frequently socializing with someone of another racial/ethnic group, only 49.9 % of seniors reported the same (Franke et al. 2010).

Finally, undergraduate students themselves are likely to report that they are not receiving opportunities for citizenship education at their respective institutions that are congruent with their civic interests. In a national survey of over 24,000 students at 23 diverse institutions, researchers found that the longer students stayed in higher education, the wider the gap between their beliefs that social responsibility should be a goal of higher education and their assessment of whether their institutions provide opportunities for growth in that area. For instance, 59 % of undergraduate seniors strongly agreed that contributing to a community *should be* a major focus of their collegiate experience, although only 38 % believed that contributing to a community *was* a major focus at their institutions (Dey et al. 2009). Furthermore, only 33.0 % of students believed that administrators publicly advocate the need for students to become active and involved citizens and that only 35.8 % of faculty advocated the same message (Dey et al. 2009).

These persistent patterns are distressing and, we argue, should compel institutions to invest more efforts into meeting their civic missions. The purpose of this volume is to serve as a catalyst toward those reforms and strategies by providing researchers, administrators, and policymakers at public research universities with information they can utilize to benchmark their institutional efforts, examine the benefits of students' participation in civic-related endeavors at research universities, and critically analyze their current citizenship education practices.

STARTING A CONVERSATION: CONTRIBUTIONS OF THIS VOLUME

The first section of the volume addresses institutional conditions that frame undergraduates' civic and citizenship engagement at research universities. The book begins with a chapter using data from the 2010 University of California Undergraduate Experience Survey (UCUES). Kim, Franco, and Rennick investigate the higher education experiences that contribute to students' civic attitudes development and how these contributing undergraduate experiences differ by students' gender, race/ethnicity, and socioeconomic status. Their research underscores the different higher education experiences that may be effective in developing civic attitudes, as well as how students might benefit differently from those experiences across race, gender, and socioeconomic lines. In Chap. 2, Kliewer and Priest present a conceptual framework for a deliberative civic engagement designed to increase the civic leadership capacity of individuals interested in making progress on tough challenges. Using examples from a leadership seminar facilitating community-based dialogues on critical issues, they discuss how to create the necessary conditions to support forms of political learning focused on identifying common interests and values.

Chapter 3 offered by Porterfield, like Kim, Franco, and Rennick's, investigates the different impacts of civic learning opportunities on diverse student populations. Using data from the Student Engagement in the Research University (SERU) survey, Porterfield offers a needed quantitative assessment of whether classroom engagement enhances civic and community engagement among students from disadvantaged backgrounds attending large, public research universities. Also using SERU data, Chap. 4, by Williams, Soria, and Erickson, offers important insights into the rates of participation in community-engagement activities at public research universities. Looking at institutions that have received the elective Community Engagement Classification from the Carnegie Foundation for the Advancement of Teaching, this study helps us understand how participation in community engagement differs at institutions that have received the classification in comparison to those that have not.

The first section ends with the presentation of a multidimensional developmental model theorizing the development of civic engagement of undergraduates. In Chap. 5 Ponjuan, Alcantar, and Soria aim to advance our understanding of the construct of civic engagement through a critical review of the literature that captures how students develop civic-related capabilities across developmental domains. This model of civic-related capabilities is a valuable resource for practitioners, researchers, and policymakers to better understand student development of civic engagement.

In the second section of the book, we turn to discussions of undergraduate students' participation in community service and service-learning to better understand how students are involved and the outcomes developed as a result of that engagement. In the first chapter of this section, Chap. 6 of the book, Kirk and Grohs explore associations between three civic learning opportunities—living learning communities, volunteering, and service-learning—and civic attitudes. Their research affirms what we feel is a key learning from this text: explicit and intentional integration of civic learning in the undergraduate experience is essential to achieving the democratic aims with which public research universities have been charged.

In the next chapter data from the Community and Civic Engagement Module of the 2010 multi-institutional SERU survey were used to develop and test two structural equation models that estimated the potential direct and indirect effects of service-learning involvement on undergraduate students. Furco, Jones-White, Huesman, and Gorny explore students' perceptions of their academic and sociocultural development in Chap. 7. The models offer useful insights into the relationship between service-learning and students' perceptions of their citizenship and civic behaviors.

The section continues with a chapter from Soria, Johnson, and Mitchell that utilizes data from the ACT College Outcomes Survey. In this study, they investigate relationships between undergraduate students' growth in citizenship and two critical outcomes: students' development of leadership and multicultural competence.

Section two concludes with Chap. 9 that uses data from the 2014 SERU survey. Trolian, San Giovanni, and Jacobson examine relationships between community service and service-learning experiences and student satisfaction with their higher education experience. Their chapter is especially valuable in its implications, which support higher education professionals in considering strategies through social and academic experiences to improve student satisfaction.

The final section of the book offers critical perspectives on students' civic engagement and aims to challenge research universities to consider their roles in preparing students for social justice and social change work. Recognizing how many research universities are grappling with how to carry out their student development goals tied to diversity, Barrera, Kukahiko, Willner, and O'Byrne begin this section with Chap. 10 by presenting a pedagogical framework. Their critical approach begins with identity awareness aimed at supporting a focus on sociopolitical development in service-learning. Student activism is rarely considered in discussions of service-learning and community engagement, but Chap. 11 by Heinecke, Cole, Han, and Mthethwa reminds us that dissent and activism are important expressions of civic leadership. In their qualitative study, conflicting definitions of democracy and citizenship are uncovered. The authors call for research universities to engage in introspection and self-study to understand how campus culture may limit students' abilities to take civic action in service of social justice.

Mitchell and Soria conclude this section with Chap. 12, a study utilizing SERU survey data that explores how students characterize their community service and service-learning experiences. They look at relationships between how students' characterize their community-engagement activity (e.g., charity, empowering others, social change, social justice) and their self-reported development of outcomes considered essential to preparing students for active engagement in a diverse democracy.

As the book concludes, we hope that this volume serves to further the conversation about the role of public research universities in the civic engagement movement. Several chapters in this text present research using large data sets that provide significant insight into community-engaged practice and its resulting outcomes that can be used to advance research and practice. The models and frameworks offered highlight how public research universities have responded to the challenges of the *Wingspread Declaration* and *Crucible Moment* revealing the challenges of community-engaged practice and the possibilities to strengthen our work. We encourage readers to engage deeply with this text, connect with the ideas that resonate most with their unique institutional contexts, reconsider the roles of research universities in preparing undergraduates for critical public-centered work, and enhance university programs to better prepare undergraduates with the civic capacities needed to sustain our democracy.

References

Benson, L., Harkavy, I., & Hartley, M. (2005). Integrating a commitment to the public good into the institutional fabric. In A. Kezar, T. Chambers, & J. Burkardt (Eds.), *Higher education for the public good: Emerging voices from a national movement* (pp. 185–216). San Francisco, CA: Jossey-Bass.

Bernstein, A., & Cock, J. (1997, November 14). Educating citizens for democracies young and old. *The Chronicle of Higher Education*, p. B6.

Bok, D. (2006). *Our underachieving colleges: A candid look at how much students learn and why they should be learning more.* Princeton, NJ: Princeton University Press.

Boyte, H., & Hollander, E. (1999). *Wingspread declaration on renewing the civic mission of the American research university.* Providence, RI: Campus Compact.

Brubacher, J. S., Rudy, W., et al. (1997). *Higher education in transition: A history of American colleges and universities* (4th ed.). New Brunswick, NJ: Transaction Publishers.

Carnegie Community Engagement Classification. (2015). *How is "community engagement" defined?* Boston, MA: University of Massachusetts Boston, New England Resource Center for Higher Education. Retrieved from http://nerche.org/index.php?option=com_content&view=article&id=341&Itemid=92#CE%20def.

Chambers, A. C. (2005). The special role of higher education in society: As a public good for the public good. In A. J. Kezar, A. C. Chambers, & J. Burkhardt (Eds.), *Higher education for the public good: Emerging voices from a national movement* (pp. 3–22). San Francisco, CA: Jossey-Bass.

Checkoway, B. (2001). Renewing the civic mission of the American research university. *Journal of Higher Education, 72*(2), 125–147.

Colby, A., Ehrlich, A., Beaumont, E., & Stephens, J. (2003). *Educating citizens: Preparing America's undergraduates for lives of moral and civic responsibility.* San Francisco, CA: Jossey-Bass.

Dewey, J. (1916). *Democracy and education.* New York, NY: Free Press.

Dey, E. L., Barnhardt, C. L., Antonaros, M., Ott, M. C., & Hopsapple, M. A. (2009). *Civic responsibility: What is the campus climate for learning?* Washington, DC: Association of American Colleges and Universities.

Duderstadt, J. J., & Womack, F. W. (2003). *The future of the public university in America: Beyond the crossroads.* Baltimore, MD: The Johns Hopkins University Press.

Eagan, K., Bara Stolzenberg, E., Ramirez, J. J., Aragon, M. C., Ramirez Suchard, M., & Hurtado, S. (2014). *The American freshman: National norms fall 2014.* Los Angeles, CA: University of California Los Angeles, Higher Education Research Institutes.

Ehrlich, T. (Ed.). (2000). *Civic responsibility in higher education.* Phoenix, AZ: Oryx Press.

Finley, A. (2012). *Making progress? What we know about the achievement of liberal education outcomes.* Washington, DC: Association of American Colleges and Universities.

Franke, R., Ruiz, S., Sharkness, J., DeAngelo, L., & Pryor, J. (2010). *Findings from the 2009 administration of the College Senior Survey (CSS): National aggregates.* Los Angeles, CA: University of California Los Angeles, Higher Education Research Institutes.

Hollander, E. L. (2011). Civic education in research universities: Leaders or followers? *Emerald Education + Training, 53,* 166–176.

Hurtado, S., Ruiz, A., & Whang, H. (2012). Assessing students' social responsibility and civic learning. Presented at the Association for Institutional Research: New Orleans, LA.

Jacoby, B. (Ed.). (2009). *Civic engagement in higher education: Concepts and practices.* San Francisco, CA: Jossey-Bass.

Kerr, C. (2001). *The uses of a university.* Boston, MA: Harvard University Press.

Kezar, A. J., Chambers, A. C., & Burkhardt, J. (Eds.). (2005). *Higher education for the public good: Emerging voices from a national movement* (1st ed.). San Francisco, CA: Jossey-Bass.

Levine, P. (2007). *The future of democracy: Developing the next generation of American citizens.* Lebanon, NH: Tufts University Press.

McDowell, G. R. (2001). *Land-grant universities and extension into the 21st century: Renegotiating or abandoning a social contract.* Ames, IA: Iowa State University Press.

Newman, F. (1985). *Higher education and the American resurgence. A Carnegie Foundation special report.* Princeton, NJ: Princeton University Press.

Nodding, N. (2000). Education as a public good. In A. Anton, M. Fisk, & N. Holstrom (Eds.), *Not for sale: In defense of public goods* (pp. 279–294). Boulder, CO: Westview Press.

Smith, W., & Bender, T. (2008). Introduction. In W. Smith & T. Bender (Eds.), *American higher education transformed, 1940–2005: Documenting the national discourse* (pp. 1–11). Baltimore, MD: The Johns Hopkins University Press.

Thomas, N. L. (2010). Why it is imperative to strengthen American democracy through study, dialogue and change in higher education. *Journal of Public Deliberation, 6*(1), 1–14.

PART I

Institutional Conditions Framing Undergraduates' Civic and Citizenship Engagement at Research Universities

Civic Attitudes Development Among Undergraduate Students at American Research Universities: An Examination by Student Gender, Race/Ethnicity, and Socioeconomic Status

Young K. Kim, Marla A. Franco, and Liz A. Rennick

Postsecondary education in the USA has long been charged with fostering the intellectual development and civic responsibility of undergraduates (Pascarella and Terenzini 2005). Although reduced attention to fostering civic responsibility occurred during the industrialization and educational specialization of the nineteenth century, focus on the development of civic attitudes among undergraduate students has regained priority as institutions respond by promoting students' understanding of and commitment to local, national, and global communities (Colby et al. 2003; Sax 2004). Despite this resurgence among higher education institutions to focus on developing civic attitudes, a recent report by the US Department of Education (2012) conveyed a lack of clarity as to whether civic opportunities for students lead to an increase in students' civic readiness. Even less is known about the development of civic attitudes across different gender, racial, and socioeconomic subgroups of students—especially

© The Editor(s) (if applicable) and The Author(s) 2016
K.M. Soria, T.D. Mitchell (eds.), *Civic Engagement and Community Service at Research Universities*,
DOI 10.1057/978-1-137-55312-6_2

as they might exist at large, American public research universities, which have been explicitly charged with promoting such outcomes in their students (Boyte and Hollander 1999).

This chapter examines ways in which large public research universities can enhance the civic outcomes of undergraduate students. Our goal is to improve our understanding of undergraduate students' civic attitudes development by investigating not only the undergraduate experiences that contribute to students' civic attitudes development, but also how these contributing undergraduate experiences differ by students' gender, race/ethnicity, and socioeconomic status. Implications for practice go beyond traditional models of scholarship and practice, as most research and policy reports focus on repetitive inquiries related to the shortcomings of underrepresented college students (Harper 2010). As opposed to exacerbating the failure of underrepresented students by framing research, analysis, and practice using a deficit-achievement framework, more critical thought will be given in this study to examining the experiences that uniquely contribute to the development of civic attitudes among students from diverse gender, racial/ethnic, and socioeconomic groups. Specifically, the research questions guiding this study are: (1) How does the level of civic attitudes among undergraduate students at American research universities change over time during the undergraduate years? How does the change in the level of civic attitudes differ by their gender, race/ethnicity, and socioeconomic status? (2) What undergraduate experiences contribute to the development of civic attitudes among undergraduate students at American research universities? (3) How do the undergraduate experiences contributing to civic attitudes development at American research universities differ by students' gender, race/ethnicity, and socioeconomic status?

CIVIC ATTITUDES DEVELOPMENT AMONG UNDERGRADUATE STUDENTS

The development of citizenship among USA undergraduate students has been a long-standing goal of higher education (Sax 2004). Early efforts toward building civic-minded undergraduate students began in the 1800s as religiously affiliated liberal arts colleges closely tied religious and moral values to institutional missions and curricula in an effort to graduate students who were wiser and more sensitive to their moral and ethical responsibilities (Bryant et al. 2012; Pascarella and Terenzini 2005). Major shifts occurred during the 1900s with the rise of public research universities and the fragmentation of knowledge, which led to the development of a wide array of academic disciplines (Pascarella and Terenzini 2005). Such changes brought about a more diverse undergraduate student population, an expansion of curriculum beyond the classics, and the development of general education curriculum, which minimally included civic and moral education (Bryant et al. 2012). Preparing undergraduate students for lifelong active citizenship and civic engagement returned as a core outcome of higher education in the USA by the late 1900s as a result of increasing concern that students were not internalizing the civic missions of higher education institutions (O'Leary 2014). Many USA higher education institutions are reevaluating their civic functions (Colby et al. 2003) and increasingly applying their intellectual and financial resources to developing civically educated undergraduate students who are prepared to address pressing local, national, and global issues (Pew Partnership for Civic Change 2004).

Impact of Undergraduate Experiences on Students' Civic Attitudes

Evidence suggests that the development of civic attitudes is enhanced by students' degree of involvement during higher education (Sax 2000); therefore, many higher education institutions seek to enhance a sense of social concern among their students using both curricular and co-curricular forms of involvement (Colby et al. 2000). While some institutions have developed intentional and broad-based strategies for developing civic attitudes among their students, others have taken less comprehensive and more mixed approaches (Colby et al. 2000). In general, citizenship development among undergraduate students is fostered by certain types of civic, peer, faculty, and academic involvement, often resulting in increased commitment to helping others in difficulty, influencing social values and the political structure, and participating in community-action programs (Sax 2000).

All students benefit from participating in institutional involvement that is educationally meaningful; however, some researchers have found that certain student subgroups experience greater gains from select types of involvement compared to their peers (Feagin et al. 1996; Kim et al. 2014; Swail et al. 2005). For example, female undergraduates reported higher levels of civic and social values after 4 years of higher education than their male peers (Astin and Antonio 2004). Kim et al. (2014) found that gains in civic outcomes were experienced by students from all racial and ethnic subgroups, although Latino students reported experiencing the greatest gains in the development of civic attitudes compared to their peers from other racial groups. The study also found that students' socioeconomic status uniquely shapes their development in civic outcomes during higher education. Focusing on some major types of institutional involvement found to be related to undergraduates' civic development, the next section summarizes findings of the effects of college students' institutional involvement on their civic outcomes.

Undergraduates' Student Satisfaction and Belonging

Undergraduates' satisfaction and belonging are among the most traditional predictors of civic outcomes because students' perceived investment and membership in the campus community may encourage them to develop pro-social behaviors and values that are aligned with those of their peers and faculty (Hurtado et al. 2012). In a study using multiple datasets, researchers assessing undergraduates' social responsibility and civic learning found that students' sense of belonging positively predicted their understanding of self and others, civic awareness, pluralistic orientation, social agency, and civic engagement (Hurtado et al. 2012). While self-reported levels of sense of belonging and satisfaction have been found to be greatest among White students compared to their peers from other racial groups, Latino students' sense of belonging and satisfaction with their undergraduate experience has been found to positively predict their civic outcomes (Kim et al. 2014). Therefore, research suggests that students who experience varying levels of belonging and satisfaction may differentially develop civic outcomes.

Civic Involvement

According to data from the Cooperative Institutional Research Program (CIRP) Freshman Survey, approximately 75 % of undergraduate freshmen in 1998 reported volunteering on a weekly basis compared to approximately 63 % in 1988 (Sax 2000). Along with this increase in time spent volunteering among undergraduates, research suggests that frequent engagement in volunteer work positively influences the development of civic values among undergraduate students (Hurtado and DeAngelo 2012; Lott II 2013; Sax 2000). Astin and Sax (1998) used CIRP data to examine the effects of service participation on the development of civic responsibility. Findings revealed that involvement in service positively affected students' civic-responsibility outcomes, including students' commitment to participate in a community-action program, help others who are in difficulty, promote racial understanding, become involved in programs to clean the environment, serve the community, and influence social values and political structure (Astin and Sax 1998). These findings are supported by Astin et al. (1999) study on the postgraduate effects of undergraduates' volunteering. Findings suggest that, even after controlling for students' inputs and other confounding variables, participation in service positively influenced students' commitment to helping others in difficulty and promoting racial diversity even after graduating from higher education.

Peer Involvement

Undergraduate campuses offer interpersonal environments both in and outside of the classroom, which influence socialization and student development and have been found to mediate institutional-level peer group effects (Antonio 2004). Peer engagement outside of the classroom often occurs within the setting of student clubs and organizations. Estimates from the 2010 National Survey of Student Engagement (NSSE) indicate that 53 % of undergraduate students spend at least an hour or more per week participating in student clubs and organizations and 80 % of students participate in at least one academically affiliated organization by the end of their senior year (Dugan and Komives 2007). Researchers suggest the role-taking opportunities that often accompany co-curricular engagement are important for developing principled moral reasoning among undergraduate students (Lind 1997). Civic attitudes development has also been found to occur among certain types of friendship networks. Low-density friendship networks, characterized by multiple independent friendships among a widely diverse student composition who do not typically interact with one another, have been shown to significantly and positively affect undergraduates' moral reasoning levels (Derryberry and Thoma 2000). These findings suggest that low-density friendship networks provide students with a more diverse social environment, which allows for greater exposure to different ideas, values, and experiences (Derryberry and Thoma 2000). Sax's (2000) study on undergraduates' citizenship development confirms such findings. An increased sense of empowerment and community involvement was found to be positively affected by belonging to a diverse peer group (i.e., socioeconomic diversity, racial/ethnic diversity) (Sax 2000). Therefore, sociability across race through peer groups contributes to students' sense of civic responsibility, cultural awareness, service to the community, faith formation, and understanding of others (Astin and Antonio 2004).

Faculty Involvement

Student-faculty interactions, both inside and outside the classroom, are critical experiences found to develop undergraduate student outcomes, including civic outcomes (Astin 1993; Checkoway 2001; Pascarella et al. 1988). A meta-analysis by Hurtado and DeAngelo (2012) linked diversity and civic-minded practices with student outcomes. Review of the literature revealed that faculty engaged in civic-minded practices, such as engaging undergraduates on their research project, also typically engage in student-centered practices which can lead to civic attitudes development among students. Astin's (1993) analysis of students' attitudes toward social issues revealed that student-faculty interaction contributed toward increasing social activism among students, as well as positively affected students' beliefs and values regarding liberalism, libertarianism, and feminism. Yet, when quality of faculty instruction in the major and students' research or creative projects experience was explored, no significant effects were found on students' civic outcomes (Kim et al. 2014). Additionally, Pascarella et al. (1988) suggested that undergraduate students benefited differently from student-faculty interaction as it relates to civic outcomes. For example, White students' familiarity with faculty and staff positively influenced their development of humanitarian and civic values, yet that was not the case for African American undergraduates.

Academic Involvement

Research suggests there is a link between academic involvement and student development in civic attitudes (Astin 1993; Kim et al. 2014; Pascarella and Terenzini 2005). Academic involvement such as time spent studying, completing homework, and attending class and labs have been shown to positively contribute to promoting students' racial understanding (Astin 1993), commitment to social activism (Sax 2004), and social awareness (Schreiner and Kim 2011). Curricular activities such as taking ethnic and women's studies courses, majoring in social science, frequently performing community service as part of a class, and participating in study abroad have all been shown to foster civic awareness and skills needed for students to participate in a diverse democracy (Hurtado and DeAngelo 2012; Lott II 2013). Additionally, students' academic involvement and initiative, critical-reasoning classroom activity, and elevated academic effort were found to positively predict civic outcomes (Kim et al. 2014). Such forms of academic engagement have been shown to empower students and foster their self-discovery, which often creates ideal conditions for civic attitudes development among undergraduates (Lott II 2013).

METHODS

Data Source

For this quantitative study, we used data from the 2010 University of California Undergraduate Experience Survey (UCUES). The UCUES is distributed online to all students system-wide on a biennial basis and is administered by the Center for Studies in Higher Education at the University of California, Berkeley, and the University of California Office of the President. The 2010 survey was administered to all undergraduate students across all ten University of California campuses, yielding a response rate of 43 %, or 74.410 responses. Since our study was designed to examine "development" or "gains" in civic attitudes among students after they were fully exposed to university experiences, the sample was limited to junior and senior undergraduate students. We cleaned our data to meet the statistical assumptions of the study and the final sample size for the data analysis was 31,432.

Participants

Participants in this study included 56 % female students and 40 % male students. Participants also included 2.3 % African American students, 14 % Latino, 39 % Asian American, and 34 % White. Some racial/ethnic groups, including Native Americans, were severely underrepresented in our data; hence, they were excluded from this study for the purpose of data analysis. Students with middle-class family backgrounds were in the majority, representing 39 % of the sample, while students from low-income or working-class families made up 35 % of the sample and students from wealthy, professional, or upper-middle-class families made up 24 % of the sample.

Variables

The dependent variable of this study was students' level of civic attitudes at their junior or senior year, as measured by a factor scale that included three individual survey items that assessed students' ability to (1) appreciate, tolerate, and understand racial and ethnic diversity, (2) appreciate cultural and global diversity, and (3) understand the importance of personal social responsibility. To control for the level of civic attitudes upon entering the university, we also utilized an identical factor scale that measured students' retrospective self-assessment of civic attitudes when they entered the institutions. Table 2.1 displays the factor loadings and reliability estimates of both pretest and posttest civic attitudes factor scales.

The independent variables of the study included a broad range of higher education environments and experiences thought to impact students' development. They included three factor scales that represented campus climate for diversity (i.e., climate personal characteristics, freedom to express beliefs, climate of respect for personal beliefs); a factor scale for students' satisfaction and sense of belonging; an individual survey item

Table 2.1 Factor loadings and internal consistency on civic attitudes measures

Factor and survey items	Factor loading	Internal consistency (α)
Civic attitudes factor scale: posttest		0.84
Please rate your level of proficiency in the following areas when you started at this campus and now (current ability level):		
Ability to appreciate, tolerate, and understand racial and ethnic diversity	0.90	
Ability to appreciate cultural and global diversity	0.88	
Understanding the importance of personal social responsibility	0.84	
Civic attitudes factor scale: pretest		0.86
Please rate your level of proficiency in the following areas when you started at this campus and now (started ability level):		
Ability to appreciate, tolerate, and understand racial and ethnic diversity	0.91	
Ability to appreciate cultural and global diversity	0.88	
Understanding the importance of personal social responsibility	0.85	

Note: All contributing items of the factor scales were measured by a six-point Likert scale, ranging from 1 = very poor to 6 = excellent for civic involvement (i.e., community service or volunteer work); individual survey items for peer involvement (i.e., participation in clubs or organizations, socializing with friends, working with a group of students outside of class, helping a classmate understand material better); two factor scales for faculty involvement (i.e., faculty involvement with academics; research engagement with faculty); and four variables for academic involvement (i.e., active learning environments factor scale, high-order cognitive activities factor scale, raised standards for acceptable effort due to high standards of a faculty member, extensively revised a paper at least once before submitting for a grade).

We also controlled for a number of student-background characteristics, including gender, race/ethnicity, socioeconomic family background, parental education level, immigrant status, language heritage, and transfer status. Finally, we controlled for students' major as represented in one of five academic disciplines: (1) social sciences, (2) engineering and computer sciences, (3) physical and biological sciences, (4) arts and humanities, and (5) professional schools. Variable definitions and coding schemes may be found in Table 2.2. Factor loadings and reliability estimates of composite measures utilized in this study may be found in Table 2.3.

Analysis

We used IBM SPSS Statistics version 23 to analyze data. To meet the assumptions of our statistical methods, we cleaned our data to address missing values, outliers, univariate and multivariate normality, and homoscedasticity. To answer our first research question about the differences in the development (or change) of civic attitudes during higher education across different student subgroups (i.e., gender, race, socioeconomic subgroups), we conducted a series of paired samples t-tests, independent samples t-tests, and ANOVAs. For the second research question concerning undergraduate experiences that contribute to the development of civic attitudes, we conducted hierarchal multiple regression analyses using our aggregate sample. Informed by Astin's (1993) Inputs-Environments-Outcomes model, we conducted regression analyses using five blocks of independent variables: (1) pretest variable, (2) student-background characteristics, (3) academic discipline, (4) campus climate for diversity, and (5) undergraduate experiences. To begin, we conducted a hierarchical multiple regression analysis on the aggregate sample using the forward method in order to identify undergraduate experience variables that significantly contributed to our

Table 2.2   Variable definitions and coding schemes

Variables	Coding schemes
Student background characteristics	
Gender	1 = female, 2 = male
Ethnicity	
African American, Latino, Asian American, White	All dichotomous: 0 = no, 1 = yes
Socioeconomic status	1 = low income or working class; 2 = middle class; 3 = wealthy, upper-middle, or professional class
Language heritage	0 = English is not native language
	1 = English is native language
Immigrant status	0 = US Born, 1 = Immigrant
Transfer status	0 = Native or lower division transfer student
	1 = Upper division transfer student
Academic discipline (Ref: Social sciences)	
Engineering and computer sciences	All dichotomous: 0 = no, 1 = yes
Physical and biological sciences	
Social sciences	
Professional schools	
Climate for diversity	
Climate for personal characteristics	Factor scale (range 0–8)
Freedom to express beliefs	Factor scale (range 0–8)
Freedom to express political beliefs	Factor scale (range 0–8)
College experiences	
Satisfaction and sense of belonging	Factor scale (range 1–6)
Community service or volunteer work	Hours per week: 1 = 0 h, 2 = 1–5 h, 3 = 6–10 h, 4 = 11 or more hours
Participation in clubs or organizations	Hours per week: 1 = 0 h, 2 = 1–5 h, 3 = 6–10 h, 4 = 11 or more hours
Worked with group of students outside of class	Likert scale: 1 = never, 6 = very often
Helped classmate understand material better	Likert scale: 1 = never, 6 = very often
Raised standard for acceptable effort due to high standards of a faculty member	Likert scale: 1 = never, 6 = very often
Extensively revised a paper at least once before submitting for grade	Likert scale: 1 = never, 6 = very often
Involved in faculty research projects	0 = no, 1 = yes
Active learning environments	Factor scale (range 1–6)
Student-faculty interaction	Factor scale (range 1–6)
High order cognitive activities	Factor scale (range 1–6)

Note: For information on factor loadings and internal reliability on factor scales, please see Table 2.3.

Table 2.3 Factor loadings and internal consistency on scale items

Factor and survey items	Factor loading	Internal consistency (α)
Climate for personal characteristics[a]		0.86
Indicate how strongly you agree or disagree with each of the following statements (Likert scale: 1 = strongly disagree, 6 = strongly agree):		
Students are respected here regardless of their economic or social class	0.86	
Students are respected here regardless of their gender	0.88	
Students are respected here regardless of their race or ethnicity	0.88	
Students are respected here regardless of their sexual orientation	0.68	
Freedom to express beliefs[a]		0.82
Indicate how strongly you agree or disagree with each of the following statements (Likert scale: 1 = strongly disagree, 6 = strongly agree):		
I feel free to express my political beliefs on campus	0.91	
I feel free to express my religious beliefs on campus	0.91	
Climate of respect for personal beliefs[a]		0.81
Indicate how strongly you agree or disagree with each of the following statements (Likert scale: 1 = strongly disagree, 6 = strongly agree):		
Students are respected here regardless of their religious beliefs	0.86	
Students are respected here regardless of their political beliefs	0.89	
Satisfaction and sense of belonging		0.84
Please rate your level of satisfaction with the following aspects of your university education (Likert scale: 1 = very dissatisfied, 6 = very satisfied):		
Satisfaction with the overall academic experience	0.80	
Satisfaction with the overall social experience	0.76	
Satisfaction with the value of your education for the price you are paying	0.70	
Please rate your level of agreement with the following statements (Likert scale: 1 = strongly disagree, 6 = strongly agree):		
Knowing what I know now, I would still choose to enroll at this campus	0.84	
I feel that I belong at this campus	0.84	

(continued)

Table 2.3   (continued)

Factor and survey items	Factor loading	Internal consistency (α)
Student–faculty interaction		0.76
How frequently during this academic year have you done each of the following? (*Likert scale: 1 = never, 6 = very often*):		
Talked with the instructor outside of class about course material	0.83	
Communicated with a faculty member by email or in person	0.81	
Worked with a faculty member on an activity other than coursework	0.71	
Taken a small research-oriented seminar with faculty	0.68	
Active learning environments		0.90
How frequently have you done each of these activities during this academic year? (*Likert scale: 1 = never, 6 = very often*):		
Asked an insightful question in class	0.90	
Brought up ideas or concepts from different courses during class discussions	0.89	
Contributed to a class discussion	0.88	
Interacted with faculty during lecture class sessions	0.81	
Found a course so interesting that you did more work than was required	0.70	
Made a class presentation	0.58	
Higher order cognitive activities		0.89
Thinking back on this academic year, how often have you done each of the following? (*Likert scale: 1 = never, 6 = very often*):		
Examined how others gathered and interpreted data and assessed the soundness of their conclusions	0.86	
Reconsider own position after assessing other arguments	0.83	
Incorporate ideas or concepts from different courses when completing assignments	0.76	
Used facts and examples to support your viewpoint	0.63	
Thinking back on this academic year, how often were you REQUIRED to do the following? (*Likert scale: 1 = never, 6 = very often*):		
Create or generate new ideas, products, or ways of understanding	0.70	
Judge the value of information, ideas, actions, and conclusions based on the soundness of sources, methods, and reasoning	0.65	

[a]Factor scales were developed by the Center for Studies in Higher Education, UC Berkeley

outcome measure (i.e., students' civic attitudes) and remove those that did not. Once we identified the most parsimonious model, we again conducted a hierarchical multiple regression analysis using the enter method. Then, to examine how the strength of the relationship between those significant undergraduate experiences and civic attitude development varies by students' gender, race/ethnicity, or socioeconomic background (third research question), we disaggregated the data and conducted a series of hierarchical multiple regression analyses using the same exploratory techniques we used for the aggregate sample.

RESULTS

Patterns of Civic Attitudes Development

All students in our sample, regardless of their gender, race/ethnicity, or socioeconomic background, made significant gains in their civic attitudes during their time in higher education; however, there were some statistically significant differences in students' mean scores at the first year, mean scores in their third or fourth year, and mean gains from the first year to their third or fourth year. Those differences are discussed in Table 2.4 and below.

Gender
The women in our study indicated higher mean scores of civic attitudes than men at both the freshman and junior or senior years. In other words, female undergraduates appear to have entered higher education with higher levels of civic attitudes than male students. Female students also experienced slightly larger gains than male students during their undergraduate experiences, indicating that women may benefit more than men from their undergraduate experiences in terms of civic attitudes development.

Race/Ethnicity
African American students in our study reported the highest mean scores of civic attitudes both at the freshman and junior or senior years, while Asian American students indicated the lowest scores at both the freshman and junior or senior years. That is, it appears that the African American students entered higher education with a higher level of civic attitudes than students of other races/ethnicities. It also appears that Asian American students entered higher education with the lowest level of civic attitudes;

Table 2.4   Differences on gains in civic attitudes factor scale by gender, race/ethnicity, and socioeconomic status

Background characteristics	Mean at Freshman year	SD	Mean at junior or senior year	SD	Mean gains	SD
Gender						
Female (n = 17,607)	4.61	0.91	5.15	0.73	0.54	0.73
Male (n = 12,342)	4.38	0.93	4.89	0.81	0.52	0.80
Race/ethnicity						
African American (n = 735)	4.75	0.93	5.33	0.65	0.59	0.72
Latino (n = 4396)	4.55	0.96	5.21	0.71	0.66	0.81
Asian American (n = 12,113)	4.39	0.94	4.94	0.80	0.55	0.72
White (n = 10,670)	4.60	0.88	5.08	0.74	0.48	0.70
Socioeconomic background						
Low income/working class (n = 10,873)	4.47	0.97	5.05	0.79	0.58	0.78
Middle class (n = 12,073)	4.53	0.90	5.03	0.76	0.50	0.69
Upper middle/wealthy (n = 7444)	4.56	0.90	5.05	0.77	0.49	0.70

Note 1: Paired samples t-tests show that all longitudinal changes were significant ($p < 0.001$) within all subgroups: t scores varied as follows: female, $t = 154.72$; male, $t = 129.60$; African American, $t = 20.95$; Latino, $t = 50.93$; Asian-Filipino-Pacific Islander, $t = 77.65$; White, $t = 64.71$; low income or working class, $t = 71.38$; middle class, $t = 74.07$; upper-middle/professional/wealthy class, $t = 56.98$
Note 2: ANOVA or independent samples t-test results indicated significant differences in mean gain scores (mean change between freshman and junior/senior year) between all gender, racial/ethnic, and socioeconomic subgroups. F ratio scores or t scores and p values varied by subgroups: gender, $t = 2.54$, $p < 0.05$; race/ethnicity, $F = 69.103$, $p < 0.001$; socioeconomic status, $F = 40.23$, $p < 0.001$

however, African American students did not indicate the most gains in civic attitudes during higher education, nor did Asian American students indicate the least gains. Instead, Latino students reported the most gains in civic attitudes during college, and White students indicated the least gains during their higher education experiences.

Socioeconomic Status

Students from wealthier family backgrounds indicated the highest level of civic attitudes upon entering higher education, while students with the lowest-income family backgrounds indicated the lowest level of civic attitudes upon entering higher education; however, the lowest-income students in our study appear to have "caught up" with other students as mean scores at the junior or senior year were nearly identical across all socioeconomic groups.

College Experiences Contributing to Civic Attitudes Development

After controlling for students' input characteristics and academic discipline in the aggregate sample, a number of undergraduate experiences were found to impact civic attitudes development among undergraduates (Table 2.5). Undergraduate experiences that positively affected students' civic attitudes development included a favorable campus climate for diversity, civic involvement, undergraduates' satisfaction and sense of belonging, peer involvement, and academic involvement. Among these undergraduate experiences, students' satisfaction and sense of belonging and their academic involvement were the strongest positive predictors of civic attitudes development. Peer involvement was shown to have a small but positive effect on civic attitudes development. While research engagement with faculty was found to have a small negative effect on civic attitudes development, faculty involvement with academics had no impact on civic attitudes development.

Conditional Effects of Undergraduate Experiences on Civic Attitudes Development

When the sample was disaggregated by gender, racial/ethnic, and socioeconomic subgroups, several conditional effects of undergraduate experiences on civic attitudes development were observed (refer to Table 2.5). While most of the undergraduate experiences had similar effects on civic attitudes development across the different student subgroups, albeit with varying degrees of influence, the effects of some other undergraduate experiences were found to be conditioned by various student characteristics.

Gender-Based Conditional Effects

Two factor scales representing campus climate for diversity were found to impact civic attitudes development among students in the aggregate sample; however, when the sample was disaggregated by gender, we found that the campus climate of respect for personal beliefs in religious or political matters was a significant predictor of civic attitudes development among male students but not among female students. The same pattern was observed in academic involvement: male students appeared to benefit from extensively revising papers while female students did not. Opposite-gender-based conditional patterns were observed for peer involvement: participation in student clubs or organizations seemed to impact civic attitudes development for female students but not for male students. In the aggregate sample, we observed that involvement with faculty research was

Table 2.5 Results of regression analyses on civic attitudes factor scale by gender, race/ethnicity, and socioeconomic background

	All students	Gender		Race/ethnicity				Socioeconomic background		
		Female	Male	AA	LAT	ASI	WH	Low income	Middle class	Upper middle/wealthy
Block 1: pretest										
Pretest variable	0.60***	0.61***	0.60***	0.65***	0.56***	0.62***	0.61***	0.58***	0.62***	0.61***
Block 2: student background										
Gender (Male)	-0.05***			-0.04	-0.07***	-0.04***	-0.05***	-0.04***	-0.04***	-0.05***
Race/ethnicity (REF=White)										
African American	0.03***	0.04***	0.03***					0.03**	0.04***	0.03***
Latino	0.06***	0.07***	0.05***					0.07***	0.03***	0.02*
Asian American		0.02*	0.01					-0.02*	0.02*	0.03**
Social Class (REF=Wealthy)										
Working/low income	0.03***	0.02**	0.03**	-0.02	0.05***	0.01	0.02**			
Parental education level (AA degree or more)				-0.01	-0.04**	0.01	-0.03***	-0.01	-0.01	-0.03**
Immigrant status		-0.01	-0.03**							
English language heritage		0.02	-0.04***							
Transfer status (transfer student)	-0.07***	-0.06***	-0.07***	-0.08*	-0.08***	-0.06***	-0.07***	-0.09***	-0.07***	-0.03**

	All students	Gender			Race/ethnicity				Socioeconomic background		
		Female	Male	AA	LAT	ASI	WH	Low income	Middle class	Upper middle/ wealthy
Block 3: academic discipline (Ref= social sciences)											
Engineering and computer sciences	-0.08***	-0.06***	-0.09***	-0.06	-0.08***	-0.10***	-0.07***	-0.08***	-0.08***	-0.09***
Physical and biological sciences	-0.08***	-0.08***	-0.06***	-0.02	-0.08***	-0.08***	-0.07***	-0.07***	-0.08***	-0.06***
Professional schools	-0.02***	-0.01*	-0.02**	-0.02	-0.01	-0.04***	0.01	-0.02*	-0.03**	-0.01
Block 4: climate for diversity											
Freedom to express beliefs†	0.06***	0.08***	0.04**	0.04	0.09***	0.07***	0.08***	0.07***	0.08***	0.08***
Climate of respect for personal beliefs†	0.02**	0.01	0.04**							
Block 5: college experiences											
College student satisfaction											
Satisfaction and sense of belonging†	0.10***	0.10***	0.11***	0.10**	0.08***	0.11***	0.10***	0.11***	0.11***	0.09***

(continued)

Table 2.5 (continued)

	All students	Gender		Race/ethnicity				Socioeconomic background		
		Female	Male	AA	LAT	ASI	WH	Low income	Middle class	Upper middle/wealthy
Civic involvement										
Community service or volunteer work	0.05***	0.04***	0.05***	−0.01	0.04**	0.04***	0.06***	0.04***	0.05***	0.06***
Peer involvement										
Participation in clubs or organizations	0.02***	0.04***	0.01	0.08*	0.04**	0.04***	−0.01	0.04***	0.02**	0.01
Socializing with friends	0.03***	0.02***	0.05***	0.01	0.04**	0.04***	0.03**	0.04***	0.02**	0.05***
Worked with group of students outside of class				0.02	0.01	0.03**	0.01			
Helped classmate understand material better	0.01**									
Faculty involvement										
Involved in faculty research projects	−0.02**	−0.02**	−0.01	0.03	−0.02	−0.01	−0.02*	−0.02*	−0.01	−0.02

	All students	Gender		Race/ethnicity				Socioeconomic background		
		Female	Male	AA	LAT	ASI	WH	Low income	Middle class	Upper middle/wealthy
Academic involvement										
Active learning environments†	0.06***	0.08***	0.06***	0.09*	0.10***	0.06***	0.06***	0.09***	0.06***	0.07***
High order cognitive activities†	0.09***	0.09***	0.09***	0.05	0.10***	0.09***	0.09***	0.10***	0.08***	0.09***
Raised standard for acceptable effort due to high standards of a faculty member	0.06***	0.07***	0.06***	0.05	0.06***	0.06***	0.06***	0.06***	0.06***	0.07***
Extensively revised a paper at least once before submitting for grade	0.01*	0.01	0.02**	−0.01	0.01	0.01	0.02**	0.01	0.02**	0.01
Adjusted R^2	0.52	0.52	0.50	0.47	0.44	0.53	0.51	0.51	0.53	0.52

$*p < 0.01$, $**p < 0.01$, $***p < 0.001$

Note 1: Results reflect standardized regression coefficients

Note 2: Sample sizes varied as follows: female ($n = 14,216$), male ($n = 9864$), African American ($n = 582$), Latino ($n = 3608$), Asian American ($n = 10,286$), White ($n = 9223$), low income ($n = 8378$), middle class ($n = 9501$), upper-middle or wealthy class ($n = 5874$)

a negative predictor of civic attitudes development; however, in the sample disaggregated by gender, we observed that the effect was only true for female students and had no significant effect on male students.

Race/Ethnicity-Based Conditional Effects
Unlike the other races/ethnicities in our study, African American students appeared not to benefit in terms of their civic attitudes development from undergraduate experiences in some areas of campus climate for diversity (i.e., freedom to express religious or political beliefs on campus), civic involvement (i.e., community service or volunteer work), some aspects of peer involvement (i.e., socializing with friends), and some aspects of academic involvement (i.e., higher order cognitive activities, raising standards for acceptable effort due to high standards of faculty). On the other hand, Asian American students' civic attitudes development appeared to benefit from one aspect of peer involvement (i.e., working with a group of students outside of class), while their peers in other racial/ethnic groups did not. White students were the only group who were positively affected by certain aspects of academic involvement (i.e., the practice of extensively revising papers at least once before submitting for a grade) and negatively affected by research engagement with faculty.

Conditional Effects by Socioeconomic Status
Differential effects of peer, faculty, and academic involvement were also observed when the data were disaggregated by socioeconomic background. When it comes to peer involvement, it appears that lower-income and middle-class students who participated in clubs or organizations tended to report higher gains in civic attitudes development; however, this finding did not emerge for wealthier students in our sample. When it comes to academic involvement, middle-class students who engaged in the act of extensively revising papers at least once prior to submitting for a grade also reported higher gains in civic attitudes development. The positive effect was not the case for lower-income or wealthier students. For low-income students, we also observed that participation in faculty research appeared to have a small but significant negative effect on civic attitudes development.

DISCUSSION AND PRACTICAL IMPLICATIONS

Results of this study are unique in that we examined the conditional effects of undergraduate experiences on civic attitudes development across different gender, race/ethnicity, and socioeconomic subgroups.

Several other studies have examined civic attitudes development among undergraduates (Bowman et al. 2015; Hurtado and DeAngelo 2012; Hurtado et al. 2012). Our study, however, sheds light on how the impact of higher education experiences on civic attitudes development is conditioned by student characteristics (i.e., gender, race/ethnicity, socioeconomic background) at public research universities.

Results of comparative analyses in this study revealed stark differences regarding the development of civic attitudes during higher education. For example, we found that White students tended to obtain the least gains in their civic attitudes during their time in higher education compared to those among their peers of other races/ethnicities. Latino students appeared to obtain the largest gains in civic attitudes compared to their peers, a finding consistent with Lott II's (2013) study.

In another study, Asian American freshman students were found to be more civically engaged and were more likely to hold civic values, including in the area of racial understanding, compared to the national average (Park et al. 2008). While this finding is contradictory to the results of our study, we can assume that the lower levels of civic attitudes observed among Asian American students of our sample may be related to the unique nature of our dataset (e.g., highly selective institutions, public 4-year research universities). Nevertheless, results from our regression analyses suggest several ways to improve civic attitudes outcomes among Asian American students. In our study, sense of belonging and satisfaction appeared to be among the best predictors of civic attitudes development among Asian American students; however, our analyses also revealed that Asian American students in our study had the lowest mean score in sense of belonging and satisfaction compared to their peers of other racial/ethnic groups. That is, Asian American students were less likely to feel that they belonged on campus (despite being the majority), raising questions about the effort that public research institutions are making on behalf of this group of students. This finding is even more perplexing, given that Asian American students are the majority within the University of California system. These findings should initiate a more purposeful and proactive approach to developing a sense of satisfaction and belonging among this group of students.

The picture becomes more complex when dissecting the implications of these results for White students. As the dominant group in a country that is increasingly becoming more diverse and continues to struggle with racial inequities, strife, and misunderstanding, it becomes especially incumbent upon educational institutions with a mission toward civic-minded outcomes to proactively engage the dominant or advantaged group in their development of global and racial understanding and appreciation, as well as a full appreciation of their own social agency. This appreciation is even more important when considering that, according to the US Census (2012), the White majority is in steady decline and is projected to end by 2043. Although full discussion of this topic is beyond the scope of this chapter, it is worth noting that students from dominant or advantaged groups may in their futures act as agents that either reinforce or challenge oppressive practices and policies through civic engagement and leadership. The results of this study are, therefore, especially concerning for White students who ideally should be reflecting development in civic attitudes at levels equivalent to students of other races/ethnicities.

The examination of the conditional effects also revealed that African American students do not appear to benefit in terms of their civic attitudes development from many types of institutional involvement compared to their peers. There may be more than one possible explanation for these results; for example, our findings indicated a few variables that contributed to African American students' civic attitudes development during their time in higher education, including participation in clubs or organizations. Perhaps, at least for their civic attitudes development, African American students seem to benefit more from their experiences with a group of homogenous peers than those with students of other races/ethnicities. Another possible explanation is that a great deal of their development in civic attitudes occurred prior to attending the institution. It makes more sense that, for many African American undergraduate students, civic attitudes development occurs in the everyday context of facing racial challenges much more than in an educational or college context. Theoretically, this means that we are missing some confounding precollege experiences that help explain civic attitudes development among African American college students. More research should focus on the qualitative aspects of college experiences on civic attitudes development to gain a deeper understanding of internal processes and more nuanced experiences attributed to civic attitudes development.

Our findings also revealed some differences between male and female students. Similar to previous research (Astin and Antonio 2004), our results indicated that women gained more in civic attitudes development during higher education than men. In addition, the mean score at the end of their junior or senior year indicated that women perceived their civic attitudes at significantly higher levels than men. Our regression analyses also illuminate some areas of significant impact on civic attitudes development for men. In particular, male students were the only subgroup in our study to show that a campus climate of respect for personal beliefs (i.e., religious, political) had a significant and positive effect on civic attitudes development. It seems that male students at American public research universities uniquely benefit from campus climates that value diverse political and religious beliefs or that regard those beliefs as worthy. In addition, we also found that, unlike the women in our study, men benefited in terms of civic attitudes development from participation in clubs and organizations. Our analyses revealed that while there was no statistical difference in participation in clubs and organizations between male and female students, participation overall was quite low. Roughly 43 % of the men and women in our study did not participate in such activities at all, revealing perhaps a missed opportunity for American public research institutions to meet the goals of their civic missions.

Although this study was more interested in examining the conditional effects, it also identified some undergraduate environments and experiences that were beneficial to *all* students. Namely, all students appeared to benefit in terms of their civic attitudes development from a campus climate where they felt comfortable in expressing religious and political beliefs, a finding that further clarifies previous research on the benefits of diversity on the development of civic outcomes. Studies have demonstrated that positive interactions with diverse peers is positively related to civic outcomes among undergraduates (Astin and Antonio 2004; Bowman et al. 2015; Engberg 2007; Hurtado and DeAngelo 2012; Hurtado et al. 2002; Lott II 2013). The findings from this study support and expand the previous findings on the positive link between students' diversity engagement (mostly "behavioral" aspect of diversity) and their civic outcomes by underscoring the influence of campus diversity climate ("psychological" aspect of diversity) on these outcomes.

Additionally, all students seemed to benefit from their satisfaction with their undergraduate experience and their sense of belonging on campus, mirroring previous research on Latino students' civic attitudes development (Kim et al. 2014) and further elucidating the benefits for students with varying characteristics (i.e., gender, race/ethnicity, socioeconomic background) at public research institutions. Students who experience a sense of satisfaction with the overall higher education experience, overall social experience, and value of their education and students who acquire a sense of belonging are all more likely to develop positive civic attitudes during college, indicating another area of interest for American public research institutions to meet their civic missions.

Previous research has extolled student-faculty interaction as one of the critical influences of a broad range of positive student outcomes, including civic outcomes (Astin 1993; Checkoway 2001; Pascarella et al. 1988). It was interesting to find in our study that student–faculty interaction on academic matters appeared to have no statistically significant effect or, in the case of participation in faculty research, a small negative effect on civic attitudes development. This finding was also the case in a previous study by Hurtado and DeAngelo (2012) who also found that student–faculty interaction was not a significant predictor of pluralistic orientation. Both our study and the Hurtado and DeAngelo study utilized factor scales to represent student–faculty interaction and perhaps examining individual survey items might illuminate more nuanced effects of faculty interaction on students' civic outcomes. Because of the critical influence of faculty on student development and undergraduate outcomes, it is also promising to employ a qualitative approach to investigate how and why student–faculty interaction uniquely shapes undergraduates' civic outcomes development.

Fostering Civic Outcomes Among Undergraduate Students

The results of this study underscore not only the ways in which a variety of undergraduate experiences at research universities might be effective in the development of civic attitudes but also how different student subgroups might benefit more or less from those experiences. As Bowman (2011) pointed out, disaggregating data to better understand the conditional effects of undergraduate experiences on civic outcomes provides a more nuanced understanding of student development that helps practitioners develop optimally effective interventions. We hope that the findings of this study provide that understanding and direction. Thus, based on our findings, we recommend the following institutional conditions for developing civic attitudes:

- Given the general positive effects of participating in active learning environments on the development of civic attitudes among *all* students, faculty should be encouraged and provided with the tools needed to create such dynamic learning environments.

- Campus climates in which students feel free to express their personal beliefs are likely to produce gains in civic attitudes among most students; therefore, institutions should be intentional about creating climates that feel safe for students of all backgrounds to engage in this high impact practice.
- Given the general positive effects of satisfaction and sense of belonging on the development of civic attitudes among *all* students, institutional professionals should be more aware of the levels of satisfaction and sense of belonging experienced by various student subgroups and be more intentional about fostering such positive institutional and academic connections among a diverse student body.
- Asian American students reported the lowest mean scores of satisfaction and sense of belonging, which is alarming given that they account for the racial/ethnic majority in the UC. The predictive strength of sense of belonging and satisfaction for civic attitudes development among Asian Americans shows great promise as an institutional strategy for furthering its civic mission.
- White students reported experiencing the lowest gains in civic attitudes from freshman to junior or senior year. Higher education researchers and professionals should facilitate environments where White students can proactively engage in their development of global and racial understanding and appreciation so that they are more prepared to civically engage in a complex and multicultural society.

Furthermore, higher education leaders must recognize that not all students experience the same levels of involvement, nor do they benefit from such participation in the same way. Higher education institutions must be accountable for the civic development of all college and university students and committed to ensuring that institutional involvement is designed to be responsive to the unique needs of a diverse undergraduate student population. Based on our findings, we recommend the following strategies for increasing institutional involvement and their accompanying benefits for certain undergraduate subgroups:

- *Civic involvement*: Institutions could benefit by acknowledging broader forms of civic engagement that could be occurring among African American students outside of higher education's traditional civic and educational engagement models.

- *Peer involvement*: Participation in clubs and organizations and socializing with friends contributed greatly to the significant gains in civic attitudes among low-income/working-class students. In addition, participation in clubs or organizations was a significant predictor of civic attitudes development among African American students, while other forms of peer interaction were not. Hence, institutions must ensure that such involvement opportunities continue to be accessible to these student subgroups.
- *Faculty involvement*: Clearly, this form of involvement was not a significant indicator of civic attitudes development among all students, and for some student subgroups the experience actually produced negative effects. Given the contrary findings of previous studies, more research is needed to understand how the impact of faculty on students' civic attitudes development is conditioned by institutional type and selectivity.
- *Academic involvement*: Male students reported both the lowest mean scores during their freshman and junior or senior years as well as in gains made throughout higher education compared to their female peers. All four academic involvement items demonstrated a strong positive effect on males' civic attitudes development and should therefore be seen as evidence-based strategies for enhancing civic-mindedness among males.

Overall, findings of this study suggest that not only do select undergraduate experiences contribute to students' civic attitudes development, but that the nature of the contribution is conditioned by various student characteristics. Therefore, higher education institutions should acknowledge the undergraduate experiences that uniquely shape the development of civic attitudes among students from diverse gender, race, and socioeconomic groups in order to maximize the positive influence of institutional involvement on civic attitudes development for all students.

REFERENCES

Antonio, A. L. (2004). The influence of friendship groups on intellectual self-confidence and educational aspirations in college. *The Journal of Higher Education, 75*(4), 446–471.

Astin, A. W. (1993). *What matters in college? Four critical years revisited*. San Francisco, CA: Jossey-Bass.

Astin, H. S., & Antonio, A. L. (2004). The impact of college on character development. *New Directions for Institutional Research, 122*, 55–64. doi:10.1002/ir.109.

Astin, A. W., Sax, L. J., & Avalos, J. (1999). Long-term effects of volunteerism during the undergraduate years. *The Review of Higher Education, 22*(2), 187–202.

Astin, A. W., Sax, L. J., & Sax, L. J. (1998). How undergraduates are affected by service participation. *Journal of College Student Development, 39*(3), 251–263.

Bowman, N. A. (2011). Promoting participation in a diverse democracy: A meta-analysis of college diversity experiences and civic engagement. *Review of Educational Research, 81*(1), 29–68. doi:10.3102/0034654310383047.

Bowman, N. A., Park, J. J., & Denson, N. (2015). Student involvement in ethnic student organizations: Examining civic outcomes 6 years after graduation. *Research in Higher Education, 56*(2), 127–145. doi:10.1007/s11162-014-9353-8.

Boyte, H., & Hollander, E. (1999). *Wingspread declaration on renewing the civic mission of the American research university.* Providence, RI: Campus Compact.

Bryant, A. N., Gayles, J. G., & Davis, H. A. (2012). The relationship between civic behavior and civic values: A conceptual model. *Research in Higher Education, 53*(1), 76–93. doi:10.1007/s11162-011-9218-3.

Checkoway, B. (2001). Renewing the civic mission of the American research university. *The Journal of Higher Education, 72*(2), 125–147.

Colby, A., Ehrlich, T., Beaumont, E., Rosner, J., & Stephens, J. (2000). Higher education and the development of civic responsibility. In T. Ehrlich (Ed.), *Civic responsibility and higher education* (pp. xxi–xliii). Phoenix, AZ: The Oryx Press.

Colby, A., Ehrlich, T., Beaumont, E., & Stephens, J. (2003). *Educating citizens: Preparing America's undergraduates for lives of moral and civic responsibility.* Hoboken, NJ: Jossey-Bass.

Derryberry, P., & Thoma, S. (2000). The friendship effect: Its role in the development of moral thinking in students. *About Campus, 5*(2), 13–18.

Dugan, J. P., & Komives, S. R. (2007). *Developing leadership capacity in college students: Findings from a national study. A report from the multi-institutional study of leadership.* College Park, MD: National Clearinghouse for Leadership Programs.

Engberg, M. E. (2007). Educating the workforce for the 21st century: A cross-disciplinary analysis of the impact of the undergraduate experience on students' development of a pluralistic orientation. *Research in Higher Education, 48*(3), 283–317. doi:10.1007/s11162-006-9027-2.

Feagin, J. R., Hernan, V., & Nikitah, I. (1996). *The agony of education: Black students at White colleges and universities.* New York, NY: Routledge.

Harper, S. R. (2010). An anti-deficit achievement framework for research on students of color in STEM. *New Directions for Institutional Research, 148*, 63–74. doi:10.1002/ir.

Hurtado, S., & DeAngelo, L. (2012). Linking diversity and civic-minded practices with student outcomes. *Liberal Education, 98*(2), 14–23.

Hurtado, S., Engberg, M. E., Ponjuan, L., & Landreman, L. (2002). Students' precollege preparation for participation in a diverse democracy. *Research in Higher Education, 43*(2), 163–186. doi:10.1023/A:1014467607253.

Hurtado, S., Ruiz, A., & Whang, H. (2012). *Assessing students' social responsibility and civic learning.* Paper presented at the Annual Forum of the Association for Institutional Research, New Orleans, LA.

Kim, Y. K., Rennick, L. A., & Franco, M. (2014). Latino college students at highly selective institutions: A comparison of their college experiences and outcomes to other racial/ethnic groups. *Journal of Hispanic Higher Education, 13*(4), 245–268. doi:10.1177/1538192714532815.

Lind, G. (1997). *Educational environments which promote self-sustaining moral development.* Konstanz, Germany: University of Konstanz.

Lott, J. L., II. (2013). Predictors of civic values: Understanding student-level and institutional-level effects. *Journal of College Student Development, 54*(1), 1–16.

O'Leary, L. S. (2014). Civic engagement in college students: Connections between involvement and attitudes. *New Directions for Institutional Research, 162,* 55–65. doi:10.1002/ir.

Park, J. J., Lin, M. H., Poon, O. A., & Chang, M. J. (2008). Asian American college students and civic engagement. In P. M. Ong (Ed.), *The state of Asian America: Trajectory of civic and political engagement* (pp. 75–97). Los Angeles, CA: LEAP Asian Pacific American Public Policy Institute.

Pascarella, E. T., Ethington, C. A., & Smart, J. C. (1988). The influence of college on humanitarian/civic involvement values. *Journal of Higher Education, 59,* 412–437.

Pascarella, E. T., & Terenzini, P. T. (2005). *How college affects students.* San Francisco, CA: Jossey-Bass.

Pew Partnership for Civic Change. (2004). New directions in civic engagement: University avenue meets main street. http://www.civicchange.org/resources/newdirections.html.

Sax, L. (2000). Citizenship development and the American college student. In T. Ehrlich (Ed.), *Civic responsibility and higher education* (pp. 3–18). Phoenix, AZ: The Oryx Press.

Sax, L. (2004). Citizenship development and the American college student. *New Directions for Institutional Research, 122,* 65–80. doi:10.1002/ir.110.

Schreiner, L. A., & Kim, Y. K. (2011). Outcomes of a Christian college education: A comparison of CCCU students' gains to the national aggregate. *Christian Higher Education, 10,* 324–352. doi:10.1080/15363759.2011.577714.

Swail, W. S., Cabrera, A. F., Lee, C., & Williams, A. (2005). *Part III: Pathways to the bachelor's degree for Latino students.* Washington, DC: The Educational Policy Institute.

U.S. Census Bureau. (2012). *U.S. Census Bureau projections show a slower growing, older, more diverse national a half century from now [Press release]*. Washington, DC: U.S. Census Bureau. https://www.census.gov/newsroom/releases/archives/population/cb12-243.html.

U.S. Department of Education. (2012). *Advancing civic learning and engagement in democracy: A roadmap and call to action*. Washington, DC: U.S. Department of Education. http://www.census.gov/compendia/statab/2012/tables/12s0281.pdf.

CHAPTER 3

Creating the Conditions for Political Engagement: A Narrative Approach for Community-Engaged Scholarship and Civic Leadership Development

Brandon W. Kliewer and Kerry L. Priest

The challenges facing our world require a new kind of leadership and commitment to participation in civic life (Harward 2013; Levine and Soltan 2013; Mathews 2014). Education that supports meaningful democratic engagement necessitates a shared commitment to deep, theoretical, and practical understandings of the values and processes of democracy (Saltmarsh and Hartley 2011). Public engagement, academic service-learning, and community-engaged scholarship are examples of types of educational practices that promote learning linked to citizenship, civic-mindedness, and socially responsible leadership development (Dugan et al. 2013; Steinberg et al. 2011). The transformative potential of community-engaged practices hinges on the ability not only to cultivate the personal and civic capacity of individuals, but also to create conditions for democracy to thrive more widely in society (Kliewer 2013). The latter cannot be accomplished through only *learning about* and *minimally experiencing* values and processes of democratic engagement in the context of neatly structured courses, programs, or partnerships.

© The Editor(s) (if applicable) and The Author(s) 2016   47
K.M. Soria, T.D. Mitchell (eds.), *Civic Engagement and Community Service at Research Universities*,
DOI 10.1057/978-1-137-55312-6_3

Forms of community-engaged scholarship that expand spaces of civic learning are necessary in order for large public universities to make progress toward the vision of public engagement set forth by the *Wingspread Declaration*. For students, faculty, and institutions to become "agents of democracy" (Boyte and Hollander 1999, p. 7) requires leadership: more specifically, exercising leadership by creating conditions that enable individuals and groups to share the responsibility for making progress on civic challenges (Chrislip and O'Malley 2013; Ganz 2010). Indeed, exercising civic leadership (i.e., leadership as engagement in democracy for the purpose of advancing democracy) requires a commitment to shared purpose and to the common good, as well as an ability to navigate the uncertainty and messiness of civic work (Chrislip and O'Malley 2013; Ganz 2010).

The project of civic leadership exists within the larger adaptive leadership framework (Chrislip and O'Malley 2013; Heifetz et al. 2009) and presumes the activity of leadership should be reform oriented and that it does not require individuals to act from a position of formal authority. This chapter presents an approach to civic leadership education and development that accounts for the political. *The political* is the space in which groups of people negotiate power and choice (Wolin 2004). Power, understood from a postmodern perspective, includes power *over*, power *with*, power *to*, and power *within* (Rowlands 1997). Choice is simply the representation between different values, interests, and positions (Nabatchi and Leighninger 2015). Decoupling civic leadership education from neatly organized civic learning infrastructure releases the work into *the political* in potentially transformative ways. Public research universities have a responsibility not only to citizenship and civic learning, but also to create the capacity of individuals and communities to productively respond to political contestation.

Many American public universities use approaches to civic engagement and service-learning that introduce students and community members to preexisting civic learning infrastructure (Harkavy 2006; Harkavy et al. 2011; Hartley and Harkavy 2011). By preexisting civic learning infrastructure we mean negotiated partnerships that are entirely conceived by faculty, staff, and/or community-engagement professionals. Of course, structured service experiences that lay the groundwork for more developmentally challenging civic work are appropriate in certain circumstances, such as first-year experience courses (e.g., Priest et al. 2015). However, within more advanced learning contexts (e.g., upper-level courses, adult learning spaces, and collaborative forms of community-engaged scholarship), such traditional, highly structured, and controlled approaches to civic education and civic leadership development can sterilize the messiness involved in civic work, at best, and can perpetuate a range of stereotypes associated with civic work, at worst. Removing the "messiness" from civic work can be efficient and affirming from an administrative perspective. Such protection, direction, and order undermine the type of learning necessary to maneuver and manage politically contested spaces. Instead, it perpetuates transactional community–campus partnerships: civic learning presumes that all values and processes of democratic engagement are cumulative and linear and that civic learning is—and should be—insulated from external critique. In many cases preexisting civic learning infrastructure promotes civic work that is transactional and has resolved potentially politically contested aspects of the work before stakeholders even interact.

Consequently, the well-intentioned infrastructure that often informs civic learning can actually limit the development of students' higher-order civic leadership desires, motivations, skills, and dispositions. They may view civic engagement as merely a noble gesture, without attention to—or understanding of—the moral, social, and political aspects of engagement (Berger 2010). Current approaches to political and civic learning may therefore develop civic-minded graduates who still lack the tacit knowledge, motivations, and practices necessary to intervene in less-than-ideal civic situations. For example, a student participating in a course that uses service-learning may demonstrate the ability to work across differences within a neatly structured community-engagement experience; however, when attempting to exercise inclusive leadership in a business setting that marginalizes segments of the community at the intersection of class and race, they find themselves unable to effectively intervene because they lack the contextual ability to navigate the political contestation associated with marginalization. This example highlights the realities of civic-minded work, which require a more sophisticated set of skills that include working through political contestation to surface common interests and values.

Through our own experience as leadership educators and community-engaged scholars at a large public university, we have developed a deliberative civic engagement framework that positions the political at the center of civic leadership education and development, rather than having points of political contestation negotiated before community is convened to engage in civic work. Integrating elements of community organizing and civic studies (Ganz 2010; Harward 2013; Levine and Soltan 2013; Levy 2013), our approach to civic leader development through community-engaged scholar-ship aims to improve the quality of collective action and decision-making by creating the space for a contextual, community-driven experience that emerges from the political realities of civic challenges.

In this chapter, we outline the rationale for this civic leadership approach by unpacking literature related to deliberative democracy, community-engaged scholarship, and deliberative civic engagement. Next, we offer a narrative framework that can be applied to upper-level civic leadership courses designed to advance civic and political learning outcomes. We locate the theoretical framework within LEAD 405: Leadership in Practice, an upper-level civic leadership course that was offered by the Staley School of Leadership Studies at Kansas State University in the spring semester of 2015. Our work is contextualized within the land-grant tradition, and also an undergraduate leadership studies minor program. The public narra-tive principles associated with the framework (Ganz 2010) are illustrated through the civic work associated with the course. We conclude the chapter with a general discussion of how this approach creates the conditions for an improved civic and political imagination that is necessary to make prog-ress on the tough challenges of the twenty-first century, including specific insights for scholar-practitioners at large public research universities.

DELIBERATIVE DEMOCRACY

Institutions of higher education have historically played a role in cultivat-ing the necessary conditions of democracy and citizenship (Hatcher 1997; Saltmarsh 1996). The underlying presumption is that public education equips students not only with skills, behaviors, and dispositions necessary for democratic engagement, but also with educational practices that have the potential to create the conditions necessary for democracy to flourish in community. Democracy from this perspective is more than a form of government: it is a strategy for sustainable collective action and decision-making in social, political, economic, environmental, and cultural arenas. In a sense democracy becomes an art—a way of being and, at a general level, a way of understanding self in relation to others (Colby et al. 2003). Our understanding of democracy is positioned under the deliberative democracy framework (Gutmann and Thompson 2010; Habermas 1996; Offe and Preuss 1991; Young 2000).

Gutmann and Thompson (2010) distinguished deliberative democracy from other models of democracy in three ways. First, the principles and processes that determine deliberative democracy practices are constantly being reevaluated, which means that points of political contestation, understandings of individual rights, values, and procedural questions are always open to debate and reconsideration. Second, the model assumes that public positions are not fixed. Influencing and creating the conditions to influence viewpoints allow leadership activity to enter the model. Third, the model allows the deliberative process to produce multiple interpretations of individual rights (Gutmann and Thompson 2010). Integrating this broader understanding of democracy within higher education creates the space to include values and processes of democratic engagement into knowledge creation, dissemination, and mobilizing efforts.

THE FIT OF COMMUNITY-ENGAGED SCHOLARSHIP WITHIN THE DELIBERATIVE DEMOCRACY MODEL

Community-engaged scholarship "consists of (1) research, teaching, integration, and application scholarship that (2) incorporate reciprocal practices of civic engagement into the production of knowledge" (Barker 2004, p. 124). Sandmann (2006) noted that "scholarship is *what* is done, engaged scholarships is *how* it is done, and for the common or public good *toward what end it is done*" (p. 82). Community-engaged scholarship in the form of deliberative civic engagement is, therefore, both process and product, informed by a values orientation for the common or public good. Thus, the values and processes associated with community-engaged scholarship are positioned to advance the practices of deliberative democracy.

The two main values of deliberative democracy that inform our approach to community-engaged scholarship are political equality and deliberation. *Political equality* theoretically assumes that each person has an equal chance of participating in decision-making processes and an equal chance of influencing the outcome of a collective decision (Fishkin 2009). The value of equity is demonstrated through "processes that enable citizens, civic leaders, and governmental officials to come together in public spaces where they can engage in constructive, informed, and decisive dialogue about important public issues" (Nabatchi 2012 p. 7). Civic engagement activity is considered *deliberative* when it allows for careful consideration of public issues among community members. More specifically, deliberative civic engagement includes the following four components: (1) a "demographically representative set of peoples," (2) facilitates small group discussions "designed to move talk towards action," (3) provides the opportunity to "compare values and experiences in relation to relevant policy, positions, and information," and (4) functions with an intention to "produce outcomes that more closely align systems, organizations, and institutions with the attitudes and behaviors of citizens" (Leighninger 2012, p. 20). This model of deliberative democracy includes a space for exercising leadership because it is assumed that individuals' political positions and interests are not fixed; rather, they can be influenced through collaborative forms of civic leadership. Furthermore, deliberative democracy allows community-engaged scholarship or engaged discovery to be located within community as a leadership activity. Questions of knowledge, knowledge creation, dissemination, and evaluation are redefined as potential interventions needed to change systems, organizations, and institutions in society.

Political Positions and Interests

To more fully realize the benefits of civic leadership education, in the context of deliberative democracy, the activity should turn more fully toward political questions. A brand of politics that emphasizes position-taking is consistent with political polarization found in the USA (McCarty et al. 2006). Political polarization describes the movement of individuals to the ideological right and left. Functionally, political polarization makes it more difficult for political community to find a common ground of contested issues. In the USA, movement toward the political extreme and away from the middle has been consistent since the 1970s (Dimock et al. 2014). Political polarization makes it very difficult for community to surface common values and interests, and the current default political practice associated with polarization is public position-taking.

Intentional models of deliberative civic engagement and deliberative democracy allow individuals exercising civic leadership to make distinctions between political positions and interests. Public or political positions are defined by "what a person or group wants; they represent the demand being made" (Nabatchi and Leighninger 2015, p. 244). Public or political positions are inherently adversarial and anchored to points of disagreement. In contrast, interests are the "reasons—the needs, values, and concerns—underlying a position; they represent why a person or group wants something" (Nabatchi and Leighninger 2015, p. 244).

Civic leadership activity, in the context of deliberative civic engagement, is centered on creating the conditions for people to make progress by considering potential ways common interests and values overlap (Ganz 2010). An emphasis on finding overlapping interests and values place the focus of civic leadership activity on creating the conditions to work past political polarization. An intentional focus on common interests can overcome forms of disagreement associated with political positions. Individuals exercise leadership in systems, organizations, and institutions through interpersonal, structural, and/or procedural interventions (Ganz 2010). Leveraging community-engaged scholarship to create new processes, devise structural interventions, or build new interpersonal relationships is the point in which knowledge creation and dissemination inherent to community-engaged scholarship touches on political skill and activity. The structure of the deliberative civic engagement process supports disorienting political experiences. Our model assumes that, through disorienting experiences, individuals have the potential to transform the way they think about, understand, and express political activity (Mezirow 1981, 1997). Such a perspective shift can lead to a reformed civic identity and a deeper commitment to activate in civic spaces (Diaz and Perrault 2010; Horton and Freire 1990).

Personal transformation in the context of deliberative civic engagement and civic leadership can lead to a new way to interface with politics. Current political practices emphasize public position-taking, and very few structures encourage individuals to work to find some type of overlapping agreement or consensus. Longo (2013) noted that "deliberative pedagogy in the community" frames a style of education that can lead to a new kind of politics (p. 2). Academic service-learning and forms of community-engaged scholarship can create a space for civic leadership development when individuals are invited to engage in political dialogue, deconstruct traditional models of service, approach civic work from an asset-based perspective, experiment with perspective taking, and understand that civic work is a larger change movement (Koliba 2004). When these conditions are met, forms of community-engaged scholarship prepare citizens with cognitive gains, behaviors, attitudes, and skills that allow them to intervene in educational, workplace, and social arenas using values and processes associated with deliberative democracy frameworks (Diaz and Perrault 2010).

DELIBERATIVE CIVIC ENGAGEMENT FRAMEWORK FOR CIVIC LEADERSHIP DEVELOPMENT

Our framework begins with the assumption that the current political structure primarily supports public position-taking. The factors that contribute to political polarization are complex, but our framework attempts to make progress at the individual level. Specifically, we are interested in how interpersonal relationships respond and contribute to political structure. Imagining a new politics requires creating the conditions for individuals to move beyond the default behavior of position-taking to the behavior of identifying overlapping values and interests (Fig. 3.1).We draw from deliberative civic engagement strategies such as story circles and community-based arts, which have been shown to be effective tools to create such conditions (e.g., Imagining America n.d.; Leonard 2013; O'Neal 2006; O'Neal et al. 2006). The strategies were developed through our work, teaching an upper-level undergraduate leadership in practice course in the spring semester of 2015. We integrated Ganz's (2010) public-narrative approach (story of self, us, and now) into the design of a series of deliberative dialogues as a form of community-engaged scholarship for civic leadership development. The civic purpose of these forums was to increase local community members' leadership capacity, and to inform the strategic planning efforts of our collaborators, the United Way and Harvesters Community Food Network. In doing so, we also explored how community-engagement strategies contributed to students' own civic leadership development.

Twenty undergraduate students facilitated eight community conversations across six local counties. Students were challenged to engage in this work as scholar-practitioners; their role was more than just engaging in the practices of facilitation, and also included intentional participant

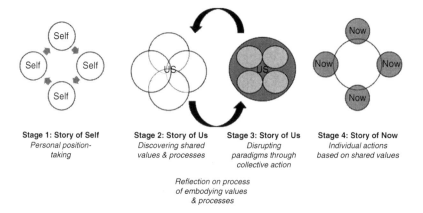

Stage 1: Story of Self
Personal position-taking

Stage 2: Story of Us
Discovering shared values & processes

Stage 3: Story of Us
Disrupting paradigms through collective action

Stage 4: Story of Now
Individual actions based on shared values

Reflection on process of embodying values & processes

Fig. 3.1   Deliberative civic engagement framework for civic leadership development

observation, data collection, reflection, and analysis. They made observations during the conversations, recorded those observations through field notes, and interpreted findings through written reflections and in-class discussion/theming. As a result of the experience, they created a variety of practical and scholarly works designed to help our community collaborators make progress on their goals. Below, we outline each of the stages within our framework (see Fig. 3.1) and provide illustrations from practice.

Stage 1: Story of Self

At this stage of the process, participants were invited into an inclusive- and intentional-designed space to tell their own story. In groups of 12 or less, participants sat in a circle with a facilitator and notetaker/timekeeper. The facilitator asked participants to consider the following prompt: *When have you observed or participated in an experience that helped to make progress on an issue or need facing our community?* Each person around the circle responded in the form of a short (1–3 minute) story. The purpose of responding in storied form, rather than traditional dialogue, is because stories translate values into action; that is, stories reveal "the choices that have made us who we are, and the values that shaped these choices" (Ganz 2010, p. 541). Thus, these individual stories are a form of public position-taking. Facilitation techniques needed to frame this stage of the process include building rapport, encouraging active listening, and creating a sense of community.

Stage 2: Story of Us Part 1 (Common Values and Processes)

Sharing personal stories served as a social transaction that honored the storyteller's past experience, and surfaced positions through the lens of values and processes (Ganz 2010). The next stage reframed the focus of the dialogue from individual positions to overlapping interests and values. Creating the conditions to identify common themes or patterns within the stories is an integral step in imagining a new approach to political activity. We specifically asked community members to identify shared values and processes of civic leadership that were surfaced by the stories, as illustrated by Stage 2 in Fig. 3.1. These themes began to surface a shared story and an emerging collective identity of the group (Ganz 2010). In practical terms, facilitators recorded themes of shared values and processes needed for leadership and change on flip chart paper. This stage relied on traditional modes of communication, knowing, and experiences (using and recording words, phrases, symbols, and images). However, in our framework, the story of us was a two-step process to disrupt common position-taking politics and moving toward a shared interest and value paradigm.

Stage 3: Story of Us Part 2 (Disrupting the Paradigm)

The story of us extended into the next stage, using an approach not common to traditional forms of deliberative civic engagement. Based on the common themes identified, participants were then asked to "embody" the values and processes of leadership and change by arranging their bodies into "story statues" (see Leonard 2013, for examples of applied theater). The rationale to support types of inclusion attached to the story statue is three-fold. First, story statues support more inclusive modes of knowing, experiencing, and being. When capturing common themes, values, experiences, and process, it is easier for some to surface those intersections in ways that feel the most natural to a person. This physical embodiment allows participants to express ideas differently, disrupting dominant patterns of communication and linear patterns of thought while generating alternative ways of communicating, knowing, and experiencing the meaning-making process. Second, the story-statues method is rooted in a collective meaning-making process that runs counter to political position-taking. In order for the story statues to represent the nuances of the conversations, participants often have to collaborate to cocreate a story statue that reflects the complexity of community. Story statues also require a commitment to the group/community that has been formed and a willingness to engage in actions that may feel risky to some participants. Third, the story-statue process also creates a jolting experience for participants that struggle to imagine a politics that moves beyond accepted paradigm of political position-taking.

Ultimately, the underlying goal of the story-statue process invites participants to apply the new mindset to community issues. This form of engagement requires an element of case-in-point facilitation, which creates the conditions for individuals to exercise leadership *in the room* (Green and McBride 2015). In this instance, participants work together to enact the values and processes they have identified as necessary for civic leadership. Through the debriefing process, the facilitator continues to support meaning-making through observation, reflection, and intervention. Thus, the stages of the story of us can be considered an iterative, generative process.

Stage 4: Story of Now (Creating "Next Stories")

The final level of public narrative in our framework is the story of now, which "articulates the urgent challenge to the values that we share that demands action now" (Ganz 2010 p. 18). Considering the shared values and processes participants have generated through the story-circle process, the facilitator asked them to identify (1) a cause or challenge they care about, (2) a role they plan in their own "circle," or sphere of influence, and (3) at least one key action step to make progress on that challenge. The overlapping space of each of these areas was referred to as the participant's "next story." Participants individually crafted their "next story" in writing, also verbally shared their plans with the group as a public commitment to exercise leadership for community change. This framing served as an acknowledgment in advance of how their individual actions would become part of a collective participation under a common interest paradigm (illustrated by the final image in Fig. 3.1).

Learning as Leadership

This deliberative civic engagement activity supported the production of community-engaged scholarship. All data collected from the community conversations (pictures, flip charts, notes, next-stories) were archived and used to create detailed field notes. The field notes were used as a way to capture the features of the community conversation and also served as the basis of data collection that were eventually used to produce scholarly artifacts that synthesized and analyzed the outcomes of the community conversation. In this way, students exercised leadership through their civic engagement and learning.

CONCLUSION

Embracing the political turn of civic leadership education, deliberative civic engagement, and community-engaged scholarship surfaces a series of new theoretical and practical questions for the field. The ecosystem of civic work activity creates the conditions to imagine new ways power, choice, and action can be managed. Reorganizing how community–campus partnerships fit within larger practices of civic activity points to the type of radical institutional change that the *Wingspread Declaration* supported. Not only was our civic work interdisciplinary, but in many ways challenges standard notions of knowing, being, and experiencing in large social–political–economic systems outside of higher education. Our framework provides an approach to not only think about teaching and learning in new ways, but illustrates emergent roles civic learning has in creating new community-centered governance structures. The next phase is to begin determining how civic leadership practices become institutionalized and normed outside of the walls of academe. The capacity to imagine alternative political practices and systems is essential to making progress on the tough challenges of the twenty-first century. Our hope is that this framework is twofold. First, we are calling on civic work practitioner-scholars to turn in toward the political dimensions of the work. Second, we hope practitioner-scholars will understand civic work and application of this framework as a strategic intervention that cultivates the capacity of collective political imagination.

The political is core to civic leadership, deliberative civic engagement, and community-engaged scholarship. The work is collective by nature and requires people to navigate structures of power and a range of choices that determine the scope and breadth of public activity. In the past, traditional forms of academic service-learning and institutions of higher education have kept political questions at arms' length. The tenuous relationship between higher education and the political can be seen in how civic learning is often operationalized in assessment and evaluation frameworks. Most civic learning approaches look to evaluate the potential for political activity, but fail to consider how learning for democracy requires the nuanced application of certain attitudes, dispositions, and behaviors. The type of learning that is required for democracy and civic leadership requires explicit acknowledgment of the political context. It is not enough to develop teaching and learning strategies that emphasize democratic skills and acknowledgment, but are removed from predominant social, political, and economic systems. Our framework calls on the field—and in particular those of us in large public universities—to position civic leadership education, deliberative civic engagement, and community-engaged scholarship activity in the political with the explicit purpose of rebuilding the capacity for political and civic association.

When civic leadership education, deliberative civic engagement, and community-engaged scholarship are leveraged to rebuild political infrastructures, practitioner-scholars push on the limits of objectivity traditionally accepted within higher education. It is important to note we are not calling for civic work to be explicitly partisan; instead, we are calling on practitioner-scholars to intentionally recognize the ways civic work has the potential to reframe the rules of politics to be more just, democratic, and sustainable. Our framework models a way in which civic leadership, deliberative civic engagement, and community-engaged scholarship can be organized to reframe how community understands politics.

Redefining both formal and informal rules of politics requires cultivating a robust collective political imagination. Many communities in the USA find it easier to imagine political and civic catastrophe compared to the mindset required to envision a significantly altered social, political, and economic reality that is more just, democratic, and sustainable. A powerful and dynamic civic and political imagination is what is required to make progress on the tough challenges of the twenty-first century. Recognizing the central role of civic and political imagination elevates the importance of learning in civic leadership and democracy work.

In the current context, authentic learning is an act of civic leadership for democracy. Our framework not only recognizes learning as central to our twenty-first-century democracy but also illustrates the scope and breadth of political activity embedded within civic leadership education, deliberative civic engagement, and community-engaged scholarship. Student learning is absorbed into the larger project of community impact and community-capacity building. The political turn requires practitioner-scholars to examine most assumptions that inform traditional approaches to teaching and learning. For example, students exercising leadership by facilitating in a deliberative civic engagement forum are obviously developing skills and knowledge associated with course objectives.

In many ways, students' learning is framed and evaluated in relation to their academic courses; however, in our suggested framework, students' learning is given context because the facilitation has to respond to real moments of political contestation in community. Learning in the context of deliberative civic engagement and community-engaged scholarship becomes a civic leadership activity when participants are given the space to experiment with interventions that respond to contextual features of deliberation. Learning is not understood through the lens of the academic course; instead, learning becomes a leadership activity that is focused on creating the conditions for an alternative social, political, and economic reality. It is this type of civic leadership activity that can motivate a civic and political imagination toward a more just, democratic, and sustainable world.

REFERENCES

Barker, D. (2004). The scholarship of engagement: A taxonomy of five emerging practices. *Journal of Higher Education Outreach and Engagement, 9*(2), 123–138.

Berger, B. (2010). *Attention deficit democracy: The paradox of civic engagement.* Princeton, NJ: Princeton University Press.

Boyte, H., & Hollander, E. (1999). *Wingspread declaration on renewing the civic mission of the American research university.* Providence, RI: Campus Compact.

Chrislip, D. D., & O'Malley, E. (2013). *For the common good: Redefining civic leadership.* Wichita, KS: Kansas Leadership Center Press.

Colby, A., Ehrlich, T., Beaumont, E., & Stephens, J. (2003). *Educating citizens: Preparing America's undergraduates for lives of moral and civic responsibility.* San Francisco, CA: Jossey-Bass.

Diaz, A., & Perrault, R. (2010). Sustained dialogue and civic life: Post-college impacts. *Michigan Journal of Community Service Learning, 17*(1), 32–43.

Dimock, M., Kiley, J., Keeter, S., & Doherty, C. (2014). *Political polarization in the American publics.* New York, NY: Pew Research Center.

Dugan, J. P., Kodama, C., Correia, B., & Associates. (2013). *Multi-institutional study of leadership insight report: Leadership program delivery.* College Park, MD: National Clearinghouse for Leadership Programs.

Fishkin, J. (2009). *When people speak: Deliberative democracy and public consultation.* Oxford: Oxford University Press.

Ganz, M. (2010). Leading change: Leadership, organization, and social movements. In N. Noharia & R. Khurana (Eds.), *Handbook of leadership theory and practice: A Harvard Business School centennial colloquium* (pp. 527–568). Boston, MA: Harvard Business Review.

Green, C., & McBride, J. F. (2015). *Teaching leadership: Case-in-point, case studies, and coaching.* Wichita, KS: Kansas Leadership Center Press.

Gutmann, A., & Thompson, D. F. (2010). Deliberative democracy. In R. A. Couto (Ed.), *Political and civic leadership: A reference handbook* (pp. 325–332). New York, NY: SAGE Publishing.

Habermas, J. (1996). *Between facts and norms: Contributions to a discourse theory of law and democracy.* Cambridge, MA: MIT Press.

Harkavy, I. (2006). The role of university in advancing citizenship and social justice in the 21st century. *Education, Citizenship, and Social Justice, 1*(1), 5–37.

Harkavy, I., Hartley, M., Weeks, J., & Bowman, C. (2011). A renaissance in college engagement. *Educational Leadership, 68*(8), 58–63.

Hartley, M., & Harkavy, I. (2011). The civic engagement movement and the democratization of the academy. In N. V. Long & C. M. Gibson (Eds.), *From command to community: A new approach to leadership education in college and universities* (pp. 67–89). Medford, MA: Tufts University Press.

Harward, D. W. (Ed.). (2013). *Civic values, civic practices*. Washington, DC: Bringing Theory to Practice.

Hatcher, J. (1997). The moral dimensions of John Dewey's philosophy: Implications for undergraduate education. *Michigan Journal of Community Service Learning, 4*(1), 22–29.

Heifetz, R., Grashow, A., & Linsky, M. (2009). *The practice of adaptive leadership: Tools and tactics for changing your organization and your world*. Boston, MA: Harvard Business Press.

Horton, M., & Freire, P. (1990). *We make the road by walking: Conversations on education and social change*. Philadelphia, PA: Temple University Press.

Imagining America. (n.d.). *Story circles as ongoing collaborative evaluation—Roadside theater's "Story to performance."* http://imaginingamerica.org/fg-item/story-circles-as-ongoing-and-collaborative-evaluation-roadside-theaters-story-to-performance/?parent=10511.

Kliewer, B. W. (2013). Why the civic engagement movement cannot achieve democracy and justice aims. *Michigan Journal of Community Service Learning, 19*(20), 72–79.

Koliba, C. (2004). Service-learning and the downsizing of democracy: Learning our way out. *Michigan Journal of Community Service Learning, 10*(2), 57–68.

Leighninger, M. (2012). Mapping deliberative civic engagement: Pictures from a (r)evolution. In T. Nabatchi, J. G. Gastil, G. M. Weiksner, & M. Leighninger (Eds.), *Democracy in motion: Evaluating the practice and impact of deliberative civic engagement* (pp. 19–40). Oxford: Oxford University Press.

Leonard, R. H. (2013). Building home: Dramaturgy for theater as civic practice. *Public, 2*(1). http://public.imaginingamerica.org/blog/article/building-home-dramaturgy-for-theater-as-civic-practice/.

Levine, P., & Soltan, K. E. (2013). *Civic studies*. Washington, DC: Bringing Theory to Practice.

Levy, J. (2013). *Cesar Chavez: Autobiography of La Causa*. Minneapolis, MN: University of Minnesota Press.

Longo, N. (2013). Deliberative pedagogy in the community: Connecting deliberative dialogue, community engagement, and democratic education. *Journal of Public Discussion, 9*(2), Article 16. http://www.publicdeliberation.net/jpd/vol9/iss2/art16.

Mathews, D. (2014). *The ecology of democracy: Finding ways to have a stronger hand in shaping our future*. Dayton, OH: The Kettering Foundation.

McCarty, N., Poole, K. T., & Rosenthal, H. (2006). *Polarized America: The dance of ideology and unequal riches*. Boston, MA: The MIT Press.

Mezirow, J. D. (1981). A critical theory of adult learning and education. *Adult Education Quarterly, 32*(1), 3–24.

Mezirow, J. D. (1997). Transformative learning: Theory and practice. *New Directions for Adult and Continuing Education, 74*, 5–12.

Nabatchi, T. (2012). Introduction to deliberative civic engagement. In T. Nabatchi, J. G. Gastil, G. M. Weiksner, & M. Leighninger (Eds.), *Democracy in motion: Evaluating the practice and impact of deliberative civic engagement* (pp. 3–17). Oxford: Oxford University Press.

Nabatchi, T., & Leighninger, M. (2015). *Public participation for 21st century democracy.* Hoboken, NJ: Wiley.

O'Neal, J. (2006). *Using art and theater to support organizing for justice.* New Orleans, LA: Junebug Productions, Inc.

O'Neal, B., Hofmann, A., & Rao, S. (2006). *Storytelling in the name of justice.* New Orleans, LA: Junebug Productions, Inc.

Offe, C., & Preuss, U. K. (1991). Democratic institutions and moral resources. In D. Held (Ed.), *Political theory today* (pp. 143–171). Palo Alto, CA: Stanford University Press.

Priest, K. L., Bauer. T., & Fine, L. (2015). The hunger project: Exercising civic leadership *with* the community *for* the common good in an introductory leadership course. *Journal of Leadership Education, 14*(2), 218–228. DOI: 1012806/V14/I2/AB2

Rowlands, J. (1997). *Questioning empowerment: Working with women in Honduras.* London: Oxfam.

Saltmarsh, J. (1996). Education for critical citizenship: John Dewey's contribution to the pedagogy of community service learning. *Michigan Journal of Community Service Learning, 3*(1), 13–21.

Saltmarsh, J., & Hartley, M. (Eds.). (2011). *"To serve a larger purpose": Engagement for democracy and the transformation of higher education.* Philadelphia, PA: Temple University Press.

Sandmann, L. R. (2006). Scholarship as architecture: Framing and enhancing community engagement. *Journal of Physical Therapy Education, 20*(3), 80–84.

Steinberg, K., Hatcher, J. A., & Bringle, R. G. (2011). Civic-minded graduates: A north star. *Michigan Journal of Community Service Learning, 18*(1), 19–33.

Wolin, A. (2004). *Politics and vision.* Princeton, NJ: Princeton University Press.

Young, I. M. (2000). *Inclusion and democracy.* New York, NY: Oxford University Press.

CHAPTER 4

Civic and Community Engagement Impact on Economically Disadvantaged Students

Victoria Porterfield

Civic engagement through community service and political activities has been integral to the practice of higher education for over a century. Civic engagement yields benefits to the individual and society at large; however, the landscape of higher education has changed dramatically over the recent past. Many institutions are faced with urgent issues that go to the heart of what higher education is and does, and as such, the significance of civic education has essentially been placed on the back burner. Although recent attention to the decline of civic engagement has caused many universities to reevaluate their practices and recommit to practices that foster civic engagement, young adults are still voting at historically low rates (File 2013). Moreover, young individuals from disadvantaged groups, mainly lower socioeconomic status and racial/ethnic minority groups, are less engaged in community and political activities (Pasek et al. 2006). Students from disadvantaged backgrounds may not engage civically due to the lower quality of their education (Flanagan and Levine 2010; Kawashima-Ginsberg and Levine 2014) and are less likely to have parents who engage in these activities that influence students' civic behavior and social capital (Flanagan and Levine 2010; Morimoto and Friedland 2013). Therefore, civic education in colleges and universities can play a critical role for these groups—especially at large public research universities that are explicitly charged with promoting such work (Boyte and Hollander 1999).

© The Editor(s) (if applicable) and The Author(s) 2016
K.M. Soria, T.D. Mitchell (eds.), *Civic Engagement
and Community Service at Research Universities*,
DOI 10.1057/978-1-137-55312-6_4

63

A careful evaluation needs to be conducted to determine whether public research universities are adequately addressing the civic education needs of students from disadvantaged backgrounds, and if not, what they can do to improve these conditions.

CIVIC ENGAGEMENT IN THE USA

Active and strong civic engagement is an essential piece of maintaining an effective democracy. Civic engagement often incorporates both political and community engagement because it involves meeting the needs of community (community engagement) and involves political and social activism to address and solve issues (political engagement) (Chapman 2014). Therefore, these two aspects are often intertwined when discussing and/or analyzing civic engagement.

Voting is a critical component of civic engagement often referred to as one's "civic duty." Yet, in the USA, many eligible individuals do not vote or may vote without being fully informed. Higher education can play a role in improving knowledge and engagement that will better prepare eligible citizens to make informed voting choices. Since higher levels of education are positively correlated with voter registration and turnout, the important role that higher education plays in eliciting positive civic behaviors is evident (The National Task Force on Civic Learning and Democratic Engagement 2012).

Students' political civic engagement is not limited to voting. Higher education can better prepare students for roles as leaders in the community. Student government and other organizations also provide opportunities for students to learn about and engage in community service. Leadership in these groups can be good training for future roles in the community (Astin and Astin 2000; Dugan 2006; Soria et al. 2013a). Civic engagement has also been found to have positive benefits to individual students (Astin and Sax 1998; Cress et al. 2001; Knefelkamp 2008). For example, Astin and Sax (1998) found that undergraduates who participated in volunteer service programs had enhanced academic development, civic responsibility, and life skills.

Involvement with civic and/or community service also provides students with the opportunity to work with other students from different backgrounds. Enhancing diversity has become more linked with the civic mission of higher education institutions (Hurtado 2007); however, because many public secondary schools in the USA are organized regionally and often with respect to socioeconomic status and racial makeup, they tend to lack the diversity that many college and university environments offer. Therefore, attending higher education institutions may present the first opportunity that students from different backgrounds will work collectively with one another. Civic and/or community service also exposes students to a more diverse community at large. Heightened exposure to individuals from different backgrounds provides students with broader perspectives about the world around them, all of which can lead to the development of more well-rounded individuals.

Decline in Civic Engagement

Despite the importance of civic engagement in higher education during the nineteenth century and most of the past century, overall civic involvement has declined since the 1980s (Bryant et al. 2012; Pryor et al. 2007; Putnam 2000). What caused this drop in civic involvement among college and university students? A compelling argument is that competing agendas within higher education have made it more difficult to focus on the civic engagement objective. According to Wellman (2000), "Part of the reason that civic teaching and service activities are not assessed or accounted for is because these roles are not a high priority either for the institutions or their patrons" (p. 328). As financial resources have become scarce in higher education, more emphasis has been placed on areas in high demand, such as job training.

One might blame student indifference to community and political awareness for lower levels of civic and political engagement; however, student apathy does not appear to be a reason for this decline. Pryor et al. (2007) examined 40-year trends using data collected through the CIRP Freshmen Survey. The researchers found that, while there was a large deterioration of student political involvement over the course of time, aspects of community involvement such as volunteer work increased. Additionally, they found that community service activities in the last year of analysis were the highest they had been in 20 years. Therefore, students do not appear to be unconcerned about civic work; instead, they are less concerned about politics. Political disengagement is further demonstrated by declining voter participation of Americans between the ages of 18 and 24 since 1964 (File 2013). Younger Americans are also much less likely to vote compared to older age groups, particularly in nonpresidential election years (File 2013). Such evidence of political disengagement suggests that more attention needs to be paid to enhancing political involvement among college-aged youth.

Impacts on Students from Disadvantaged Backgrounds

Students from disadvantaged backgrounds—particularly students from low-income households and underrepresented minorities such as Black and Hispanic students—are perceived to be less likely to engage politically or civically. Pasek et al. (2006) surveyed over 1500 young people between the ages of 14 and 22 using the 2004 National Annenberg Risk Survey of Youth. Their findings revealed that Black and Hispanic youths and individuals from low-income households were significantly less likely to engage in political or civic activity.

The impact of the falloff in civic engagement may be the most severe for students from disadvantaged backgrounds because they may lack the early exposure to political and civic engagement that students from more affluent backgrounds receive. Since parental civic engagement is positively associated with student engagement, many students who come from disadvantaged backgrounds will have little or no civic participation because their parents are not civically engaged (Flanagan and Levine 2010).

Higher education institutions expect students to demonstrate leadership qualities and high levels of civic engagement upon entry; however, the expectation can cause a dilemma for students from disadvantaged backgrounds, such as low income, minority, and with parents who did not attend higher education. These factors make it more difficult to prepare for these entrance requirements, which are often left out of secondary schools' coursework. Morimoto and Friedland (2013) found that high school students from working-class families who were motivated to help others did not have the social or cultural capital to transform their activities into academic pursuits. Students from middle-class and wealthy backgrounds were more goal-oriented with their activities, which may stem from having a greater understanding of how to prepare for higher education.

The quality of education that fosters civic engagement can exacerbate inequalities for students from different backgrounds. For instance, Kawashima-Ginsberg and Levine (2014) surveyed over 4000 American citizens between the ages of 18 and 24 and found students who reported higher quality civics education in high school were from wealthier districts and had significantly higher levels of electoral engagement and informed voting. This research lends support to the argument that the inequality gap further marginalizes students from disadvantaged backgrounds since quality civic education is largely dependent on one's household income (Flanagan and Levine 2010).

Social networks appear to be significant in transmitting civic-mindedness to students. Family life appears to have an influence on civic behavior. Children with parents who volunteer to activist or nonactivist causes are more likely to volunteer to causes similar to their parents (Caputo 2010). Likewise, having family and close friends who vote is positively correlated with a student's intention to vote (Glynn et al. 2009). Other aspects of individuals' social networks, such as a church or place of work, can also impact students' civic behavior.

Students from higher socioeconomic backgrounds are more likely to be exposed to civic learning at earlier ages through their community and educational setting. According to Kawashima-Ginsberg (2013), the results of the National Assessment of Educational Progress (NAEP) Civics test revealed that secondary school students from affluent communities were more likely to be exposed to civic learning opportunities when compared to students from lower socioeconomic backgrounds. On the other hand, Caputo (2010) found that students from poorer backgrounds were 1.4 times less likely to volunteer to nonactivist causes when compared to students from affluent backgrounds. Since students from wealthier backgrounds are more likely to be civically involved before going into the university setting, they are less likely to be impacted by the decline of civic engagement in higher education. However, the decline in civic engagement in higher education can be detrimental to students from disadvantaged backgrounds.

Research Questions

The existence of factors that exacerbate inequalities also highlight the important potentially remedial role that higher education institutions can play in meeting the need for civic engagement. The importance of civic involvement for higher education institutions has received renewed attention; yet, civic engagement is still lower than it has been in the past. According to the literature, this is particularly true for political engagement. Voting is remarkably low for college-aged individuals, despite the rise in higher education access. About half of Americans between the ages of 18 and 29 voted in the 2008 election (Kirby and Kawashima-Ginsberg 2009); however, significant disparities in voting behaviors are evident among college and university students. While 82.5 % of White undergraduate seniors voted in the 2008 election, only 66.9 % of Asian students voted (Higher Education Research Institute 2010). In a national sample of 18–29 year olds, Latinos were reported to have a significantly lower voting rate compared to their peers from other racial and ethnic backgrounds (Center for Information and Research on Civic Learning and Engagement 2008).

Ultimately, the lack of emphasis on civic education from a college or university could have harmful effects on students, and also the nation at large; however, the research on voting behavior and community service activity reveals that students from disadvantaged backgrounds are less likely to engage civically relative to their peers, resulting in detrimental effects that could affect their academic development, civic responsibility, and life skills (Astin and Sax 1998). Since the impact of higher education may not be discernible in early undergraduate years, voting and community service behavior may change for these groups, the longer the students attend higher education. Therefore, it becomes increasingly important for colleges and universities to discover factors that encourage students from disadvantaged backgrounds to vote and the motivations that encourage these students from disadvantaged backgrounds to perform community service.

To overcome some of those barriers, faculty and staff can implement practices to encourage students from underrepresented backgrounds in developing political and civic engagement. For instance, factors such as time spent inside the classroom discussing and reflecting on social issues may reveal areas that are working well or can be improved upon to expand civic engagement at their institution; however, the efficacy of these areas in promoting students' political engagement is, to date, unknown. Therefore, the purpose of this chapter is to answer the following research questions:

1. Does discussion of and reflection upon social issues in the classroom promote voting behaviors for students from underrepresented backgrounds?
2. Does discussion of and reflection upon social issues in the classroom promote community service participation for students from underrepresented backgrounds?

DATA AND METHODS

Data Collection

The Student Experience in the Research University (SERU) survey is based at the Center for Studies of Higher Education at the University of California, Berkeley. The SERU survey is administered via email to all undergraduate students in participating institutions during the spring semester. Each student responds to a series of questions that evaluates the student's major, time use, campus climate, and satisfaction, which is followed by questions from one of four randomly assigned modules. This analysis used information from the community and civic engagement module from the 2013 administration which included questions regarding the 2012 presidential election.

A total of 109,065 students over the age of 18 from 13 large universities completed the SERU survey. These institutions are classified by the Carnegie Foundation as having very high research activity and are located across the USA, with two in the Northeast, four in the Midwest, two on the West Coast, three in the Southeast, and two in the South. The response rate for the overall survey was 30.6 %, reasonable for most student web-based surveys. However, this trend is a persistent limitation in its ability to perfectly predict the behaviors of the entire student community (Groves et al. 2009). The community and civic engagement module was completed by 10 % of all undergraduate students ($n = 10,886$). International students ($n = 426$) were removed from the dataset because they are not eligible to vote in the USA.

Respondent Profile

A description of students in this sample used for this study is reported in Table 4.1. Most students were female (61.1 %), upperclassmen (25.2 % juniors and 43.7 % seniors), White (66.2 %), and came from schools in the Southeast (35 %). Only 5.2 % of students were first-generation undergraduate students and 21.3 % came from households that had a self-reported family income below $50,000.

Variables

Dependent Variables

Voting. Students were asked whether they voted in the 2012 presidential election. The variable was dummy coded to indicate whether a student voted (1 = Yes, 0 = No).

Community service. Students were asked whether they performed community service during the academic year. The variable was dummy coded to indicate whether a student performed community service (1 = Yes, 0 = No).

Table 4.1   Respondent demographics ($n = 10,460$)

Category	Number of respondents	Percent of respondents
Gender		
Male	4049	38.9 %
Female	6391	61.1 %
Class level		
Freshmen	1198	11.5 %
Sophomore	2053	19.6 %
Junior	2639	25.2 %
Senior	4570	43.7 %
Race/ethnicity		
Black	515	4.9 %
Hispanic	1128	10.8 %
Other	1889	18.1 %
White	6928	66.2 %
Parent education		
No parent went to college	545	5.2 %
At least one parent went to college	9915	94.8 %
Household income		
Under $50,000	2228	21.3 %
$50,000–$99,999	3381	32.3 %
$100,000–$199,999	3406	32.6 %
More than $200,000	1445	13.8 %
University regions		
Southeast	3665	35.0 %
Midwest	2613	25.0 %
South	1976	18.9 %
West Coast	971	9.3 %
Northeast	1235	11.8 %

Factor Analysis Variables

The survey included items that were related to activities students might do in the classroom that would foster greater civic engagement. Researchers have found evidence for the importance of social perspective-taking among undergraduates, for example, in fostering their appreciation of diversity, community engagement, and engagement in creating social change (Johnson et al. 2015; Soria et al. 2013b). In the survey, students were asked "in the classroom, how often do you" and responded to ten items on a frequency scale of one (never) to six (very often) (Table 4.2). A factor analysis was conducted on these ten items with an oblique rotation (varimax). The Kaiser-Meyer-Olkin measure verified the sampling adequacy for the analyses (KMO = 0.92). Three components were retained with an eigenvalue greater than 0.7 and explained 83.6 % of the variance. These three components

Table 4.2 Summary of rotated factor pattern for classroom activities

Item	Social perspective-taking ($\alpha=0.90$)	Identifying challenges and solutions ($\alpha=0.92$)	Reflection and action on community issues ($\alpha=0.91$)
Appreciate the world from someone else's perspective	**0.820**	0.265	0.326
Acknowledge personal differences	**0.779**	0.153	0.371
Interact with someone with views that are different from your own	**0.756**	0.435	0.138
Discuss and navigate controversial issues	**0.663**	0.443	0.366
Implement a solution to an issue or challenge	0.176	**0.846**	0.330
Reflect upon the solution of an issue or challenge	0.335	**0.811**	0.334
Define an issue or challenge and identify possible solutions	0.440	**0.789**	0.204
Act on community or social issues	0.236	0.237	**0.864**
Reflect on your responsibility for community or social issues	0.422	0.394	**0.741**
Reflect on community or social issues as a shared responsibility	0.454	0.439	**0.674**

were identified as *social perspective-taking*, *identifying challenges and solutions*, and *reflection and action on community issues*. The rotated patterns of the three components are displayed in Table 4.2, with factor loadings above 0.60 in bold. Each component had high reliability with Cronbach's alpha ≥ 0.90. Factor scores for each component were computed using the regression method and standardized to have a mean of zero and a standard deviation of one. The range of the factor scores for *social perspective-taking* is (−3.88, 3.59), *identifying challenges and solutions* is (−3.97, 3.64), and *reflection and action on community issues* is (−3.92, 3.21).

Covariates

The demographic variables used in analyses were dummy-coded. Students were considered to come from low-income households if their annual household income was less than $50,000, which is the maximum household income for most Pell grant recipients (Baum et al. 2013). The variables of particular interest are the race/ethnic groups, first-generation students, and students from low-income households, as these students are traditionally considered to come from disadvantaged backgrounds (Flanagan and Levine 2010; Morimoto and Friedland 2013; Pasek et al. 2006). Contextual effects, such as the specific university in which students were enrolled, were also of interest.

Analytic Methods

A series of logistic regression models were estimated to predict the probabilities of voting and community service participation. Models were estimated to examine the effect of focal independent variables on the probability of voting and community service while controlling for relevant covariates, which should help make the model estimates more precise. For each dependent variable, three models were run with each model incrementally including more variables in an effort to determine how the effect of the focal variables change across models and improvements in model fit. The first model included all the focal independent variables, and the second model included all focal independent variables and all demographic covariates. The final model displayed below included regional fixed effects that control for all the unmeasured, time invariant factors within university region.

Results are reported in the form of raw coefficients, odds ratios, marginal effects, and predicted probabilities. Regression coefficients and standard errors for each variable and the corresponding odds ratios for voting and community service behavior models are displayed in Tables 4.3 (voting) and 4.4 (community service). Since the third model included all the relevant covariates and the regional fixed effects, and produced the highest pseudo R^2 for both voting and community service behavior, it was retained for interpretation. Predicted probabilities(shown in Table 4.5) were calculated to estimate the probability of an outcome occurring (voting or community service) for each independent variable based on the model. Predicted probabilities were calculated for each discrete variable holding all other variables at their means (e.g., the probability of voting for the typical female when average scores on all the other variables is 73.9 %). Predicted probabilities for the factor scores (i.e., the focal variables) show the probability of voting for students engaged in social perspective-taking, or identification of challenges and solutions or reflection/action on community issues holding all other independent variables

Table 4.3 Logistic regression of voting behavior

	Model 1		Model 2		Model 3	
	Coefficient (SE)	Odds ratio	Coefficient (SE)	Odds ratio	Coefficient (SE)	Odds ratio
Classroom activities						
Social perspective-taking	0.20 (0.02)**	1.22	0.15 (0.02)**	1.16	0.14 (0.02)**	1.15
Identifying challenges and solutions	0.08 (0.02)**	1.08	0.03 (0.02)	1.04	0.04 (0.02)	1.04
Reflection and action on community issues	−0.00 (0.02)	1.00	0.03 (0.02)	1.03	0.02 (0.02)	1.02
Demographics						
Female			0.20 (0.05)**	1.23	0.21 (0.05)**	1.24
Freshmen			−0.36 (0.07)**	0.70	−0.28 (0.07)**	0.75
Sophomore			−0.11 (0.06)	0.89	−0.10 (0.06)	0.90
Junior			−0.07 (0.06)	0.94	−0.06 (0.06)	0.95
Black (non-Hispanic)			−0.05 (0.11)	0.95	−0.05 (0.11)	0.93
Hispanic			−0.54 (0.07)**	0.58	−0.43 (0.07)**	0.65
Other race/ethnicity			−1.22 (0.06)**	0.30	−1.20 (0.06)**	0.30
First-generation college			−0.18 (0.10)	0.83	−0.15 (0.10)	0.86
Students from low-income households			−0.42 (0.05)**	0.66	−0.43 (0.06)**	0.65
Regional factors						
Southeast					0.37 (0.08)**	1.44
Midwest					0.27 (0.08)**	1.31
South					−0.42 (0.08)**	0.66
West Coast					−0.08 (0.09)	0.93
Constant	0.89 (0.02)**		1.28 (0.05)**		1.15 (0.07)**	
Pseudo R^2	0.01		0.06		0.08	

Note: *indicates statistically significant at $0.05 < p < 0.01$, ** indicates statistically significant at $p < 0.01$, unstandardized coefficients are reported. Standardized coefficients with a mean of 0 and a standard deviation of 1 were generated and yielded similar patterns between the three models

Table 4.4 Logistic regression of community service participation

	Model 1		Model 2		Model 3	
	Coefficient (SE)	Odds ratio	Coefficient (SE)	Odds ratio	Coefficient (SE)	Odds ratio
Classroom activities						
Social perspective-taking	0.21 (0.02)**	1.23	0.16 (0.02)**	1.17	0.17 (0.02)**	1.19
Identifying challenges and solutions	0.05 (0.02)	1.05	0.04 (0.02)	1.04	0.04 (0.02)*	1.04
Reflection and action on community issues	0.25 (0.02)**	1.29	0.23 (0.02)**	1.26	0.23 (0.02)**	1.26
Demographics						
Female			0.58 (0.04)**	1.79	0.59 (0.04)**	1.80
Freshmen			-0.17 (0.07)*	0.84	-0.16 (0.07)*	0.85
Sophomore			-0.00 (0.06)	0.99	0.03 (0.06)	1.03
Junior			-0.01 (0.05)	0.99	0.01 (0.05)	1.01
Black (non-Hispanic)			0.17 (0.10)	1.19	0.13 (0.10)	1.14
Hispanic			0.01 (0.07)	1.01	-0.15 (0.07)*	0.86
Other race/ethnicity			-0.02 (0.06)	0.98	0.02 (0.06)	1.02
First-generation college			-0.03 (0.10)	0.97	-0.05 (0.10)	0.95
Students from low-income households			-0.28 (0.05)**	0.76	-0.27 (0.05)**	0.76
Regional factors						
Southeast					0.46 (0.07)**	1.58
Midwest					-0.04 (0.07)	0.96
South					0.70 (0.08)**	2.02
West Coast					-0.00 (0.09)	1.00
Constant	0.68 (0.02)**		0.42 (0.04)**		0.15 (0.07)*	
Pseudo R^2	0.01		0.04		0.05	

Note: *indicates statistically significant at $0.05 < p < 0.01$, **indicates statistically significant at $p < 0.01$, unstandardized coefficients are reported. Standardized coefficients with a mean of 0 and a standard deviation of 1 were generated and yielded similar patterns between the three models

Table 4.5 Predicted probabilities and marginal effects of voting and community service

	Probability of voting ($Y=1$)	Marginal effect (SE)	Probability of community service ($Y=1$)	Marginal effect (SE)
Classroom activities				
Social perspective-taking	0.723	0.027 (0.005)**	0.671	0.038 (0.005)**
Identifying challenges and solutions	0.723	0.007 (0.005)	0.671	0.010 (0.005)*
Reflection and action on community issues	0.723	0.004 (0.005)	0.671	0.051 (0.005)**
Demographics				
Female	0.739	0.043 (0.010)**	0.719	0.132 (0.010)**
Freshmen	0.670	-0.060 (0.016)**	0.639	-0.036 (0.016)*
Sophomore	0.706	-0.021 (0.013)	0.675	0.006 (0.012)
Junior	0.715	-0.010 (0.012)	0.672	0.002 (0.012)
Black (non-Hispanic)	0.709	-0.015 (0.022)	0.698	0.029 (0.022)
Hispanic	0.639	-0.093 (0.017)**	0.640	-0.034 (0.016)*
Other race/ethnicity	0.493	-0.271 (0.013)**	0.674	0.003 (0.013)
First-generation college	0.693	-0.031 (0.021)	0.661	-0.010 (0.022)
Students from low-income households	0.651	-0.090 (0.012)**	0.622	-0.062 (0.012)**
Regional factors				
Southeast	0.768	0.072 (0.014)**	0.733	0.098 (0.015)**
Midwest	0.762	0.053 (0.015)**	0.664	-0.009 (0.012)
South	0.650	-0.089 (0.018)**	0.783	0.142 (0.015)**
West Coast	0.701	-0.016 (0.020)	0.670	-0.000 (0.020)

Note: *indicates statistically significant at $0.05 < p < 0.01$, **indicates statistically significant at $p < 0.01$

at their means. Marginal effects are also computed (Table 4.5) for each independent variable, and are interpreted as the change in the probability of voting/community service for a small change (for continuous variables) or a discrete change (in dichotomous variables) in the variable.

Additionally, predicted probabilities for ideal types of students were computed to summarize the effects of key variables. The predicted probabilities of voting and community service by student type were calculated using the significant predictors in the regression models. Due to the indistinguishability of the other ethnic/race category, these students were removed from this analysis. The maximum and minimum factor scores of classroom activities were used to determine whether these activities had an effect on civic engagement, particularly among Hispanic students and students from low-income households.

RESULTS

As mentioned above, the results are reported in the form of raw coefficients, odds ratios, as well as marginal effects and predicted probabilities. The reported results had similar trends and revealed that certain classroom activities enhanced voting and community service activity. Social perspective-taking had a significant positive effect on both voting and community service. The other two factor variables—identifying challenges and solutions and reflection/action on community issues—have positive significant effects on community service behavior, but these factors did not appear to contribute to voting behavior. According to the calculated odds ratios in Tables 4.3 and 4.4, social perspective-taking increases the odds of voting by 15 % and the odds of community service participation by 19 %. Identifying challenges and solutions in the classroom increases the odds of community service participation by 4 % and reflection and action on community issues in the classroom increases the odds of community service participation by 26 %.

Additionally, predicted probabilities in Table 4.5 demonstrate that students who engaged in social perspective-taking are predicted to have a 72.3 % probability of voting and 67.1 % probability of engaging in community service. All other independent variables are set at their mean when calculating these probabilities. The marginal effects show that a unit increase in social perspective-taking increases the probability of voting by 2.7 % and that of community service participation by 3.8 %. Also, a small increase in engaging in identifying challenges and solutions in the classroom increases the probability of community service by 1 %, while small increases in reflection and action on community issues in the classroom increases community service by 5.1 %.

The results of the model also suggest that Hispanic students and students from low-income households are both significantly less likely to vote and perform community service. Additionally, first-year students are also significantly less likely to perform these activities. Students from other non-White backgrounds are also much less likely to vote. On the other hand, females are significantly more likely to vote and perform community service.

The results of the predicted probability of voting based on student characteristics of interest and classroom engagement that were significant are shown in Table 4.6. Students who are Hispanic and from low-income households are least likely to vote when compared to students from less disadvantaged backgrounds, but their probabilities are affected by the amount of classroom civic engagement. For instance, the probability of voting for a Hispanic student from a low-income household who reported low levels of social perspective-taking was approximately 44 %, whereas the same type of student who reported high levels of social perspective-taking had a 69 % chance of voting. As the level of classroom civic engagement went from low to high, the probability for a Hispanic student from a low-income household to vote increased by 25 % where the level of engagement had less of an effect on a White student who was not from a low-income household (19 %).

The results of predicted probabilities of community service participation based on the same type of students profiled in Table 4.6 are shown in Table 4.7. Similar to voting results, students from Hispanic and low-income households are least likely to perform community service when compared to students from less disadvantaged backgrounds, but their

Table 4.6 Predicted voting rates based on classroom engagement for students from disadvantaged backgrounds

Classroom activity	Level of participation	Not low income		Low income	
		White	Hispanic	White	Hispanic
Social perspective-taking	High	0.84	0.77	0.77	0.69
	Moderate	0.76	0.67	0.67	0.57
	Low	0.65	0.54	0.54	0.44

Table 4.7   Predicted community service participation rates based on classroom engagement for students from disadvantaged backgrounds

Classroom activity	Level of participation	Not low income		Low income	
		White	Hispanic	White	Hispanic
Social perspective-taking	High	0.66	0.60	0.62	0.56
	Moderate	0.51	0.45	0.48	0.41
	Low	0.35	0.29	0.32	0.26
Identifying challenge and solutions	High	0.55	0.48	0.51	0.44
	Moderate	0.51	0.45	0.48	0.41
	Low	0.47	0.41	0.44	0.37
Reflection and action on community issues	High	0.69	0.63	0.65	0.59
	Moderate	0.51	0.45	0.48	0.41
	Low	0.30	0.25	0.27	0.22
All classroom activities	High	0.82	0.78	0.80	0.75
	Moderate	0.51	0.45	0.48	0.41
	Low	0.16	0.13	0.14	0.11

probabilities are affected by the amount of classroom civic engagement. However, the probabilities for all student types increased at the same relative rate across all three types of classroom activities separately and combined.

DISCUSSION

The results of this study suggest social perspective-taking has a significant positive effect on all students' probability of voting and participating in community service. Students who were asked to identify challenge/solutions to social problems and reflect/act on community issues in the classroom were also more likely to participate in community service.

Additionally, the results of this study suggest Hispanic students and students from lower-income households are significantly less likely to vote and perform community service—findings corroborated by previous research (Center for Information and Research on Civic Learning and Engagement 2008). Females are more likely to vote and participate in community service—findings also corroborated by prior research (Higher Education Research Institute 2010). Hispanic students and students from low-income backgrounds were more likely to participate in voting and community service if they had increased rates of social perspective-taking. These results suggest that increased opportunities to connect with classmates in the classroom and develop perspective-taking skills (e.g., appreciating the world from someone else's perspective, acknowledging personal differences, interacting with someone with views that are different from your own, and discussing and navigating controversial issues) are potentially quite powerful ways to foster civic engagement among students who traditionally have the lowest civic engagement rates compared to their peers.

For the most part, the findings in this chapter suggest that classroom activities can enhance civic engagement among students from disadvantaged backgrounds; however, the current study has some limitations. The declining response rates of undergraduate surveys have made the ability to predict the behaviors of the entire student community more questionable. Although the current response rate is in line with that of many web-based undergraduate surveys, it is important to address the limitation and its potential effect on the quality of student representation. The findings also did not yield significant negative results for Black students and students who are the first in their families to attend higher education—a finding likely due to the relatively low number of students in these categories, as well as the larger Black voter turnout during the 2008 and 2012 elections (Higher Education Research Institute 2010; Taylor 2012).

As the data in this study and previous research shows, students from disadvantaged backgrounds are less likely to be civically engaged; however, these students appear to yield greater gains in voting rates when exposed to a high level of classroom civic engagement and are also likely to increase their probability of performing community service by a substantial amount. These findings suggest that students from disadvantaged backgrounds can be greatly impacted by the university environment, particularly civically engaging activities in the classroom.

The current study demonstrates the importance that university classroom activities have on fostering overall civic engagement. Although the focus on this study is on students from disadvantaged backgrounds, it is also evident that civically engaging classroom activities enhances voting rates and community service participation for all students. The significant positive effect of all three classroom activities on community service participation as well as the significant positive effect of social perspective-taking on voting suggests that the quality of classroom activities is essential to enhance civic engagement among undergraduate students. Therefore, incorporating aspects into a classroom that can foster greater civic engagement such as discussions among students where issues are defined, reflected on, and/or acted on is encouraged whenever possible.

REFERENCES

Astin, A. W., & Astin, H. S. (2000). *Leadership reconsidered: Engaging higher education in social change*. Battle Creek, MI: W. K. Kellogg Foundation.

Astin, A. W., & Sax, L. J. (1998). How undergraduates are affected by service participation. *Journal of College Student Development, 39*(3), 215–263.

Baum, S., Bailey, T., Bettinger, E., Dynarski, S., Hauptman, A., Holzer, H., et al. (2013). *Rethinking Pell grants*. New York, NY: College Board Advocacy & Policy Center.

Boyte, H., & Hollander, E. (1999). *Wingspread declaration on renewing the civic mission of the American research university*. Providence, RI: Campus Compact.

Bryant, A., Gayles, J. G., & Davis, H. A. (2012). The relationship between civic behavior and civic values: A conceptual model. *Research in Higher Education, 53*(1), 76–93.

Caputo, R. K. (2010). Family characteristics, public program participation, and civic engagement. *Journal of Sociology & Social Welfare, 37*(2), 35–61.

Center for Information & Research on Civic Learning & Engagement (CIRCLE). (2008). *Trends by race, ethnicity and gender*. Medford, MA: Tufts University Tisch College of Citizenship and Public Service.

Chapman, C. (2014). A civic engagement graduation requirement on an urban college campus. *International Journal of Civic Engagement and Social Change, 1*(4), 1–27.

Cress, C. M., Astin, H. S., Zimmerman-Oster, K., & Burkhardt, J. C. (2001). Developmental outcomes of college students' involvement in leadership activities. *Journal of College Student Development, 42*(1), 15–27.

Dugan, J. P. (2006). Involvement and leadership: A descriptive analysis of socially responsible leadership. *Journal of College Student Development, 47*(3), 335–343.

File, T. (2013). Young-adult voting: An analysis of presidential elections, 1964–2012. *United States Census Bureau (April 2014)*. Washington, DC: U.S. Census.

Flanagan, C., & Levine, P. (2010). Civic engagement and the transition to adulthood. *Future of the Children, 20*(1), 159–179.

Glynn, C. J., Huge, M. E., & Lunney, C. A. (2009). The influence of perceived social norms on college students' intention to vote. *Political Communication, 26*(1), 48–64.

Groves, R. M., Fowler, F. J., Jr., Couper, M. P., Kepkowski, J. M., Singer, E., & Tourangeau, R. (2009). *Survey methodology* (2nd ed.). Hoboken, NJ: Wiley.

Higher Education Research Institute. (2010). *Voting behavior among college students*. Los Angeles, CA: University of California Los Angeles.

Hurtado, S. (2007). Linking diversity with the educational and civic missions of higher education. *The Review of Higher Education, 20*(2), 185–196.

Johnson, M. R., Dugan, J. R., & Soria, K. M. (2015, March). Try to see it my way: What predicts social perspective-taking among college students? Paper presented at the annual meeting of American College Personnel Association (ACPA), Tampa, FL.

Kawashima-Ginsberg, K., & Levine, P. (2014). Policy effects on informed political engagement. *American Behavioral Scientist, 58*(5), 665–668.

Kirby, E. H., & Kawashima-Ginsberg, K. (2009). *CIRCLE fact sheet: The youth vote in 2008.* Medford, MA: Tufts University Tisch College of Citizenship and Public Service.

Kawashima-Ginsberg, K. (2013). Do discussion, debate, and simulations boost NAEP civics performance? (CIRCLE Fact Sheet). Medford, MA: Center for Information and Research on Civic Learning and Engagement.

Knefelkamp, L. L. (2008). Civic identity: Locating self in community. *Diversity and Democracy, 11*(2), 1–3.

Morimoto, S. A., & Friedland, L. (2013). Cultivating success: Youth achievement, capital, and civic engagement in the contemporary United States. *Sociological Perspectives, 56*(4), 523–546.

Pasek, J., Kenski, K., Romer, D., & Jamieson, K. H. (2006). America's youth and community engagement: How use of mass media is related to civic activity and political awareness in 14- to 22-year olds. *Communication Research, 33*(3), 115–135.

Pryor, J., Hurtado, S., Saenz, V. B., Santos, J. L., & Korn, W. S. (2007). *The American freshman: Forty year trends.* Los Angeles, CA: Higher Education Research Institute, University of Los Angeles.

Putnam, R. D. (2000). *Bowling alone: The collapse and revival of American community.* New York, NY: Simon & Schuster.

Soria, K. M., Fink, A., Lepkowski, C., & Snyder, L. (2013a). Undergraduate student leadership and social change. *Journal of College and Character, 14*(3), 241–251.

Soria, K. M., Nobbe, J., & Fink, A. (2013b). Examining the intersections between undergraduates' engagement in community service and development of socially responsible leadership. *Journal of Leadership Education, 12*(1), 117–140.

Taylor, P. (2012). *The growing electoral clout of Blacks is driven by turnout, not demographics.* Washington, DC: Pew Research Center.

The National Task Force on Civic Learning and Democratic Engagement. (2012). *A crucible moment: College learning and democracy's future.* Washington, DC: Association of American Colleges and Universities.

Wellman, J. V. (2000). Accounting for the civic role: Assessment and accountability strategies for civic education and institutional service. In T. Ehrlich (Ed.), *Civic responsibility and higher education* (pp. 323–344). Phoenix, AZ: American Council on Education/Oryx Press.

CHAPTER 5

Community Service and Service-Learning at Large American Public Research Universities

Jeremy L. Williams, Krista M. Soria, and Claire Erickson

Several researchers have shown the positive impact of community service and service-learning on students' learning and development (Astin et al. 2000; Eyler and Giles 1999; Hébert and Hauf 2015; Hoy and Johnson 2013; Kuh 1995, 2008); however, amid the calls for public universities to work actively to open these opportunities for students (Boyte and Hollander 1999), little is known about the rates at which undergraduates attending large public research universities are engaging in these important endeavors although several reports suggest these universities have substandard performance on civic- and community-based initiatives (Checkoway 2001; Curley and Stanton 2012; The Research University Civic Engagement Network 2015; Weerts and Sandmann 2008, 2010).

Given the lack of data specific to public research universities, the purpose of this chapter is to highlight recent data regarding the rates at which undergraduates participate in community engagement and service-learning at these types of institutions. A second goal of this chapter is to explore whether there are differences between students' participation in community service and service-learning at research universities with a Carnegie Community Engagement Classification (2015) and at institutions without

© The Editor(s) (if applicable) and The Author(s) 2016
K.M. Soria, T.D. Mitchell (eds.), *Civic Engagement
and Community Service at Research Universities*,
DOI 10.1057/978-1-137-55312-6_5

this classification. In our analysis, we hope to discover whether the Carnegie Community Engagement designation may help administrators leverage support to increase students' community engagement.

UNDERGRADUATES' COMMUNITY ENGAGEMENT AND SERVICE-LEARNING

Researchers have documented several benefits to undergraduates' participation in community engagement efforts. For instance, undergraduates who participate in community service are more likely to "encounter new perspectives on the world through the development of connections with others" (Soria, Nobbe, & Fink, 2013, p. 119). When students encounter diversity and difference through community service and engagement, these community endeavors can act as a catalyst for reflective experience and the self-questioning of assumptions (McGowan et al. 2013). Eyler and Giles (1999) suggested that community-based endeavors can spur transformative learning opportunities for students, noting that "Transformational learning occurs when individuals confront disorienting dilemmas; perspective transformation becomes possible when this dilemma raises questions about fundamental assumptions" (p. 141).

Second, in addition to bringing their assumptions into question, students learn a greater appreciation for diversity. Consequently, changes in their interpretation of others are depicted by "the reduction of negative stereotypes" (Eyler and Giles 1999, p. 29) and inspired by a greater appreciation for diversity. Engberg and Fox (2011) found that community service participation enhanced students' sense of civic responsibility and global perspective-taking. Along with identity development, civic knowledge, and dialogue across difference, community engagement also increases students' communication skills (Astin et al. 2000) and sense of belonging at their institutions (Soria et al. 2012).

As an educational construct under community engagement, service-learning affords students the chance to connect directly with local agencies and to enact change in the community (Levesque-Bristol et al. 2010). Through this experience, student learning out of the classroom has the potential to exceed in-class learning (Tucker and McCarthy 2001). Participation in service-learning and community service at the undergraduate level has proven to have positive effects on the personal development of undergraduates by providing opportunities for students to be active positive contributors to society (Soria et al. 2013). While the literature overwhelmingly supports the positive effects of service-learning on undergraduate students (Astin et al. 2000), researchers have been interested in narrowing down which definitive measures affect students involved in service-learning and community service the most. For instance, service-learning cultivates critical thinking and problem-solving skills (Astin et al. 2000; Checkoway 2001; Moely et al. 2002), promotes community engagement and interpersonal skills (Astin et al. 2000; Gallini and Moely 2003; Hébert and Hauf 2015; Moely et al. 2002), and helps students to increase their leadership abilities (Astin et al. 2000; Hébert and Hauf 2015; Moely et al. 2002). According to Celio et al. (2011) students showed significant increase in their "attitudes toward self, attitudes toward school and learning, civic engagement, social skills, and academic achievement" (p. 174).

In other studies, researchers have looked closer at categories based on certain educational frameworks. Kilgo et al. (2014) found that students who participated in service-learning reported higher gains in outcomes associated with liberal arts education, including critical thinking, moral reasoning, inclination to inquire and learn lifelong, intercultural effectiveness, psychological well-being, and political and social involvement. There are strong commonalities found across research conducted on the effects of service-learning and community service. One such outcome of community engagement is the potential for these endeavors to unleash "powerful opportunities for students to critically consider alternate viewpoints as they form their own identities and worldviews" (Soria et al. 2013, p. 119).

Barriers to Community Engagement in Research Universities

Many researchers assert that research universities have lacked a strong emphasis in promoting and enhancing community engagement (Curley and Stanton 2012; Hoy and Johnson 2013; Weerts and Sandmann 2008, 2010). With the responsibility to solve problems on local, national, and global levels, research universities have fallen behind in providing community-focused and collaborative research and teaching (Campus Compact 2010). These types of community-focused research and teaching opportunities can provide pathways for undergraduates' engagement in community service and service-learning as well; consequently, such connections should not be overlooked in research universities.

One impediment to elevating research on engagement within the research university context is that faculty who research civic and community engagement often experience difficulty validating engagement-oriented work in their respective fields and institutions. Weerts and Sandmann (2010) suggested research universities' lethargy toward community engagement results from their larger, more complex, and more decentralized structure when compared to smaller colleges and universities. Additionally, Weerts and Sandmann described tendencies of research university faculty to limit their scholarship to traditional parameters, thus inhibiting the possibilities of collaborating with community partners. Such impediments likely reduce undergraduates' opportunities for community engagement as well.

Originally founded to strengthen a nation in its infancy, research universities have diverted focus away from collective gain in favor of allocating energies and resources toward academic departments and disciplinary societies (Checkoway 2001). In 1998, a group of university presidents, provosts, deans, faculty members, and organizational representatives convened to discuss how the civic mission fit within the context of higher education. They asserted higher education held the capability of contributing to civic engagement; however, most research universities do not perceive themselves as part of the problem or of its solution (Boyte and Hollander 1999). With a group of seasoned higher education professionals representing institutions across the USA, the attendees determined their purpose was to "formulate strategies for renewing the civic mission of the research university, both by preparing students for responsible citizenship in a diverse democracy, and also by engaging faculty members to develop and utilize knowledge for the improvement of society" (Boyte and Hollander 1999, p. 6). The group agreed to champion a restoration of the universal democratic spirit and documented their ideas in the *Wingspread Declaration on Renewing the Civic Mission of the American Research University* (Boyte and Hollander 1999).

Following the *Wingspread Declaration*, research universities still seemed to expend lesser effort toward the promotion of civic engagement than their liberal arts colleges and state university counterparts (Curley and Stanton 2012). Weerts and Sandmann (2008) suggested community partners cited the size and complexity of institutions as barriers to engagement with land grant and urban universities. Building on the tradition of the *Wingspread Declaration*, Campus Compact decided in 2005 to assemble scholars from research universities known for their distinct focus on civic work (Curley and Stanton 2012). Different from the *Wingspread Declaration*'s primary focus of increasing the democratic spirit on campus, The Research University Civic Engagement Network's (TRUCEN) near-annual meetings created space to share best practices in research university civic engagement initiatives. TRUCEN colleagues shared how their respective institutions promoted engagement on campus and throughout the community and the successes and challenges that accompanied those initiatives (Campus Compact 2010). Ultimately, this group has provided invaluable space for consistent dialogue regarding how administrators and faculty address the opportunities and unique challenges relating to civic engagement work at research-intensive institutions (Curley and Stanton 2012). Since its creation, this network has steadily increased its membership across a diverse geographical representation of research universities.

Additionally, to encourage universities to highlight their efforts in civic engagement, the Carnegie Foundation for Advancement of Teaching created a new classification in 2006 to recognize a category of community-engaged institutions that define themselves by their dedication to the ideals of public engagement (Weerts and Sandmann 2008). Carnegie defined community engagement as "the collaboration between institutions of higher education and their larger communities (local, regional/ state, national, global) for the mutually beneficial exchange of knowledge and resources in a context of partnership and reciprocity" (Carnegie Community Engagement Classification 2015, para. 12). According to Carnegie, the overall purpose of community engagement is

the partnership of college and university knowledge and resources with those of the public and private sectors to enrich scholarship, research, and creative activity; enhance curriculum, teaching and learning; prepare educated, engaged citizens; strengthen democratic values and civic responsibility; address critical societal issues; and contribute to the public good. (para. 13)

There are currently 361 institutions across the USA that hold the Community Engagement Classification (Carnegie Community Engagement Classification 2015). To achieve classification, institutions submit an application detailing whether community engagement is a priority in their mission statements, formal recognition of engagement activities happen through campus-wide awards and celebrations, and mechanisms exist for systematic assessment of community perceptions of the institution's engagement with the community. Additional questions include whether community engagement is mentioned in marketing materials, whether executive leaders promote community engagement, and whether the institutions have a coordinating infrastructure to support and advance community engagement efforts.

Despite over a decade in which institutions have received community engagement classifications, little is known about whether these classifications might be associated with increases in undergraduates' community engagement. One purpose of this study is to examine whether significant differences exist in the rates at which undergraduates participate in community engagement activities at large American public research-intensive universities who have and have not received the Carnegie Community Engagement Classification.

METHODS

Student Experience in the Research University (SERU) Survey

Headquartered at the University of California at Berkeley Center for Studies in Higher Education, the Student Experience in the Research University (SERU) survey is a multi-institutional endeavor spanning several years (Center for the Studies of Higher Education 2013). With the mission to help improve the undergraduate experience and educational processes, the project obtains longitudinal information on undergraduate experience in a research university through administering an online survey annually to undergraduate students at consortium member institutions. Of note, each of the large public research institution consortium members is also a member of the Association of American Universities (Center for the Studies of Higher Education 2013). In this chapter, we used data gathered from the 2013 SERU survey, which was administered to 14 research universities across the USA.

Measures

We utilized several items from the SERU survey in this descriptive analysis. The items were derived from a civic and community engagement survey module that was randomly assigned to 10–20 % of students depending upon institutions' preferences. In the survey, students were asked if they had ever participated in community service either on campus or off campus (yes, or no) and then were asked to estimate the total hours of service they completed during the academic year (1–10 hours, 11–20 hours, 21–50 hours, 51–100 hours, or over 100 hours). We also computed a separate variable to see whether students had participated in service both on campus and off campus.

Additionally, students who indicated participating in community service (either on or off campus) were asked to indicate whether each item on a list of 14 items represented a significant reason (Yes or No) they became involved in community service (e.g., opportunity to learn new things, belief in the particular cause). Finally, students were asked whether they had ever enrolled in a course that had a service-learning component (no; yes, during this current academic year; or yes, but not during this current academic year). Those who indicated enrollment in a service-learning course were also asked the average number of hours of service they completed for a course.

Data Analysis

We computed descriptive statistics for all institutions in the sample and then provided comparative statistics between institutions that had received the Carnegie Classification for Community Engagement ($n = 5$) and those that did not have this designation ($n = 9$). There were approximately 4200 students in the sample of institutions with the classification and 9400 students in the sample of institutions without classification. Among the institutions with the classification, responses were between 580 and 1100 students per institution and the responses were between 600 and 2600 students per each non-classified institution.

In addition to computing descriptive statistics, we also utilized chi-square tests to determine whether there may be statistically significant differences in students' rate of participation between the classified and non-classified institutions. In our results below, we noted where we observed statistically significant differences using a p-value criterion of $p < 0.05$.

RESULTS

Overall, the results of the analyses suggest that 42.3 % of undergraduates enrolled at the large public research universities in 2013 participated in community service *on campus* while 56.7 % of students reported engaging in community service *off campus* (Table 5.1). Furthermore, 32.0 % of

Table 5.1 Descriptive statistics of students' participation in community service and service-learning (average and by Carnegie Community Engagement Classification)

	Non-classified institutions		Classified institutions		Total average	
	n	%	n	%	n	%
Community service participation						
On campus only	4161	43.7	1671	39.0	5832	42.3
Off campus only	5572	58.5	2263	52.8	7835	56.7
Both on and off campus	3195	33.9	1171	27.7	4366	32.0
Any service (either on, off, or a combination)	6378	67.6	2671	63.1	9049	66.2
Average hours of all service during the academic year						
1–10 hours	2465	39.9	973	37.3	3438	39.1
11–20 hours	1315	21.3	544	20.8	1859	21.1
21–50 hours	1308	21.2	603	23.1	1911	21.7
51–100 hours	701	11.3	312	11.9	1013	11.5
Over 100 hours	389	6.3	180	6.9	569	6.5
Service-learning course participation						
Yes, during this current academic year	687	7.5	428	10.3	1115	8.3
Yes, but not during this current academic year	372	4.0	229	5.5	601	4.5
Average hours of service performed during service-learning courses						
1–10 hours	346	32.9	141	21.5	487	28.5
11–25 hours	398	37.9	186	28.4	584	34.2
26–50 hours	211	20.1	270	41.2	481	28.2
Over 50 hours	96	9.1	58	8.9	154	9.0
Significant reasons for participating in community service						
Become a better citizen and community participant	4670	74.4	2002	75.5	6672	74.7
Belief in the particular cause	4568	72.7	1989	75.1	6557	73.4
Unique or interesting opportunity arose to participate	4319	68.9	1869	70.4	6188	69.3
Change conditions in the community	3916	62.5	1658	62.7	5574	62.6
Opportunity to learn new things	3795	60.5	1624	61.2	5419	60.7
Opportunities to develop leadership skills	3571	57.0	1601	60.4	5172	58.0
Strengthen my resume for graduate school or employment	3539	56.5	1531	57.8	5070	56.9
Encouragement from friends or family	2807	44.8	1254	47.3	4061	45.5
Opportunity to enhance my academic achievement	2787	44.5	1132	42.7	3919	44.0

(*continued*)

Table 5.1   (continued)

	Non-classified institutions		Classified institutions		Total average	
	n	%	n	%	n	%
Encouragement from other students	2717	43.4	1080	40.8	3797	42.6
Location of where the work was to be conducted	2430	38.8	1117	42.2	3547	39.8
Required by my fraternity or sorority	1592	25.3	528	20.0	2120	23.7
Required as part of my academic program	1498	23.8	562	21.1	2060	23.0
Encouragement from faculty or staff	1431	22.8	609	23.0	2040	22.9

students reported participating in *both* on-campus and off-campus service. The data also suggest that, overall, 66.2 % of undergraduates at all of these research universities reported completing some community service during the academic year, regardless of whether that service was on campus, off campus, or a combination of both.

Additionally, among those students who noted they completed some service, the majority spent less than 20 hours per academic year in service (60.2 %). Further, 12.8 % of students completed service-learning courses during the current academic year or during a prior academic year, with the majority stating that they spent less than 25 h completing service while enrolled in service-learning courses (62.7 %). The top three reasons that students selected for participating in community service include to become a better citizen and community participant (74.7 %), because of holding a belief in the particular cause (73.4 %), and because a unique or interesting opportunity arose to participate (69.3 %).

In relation to the second research question, we observed statistically significant differences in students' participation in community service or service-learning courses by Carnegie Community Engagement Classification. The results suggest students enrolled at non-classified institutions were significantly ($p < 0.05$) more likely to participate in community service on campus (43.7 %) or off campus (58.5 %) compared to students enrolled at institutions with the engagement classification (39.0 % participated in on-campus service and 52.8 % in off-campus service). Additionally, students at classified institutions were also significantly ($p < 0.05$) less likely to participate in community service *both* on and off campus (27.7 %) compared to their peers enrolled at non-classified institutions (33.9 %).

When comparing the average number of students who completed any service (regardless of whether it was on campus, off campus, or a combination of both), the results suggest that non-classified institutions had a significantly higher proportion of students participating in community service (67.6 %) and Carnegie-classified institutions (63.1 %) ($p<0.05$). The data also suggest that, although proportionally fewer students at classified institutions participated in service, those students enrolled at classified institutions were significantly ($p<0.05$) likely to spend more overall time in community service than students at non-classified institutions, especially in the 21–50 h category of time: 23.1 % of students at classified institutions spent 21–50 total hours in service that academic year compared to 21.2 % of students at non-classified institutions.

Students enrolled at classified institutions were significantly ($p<0.05$) more likely to report participating in service-learning courses (15.8 % compared to 12.5 %) and were significantly ($p<0.05$) more likely to report spending more time in service while taking service-learning courses than students at non-classified institutions (e.g., twice as many students at classified institutions spent 26–50 h performing service activities while enrolled in service-learning courses). Students enrolled at classified institutions were significantly ($p<0.05$) more likely to participate in service because of encouragement from friends or family, their beliefs in a particular cause, opportunities to develop leadership skills, and the location of the work to be conducted. Students enrolled at non-classified institutions were significantly ($p<0.05$) more likely to participate in service because it was required as a part of their academic program, required by a sorority or fraternity, and encouragement from other students.

In summation, the most compelling results suggest that students at classified institutions were (1) significantly less likely to participate in community service (however, when they did participate, they were more likely to spend more time in service) and (2) students at classified institutions were significantly more likely to participate in service-learning courses (and, when they participated in those courses, they spent more time performing service than the students at non-classified institutions).

Discussion

Overall, the data suggest statistically significant, although not strong, effects of the Carnegie classification as they pertain to students' involvement in community engagement. Undergraduates enrolled at institutions recognized with the community engagement classification were more likely to enroll in service-learning courses and spend more time participating in community service; however, these students were less likely, on average, to participate in service on campus, off campus, or a combination of on campus or off campus. There were also differences in the reasons students elected to participate in service; however, overall, while these differences rose to a level of significance—a factor also influenced by the large sample sizes—the differences are not particularly large between undergraduates' participation in community engagement at Carnegie-classified institutions and those that are not classified by Carnegie. It appears, however, that students attending Carnegie-classified institutions provided more intrinsic reasons for engaging in service compared to their peers at non-classified institutions (Soria and Thomas-Card 2014).

The lack of significant differences in reasons for participating in service can be attributed to several factors; for instance, the particular region in which individual institutions reside may provide undergraduates with more (or fewer) opportunities to engage in service off campus. As observed in the data, students enrolled at classified institutions were more likely to report that they participated in service because of the location where the work was to be conducted. While there are several missing descriptors about the location—which include distance from campus, among other factors, it is simply a reality that, given their locations, some institutions may not be able to connect their students to some types of community engagement opportunities.

While students at non-classified institutions were more likely to state that they had engaged in service because it was required by their academic programs, researchers have suggested that required forms of service may actually have negative effects on students' interest in community engagement postgraduation (Soria and Thomas-Card 2014). Readers should therefore be cautious about the potential implications of requiring service in academic programs; however, amid the many benefits of individualized service-learning courses, we recommend administrators continue to offer service-learning opportunities to students without necessarily mandating enrollment in them.

RECOMMENDATIONS

The results suggest that institutions with the Carnegie Classification were more likely to have students who participated in service-learning courses. It is possibly the case that institutions undertaking the steps necessary to achieve classification have put considerable time and effort into offering more opportunities for faculty to incorporate service-learning into their curriculum. To achieve similar outcomes, we recommend that administrators work closely with their institution's community and public engagement offices to facilitate faculty understanding of and commitment to the inclusion of service in their classrooms. Administrators can also work to embed community engagement expectations within tenure and promotion guidelines so as to formally encourage faculty development and work in that area.

Administrators typically have good intentions when attempting to enhance community engagement and service-learning on and around their campus; however, at times, their message of support may seem unclear. Knefelkamp (2008) summarized several Association of American Colleges and Universities (AAC&U) reports describing the relationship between higher education leaders and student engagement stating that, although administrators want students to develop a civic identity,

> the data also reveals a gap between the ideal and real: educators want to foster civic growth, but we aren't necessarily successful in doing so. If we are truly committed to fostering civic identity in our students, we must ask ourselves some difficult questions about how we approach the educational enterprise (p. 3).

Therefore, careful consideration of how administrators propagate student community engagement holds upmost importance; for instance, we recommend that administrators spend time assessing the different types of opportunities available to students at their institutions, whether all students are provided equal access to community engagement, and how messages related to community engagement are related to students, staff, faculty, and other campus stakeholders.

Similar to the AAC&U reports mentioned above, The National Task Force on Civic Learning and Democratic Engagement (2012) presented another challenge to administrators encouraging student engagement. Commissioned by the Department of Education (DOE) and published by the AAC&U, the authors of the National Task Force's policy report, *A Crucible Moment: College Learning and Democracy's Future*, charged higher education with a call for restorative action in the areas of democratic engagement, promoting civic ethos, civic literacy, civic inquiry, and civic action on campuses (The National Task Force on Civic Learning and Democratic Engagement 2012). Of particular interest in the report, students perceived a decline their campus' valuation and promotion of contributions to the community at-large between freshman and senior years. An additional recommendation for research university administrators and leaders is to seek Carnegie Community Engagement classification for their institution. The classification can assist research university administrators in emphasizing and enhancing student learning through new pathways toward community engagement. As data from this chapter have illustrated, students attending research institutions that have received a Carnegie Classification are slightly more likely than their peers to spend more time in community service and are more likely to have participated in service-learning opportunities overall. Additionally, students at Carnegie-classified institutions are more likely to participate in service because of intrinsic motivations. While these effects are very low and limitations in data analysis prevent us from understanding whether effects observed could be attributed to other factors, overall, seeking the Carnegie Community Engagement Classification can help administrators solidify their visions for community engagement on their campuses and institutionalize their public engagement missions. In pursuing the classification, administrators and faculty can transform community engagement rhetoric into community engagement action by establishing clear procedures for ongoing assessment and measurement of engagement activities, initiating and nurturing community partnerships, recognizing community engaged work as integrated in teaching and scholarship, and aligning community engagement efforts with other institutional priorities (Carnegie Community Engagement Classification 2015).

CONCLUSION

Research universities represent a unique and crucial piece in American higher education. We opened this chapter with a brief review of previous research on the benefits and challenges research university students face when participating in community engagement and service-learning. Using data from the SERU consortium member institutions, we then compared undergraduate student community engagement and service-learning among research universities in the consortium, finding that students at Carnegie Community Engaged institutions did spend more overall time in public service. We recommend research university administrators use a variety of methods to encourage students toward community service. Through these efforts, civic service can regain prominence in the American research university.

REFERENCES

Astin, A. W., Vogelgesang, L. J., Ikeda, E. K., & Yee, J. A. (2000). *How service learning affects students.* Los Angeles, CA: Higher Education Research Institute, University of California.

Boyte, H., & Hollander, E. (1999). *Wingspread declaration on renewing the civic mission of the American research university.* Providence, RI: Campus Compact.

Campus Compact. (2010). *Annual membership survey results.* Boston, MA: Campus Compact.

Carnegie Community Engagement Classification. (2015). *How is "community engagement" defined?* Boston, MA: University of Massachusetts Boston, New England Resource Center for Higher Education. http://nerche.org/index.php?option=com_content&view=article&id=341&Itemid=92#CE%20def.

Celio, C. I., Durlack, J., & Dymnicki, A. (2011). A meta-analysis of the impact of service-learning on students. *Journal of Experiential Education, 34*(2), 164–181.

Center for the Studies of Higher Education. (2013). *SERU-AAU consortium.* Berkeley, CA: University of California, Berkeley. http://cshe.berkeley.edu/research/seru/consortium.htm.

Checkoway, B. (2001). Renewing the civic mission of the American research university. *The Journal of Higher Education, 72*(2, Special Issue: The Social Role of Higher Education), 125–147.

Curley, M. F., & Stanton, T. K. (2012). The history of TRUCEN. *Journal of Higher Education Outreach and Engagement, 16*(4), 3–10.

Engberg, M. E., & Fox, K. (2011). Exploring the relationship between undergraduate service-learning experiences and global perspective-taking. *Journal of Student Affairs Research and Practice, 48*(1), 85–105.

Eyler, J., & Giles, D. E., Jr. (1999). *Where's the learning in service-learning?* San Francisco, CA: Jossey-Bass, Inc.

Gallini, S. M., & Moely, B. E. (2003). Service-learning and engagement, academic challenge, and retention. *Michigan Journal of Community Service Learning, 10*, 5–14.

Hébert, A., & Hauf, P. (2015). Student learning through service learning: Effects on academic development, civic responsibility, interpersonal skills and practical skills. *Active Learning in Higher Education, 16*(1), 37–49.

Hoy, A., & Johnson, M. (2013). *Deepening community engagement in higher education: Forging new pathways.* London: Palgrave Macmillan.

Kilgo, C. A., Pasquesi, K., Ezell Sheets, J. K., & Pascarella, E. T. (2014). The estimated effects of participation in service-learning on liberal arts outcomes. *International Journal of Research on Service-Learning and Community Engagement, 2*(1), 18–31.

Knefelkamp, L. (2008). Civic identity: Locating self in community. *Diversity and Democracy: Civic Learning for Shared Futures, 11*(2), 1–3.

Kuh, G. D. (1995). The other curriculum: Out-of-class experiences associated with student learning and personal development. *The Journal of Higher Education, 66*(2), 123–155.

Kuh, G. D. (2008). *High-impact educational practices: What they are, who has access to them, and why they matter.* Washington, DC: Association of American Colleges and Universities. https://secure.aacu.org/PubExcerpts/HIGHIMP.html.

Levesque-Bristol, C., Knapp, T. D., & Fisher, B. J. (2010). The effectiveness of service-learning: It's not always what you think. *Journal of Experiential Education, 33*(3), 208–224.

McGowan, T. G., Bonefas, S., & Siracusa, A. C. (2013). Community engagement across the curriculum: Boyer, integration, and the challenges of institutionaliza-tion. In A. Hoy & M. Johnson (Eds.), *Deepening community engagement in higher education: Forging new pathways* (pp. 169–180). Basingstoke, UK: Palgrave Macmillan.

Moely, B. E., McFarland, M., Miron, D., Mercer, S., & Ilustre, V. (2002). Changes in college students' attitudes and intentions for civic involvement as a function of service-learning experiences. *Michigan Journal of Community Service Learning, 9*, 18–26.

Soria, K. M., Nobbe, J., & Fink, A. (2013). Examining the intersections between undergraduates' engagement in community service and development of socially responsible leadership. *Journal of Leadership Education, 12*(1), 117–140.

Soria, K. M., & Thomas-Card, T. (2014). Relationships between motivations for community service participation and desire to continue service following col-lege. *Michigan Journal of Community Service Learning, 20*(2), 53–64.

Soria, K. M., Troisi, J. N., & Stebleton, M. J. (2012). Reaching out, connecting within: Community service and sense of belonging among college students. *Higher Education in Review, 9*, 65–85.

The National Task Force on Civic Learning and Democratic Engagement. (2012). *A crucible moment: College learning and democracy's future.* Washington, DC: Association of American Colleges and Universities.

The Research University Civic Engagement Network. (2015). TRUCEN. http://compact.org/initiatives/trucen/.

Tucker, M. L., & McCarthy, A. M. (2001). Presentation self-efficacy: Increasing communication skills through service-learning. *Journal of Managerial Issues, 8*(2), 227–244.

Weerts, D. J., & Sandmann, L. R. (2008). Building a two-way street: Challenges and opportunities for community engagement at research universities. *The Review of Higher Education, 32*(1), 73–106.

Weerts, D. J., & Sandmann, L. R. (2010). Community engagement and boundary-spanning roles at research universities. *Journal of Higher Education, 81*(6), 632–657.

CHAPTER 6

Redefining Civic Engagement: A Developmental Model of Students' Civic-Related Capabilities

Luis Ponjuan, Cynthia M. Alcantar, and Krista M. Soria

Amid the background of sweeping demographic and sociocultural transformations (Toossi 2012) and increased calls for higher education to fulfill its civic mission (The National Task Force on Civic Learning and Democratic Engagement 2012), contemporary notions of civic engagement have emerged in our national discourse. Amid the resurgent interest in civic engagement, nuanced differences in how civic engagement is defined, understood, and used in the higher education literature (Einfeld and Collins 2008; Kirlin 2005; Rowan-Kenyon et al. 2008) present challenges to higher education administrators, practitioners, and researchers seeking to measure higher education's civic contributions at the national, state, and local levels. Preconceptions about the nature of civic engagement are often shaped by different academic or research lenses based on political, social, cognitive, or behavioral theories that may lead to different notions and understandings of the nature of undergraduate students' civic-related capabilities.

There is just cause for concern regarding the future of civic engagement in the nation: Americans' civic engagement has decreased significantly since the 1970s (Ehrlich 2000). Macedo et al. (2005) suggested the American democracy is at risk due to the erosion of citizens' civic involvement.

© The Editor(s) (if applicable) and The Author(s) 2016
K.M. Soria, T.D. Mitchell (eds.), *Civic Engagement and Community Service at Research Universities*,
DOI 10.1057/978-1-137-55312-6_6

The authors described American civic life as "impoverished" (p. 1) and attributed the roots of the problem to Americans' infrequent public affairs involvement, lack of knowledge regarding civic and social issues, and overall tempered enthusiasm for participation in civic life. Several policy organizations have raised awareness of these issues and have turned their attention to higher education institutions to reverse these trends (Boyte and Hollander 1999; Campus Compact 2012; The National Task Force on Civic Learning and Democratic Engagement 2012; U.S. Department of Education 2012). Such calls to action are especially salient at public research universities given their unique historical legacies and public engagement missions. The preparation of individuals for participation in a democratic society is considered a primary goal of higher education (Ehrlich 2000; Hurtado et al. 2002; Morse et al. 2005); however, even though citizens have greater access to higher education than ever before, fewer are engaging in the civic affairs of the nation (Ehrlich 2000).

Kirlin (2003) posited that an individual's civic skills are most likely acquired in a trajectory through the achievement of developmental milestones of interconnected and interrelated skills. A common tenet of student development research is the institutional role in promoting various forms of student engagement through curricular and co-curricular initiatives (Kuh et al. 2010). These initiatives are often designed to encourage development of global awareness, diversity appreciation, and civic engagement; however, even though civic engagement has been assessed in courses, curricular and co-curricular activities, and among alumni, the concept is difficult to define across the extant research literature (Beaumont 2005). In an attempt to define civic skills within the public affairs research literature, Kirlin (2005) stated, "[W]e have limited consensus about what civic engagement is, let alone how to increase it" (p. 305). While there is some consensus that civic engagement remains an important learning outcome in higher education, Kirlin (2005) highlighted the challenges associated in defining the broad concept of civic engagement across the research literature.

Pascarella et al. (1988) emphasized the long-held belief that the primary societal benefit of higher education is to cultivate an informed and engaged citizenry. The authors focused on humanitarian and civic values, which include environmental causes, concern for others, community action, and influence on political and social values and institutions. Today, civic engagement remains an important educational outcome, despite an inconsistency in defining and operationalizing this concept.

In fact, Schneider (2006) called for the integration of civic engagement to prepare students "to act as responsible stewards of democracy's core commitments" (p. 3).

The purpose of this chapter is to present a multidimensional developmental model to describe undergraduate students' civic engagement development. Civic engagement encompasses broad interrelated concepts such as citizenship, democratic outcomes, and political beliefs, and researchers have operationally defined civic engagement to reflect different values, attitudes, and behaviors. Developing a taxonomy from the civic engagement literature demonstrates these challenges. For example, earlier research focused on political attitudes and community service, while current literature has evolved these terms into concepts such as civic engagement, civic responsibility, civic involvement, civic-mindedness, civic capacity, and other democratic outcomes.

There is considerable research that shapes how we understand the complex nature of identity development as a function of the interaction between the cognitive, intrapersonal, and interpersonal domains (Baxter Magolda 2001; Kegan 1994). These scholars suggested student development requires a holistic perspective to encompass the complex nature of identity development and how these dimensions shape essential learning outcomes such as civic engagement. While civic engagement is a learning outcome utilized in the literature and scholars and policymakers often encourage the development of this learning outcome (Dey et al. 2009), there is scant evidence in the literature that explores how the interaction between these broader domains applies to this particular outcome.

We also argue that exploring the construct civic engagement using these domains expands and deepens our understanding by creating a more inclusive and comprehensive model better capturing how students develop capabilities across civic-related domains. That is, the current use of the monolithic term *civic engagement* limits our understanding of this complex learning outcome, and our model provides a nuanced discussion from solely civic engagement to civic-related capabilities. The term civic engagement can be viewed as simply as students' behavioral engagement in civic issues, even though their engagement does not necessitate developmental growth. In contrast to traditional measures of civic engagement, we specifically use the term *civic-related capabilities* to reflect a student's capability, skill, or ability in the cognitive, intrapersonal, and interpersonal domains.

King and Baxter Magolda (2005) used a similar argument to create a developmental model for intercultural maturity, noting that "Looking at intercultural maturity using a holistic perspective provides a possible explanation for the ineffectiveness of simpler, more superficial approaches to intercultural competence … because they fail to consider one or more domains (cognitive, identity, interpersonal) of development" (p. 573). Therefore, in this chapter we seek to advance our understanding of the construct civic engagement through a critical review of the literature and the development of a multidimensional model to describe the learning outcome of civic engagement. We assert that such a model, while useful in the context of research universities (the focus of this volume), can also be applied in any number of institutional contexts.

REVIEW OF THE LITERATURE

We utilized King and Baxter Magolda's (2005) theoretical framework to understand the three civic engagement developmental domains (i.e., cognitive, intrapersonal, and interpersonal). We then examined how researchers from various social science disciplines applied the civic engagement construct and found it critical to investigate how other academic disciplines view civic engagement. Finally, we present a new developmental model to describe students' civic-related capabilities across three inter-related domains.

Multidimensional Intercultural Maturity Model

King and Baxter Magolda (2005) relied predominately upon Kegan's (1994) holistic model of human development across the lifespan. Kegan argued that adults are better suited to coping and addressing complex life issues with individual development in three domains (cognitive, interpersonal, and intrapersonal). In their developmental model of intercultural maturity, King and Baxter Magolda provided a three-by-three matrix that emphasized the value of promoting and assessing intercultural maturity in a holistic manner by weaving together *cognitive, intrapersonal, and interpersonal* developmental domains (i.e., domain rows) by the trajectories of *initial, intermediate, and mature* levels of development (i.e., trajectory columns). The authors contended that students will become more competent, interculturally mature individuals if they have developed the cognitive, intrapersonal, and interpersonal capabilities necessary for effective intercultural understanding, values, and interactions. King and Baxter Magolda's model provided a holistic, comprehensive developmental framework to assist educators in promoting student development of complex and vital learning outcomes. The authors illustrated each of the intercultural maturity model's domain with excerpts from interviews of students and their previous research on student development theory.

Cognitive Domain of Intercultural Maturity
The cognitive domain of intercultural maturity is based upon the work of several cognitive theorists (Baxter Magolda 2001; Gilligan 1982; Kegan 1994; King and Kitchener 1994, 2004; Perry 1970). The cognitive domain "focuses on how one constructs one's view and creates a meaning-making system based on how one understands knowledge and how it is gained" (King and Baxter Magolda 2005, p. 574). The cognitive domain involves individuals' understanding and reflection of the world—in this model, the world of diversity issues. In King and Baxter Magolda's model, individuals in the initial level of cognitive development of intercultural maturity exhibit dualistic thinking about the world, cultures, and values of others who are different from self. The intermediate level of cognitive domain is characterized by a growing awareness of diverse perspectives. In the mature level, the desired level of the intercultural maturity outcome, individuals can see ideas from multiple perspectives.

Intrapersonal Domain of Intercultural Maturity
The intrapersonal domain describes an individual's development of identity, including values and beliefs that may be influenced by individual characteristics, such as race/ethnicity and socioeconomic status. This domain "focuses on how one understands one's own beliefs, values, and sense of self, and uses these to guide choices and behaviors" (King and Baxter Magolda 2005, p. 574). In the intercultural maturity model, the initial level of intrapersonal development of intercultural maturity describes an individual's lack of a personal value system based upon one's own individual characteristics and experiences. At this level, values are based on the reliance on others for shaping one's personal identity. The individual looks externally for acceptable definitions of identity; thus, any difference from the acceptable definition may not be welcome. The intermediate level of the intrapersonal domain is characterized by development and recognition of an identity separate from others, exploration of one's own values and culture, and acceptance of those who are different. The desired outcome,

or mature level, is described as the "capacity to create an internal self that openly engages challenges to one's views and beliefs and that considers social identities (race, class, gender, etc.) in a global and national context; integrates aspects of self into one's identity" (p. 576). Interculturally mature individuals possess an integrated identity in which values and beliefs may be reexamined and modified.

Interpersonal Domain of Intercultural Maturity
The interpersonal domain of intercultural maturity describes the ability to interact effectively and interdependently with others from diverse backgrounds (King and Baxter Magolda 2005). In the intercultural maturity model, the initial level of the interpersonal development is characterized by relationships that are self-serving, individualistic in nature and a lack of awareness of the nature of community or society and the influence of group norms. The authors noted that "Social problems are viewed egocentrically" (p. 576). The intermediate level of the interpersonal domain is characterized by development of relationships with others who are different despite continued pressure for external validation of self. Individuals begin to understand the nature of society and groups. The mature level is noted by healthy relationships with others based on diversity appreciation and an understanding of influences on societal systems.

King and Baxter Magolda (2005) used a holistic development approach to develop their model to provide a helpful way to understand and promote the complex learning outcome of intercultural maturity. This matrix serves a framework for our analysis and discussion of the research articles on civic engagement.

Cognitive Domain in Civic-Related Capabilities Model

A brief review of the literature revealed that the cognitive domain of undergraduates' civic engagement included many related constructs: civic knowledge, skills, and abilities that support civic engagement in a complex world, with infinite points of view, diverse value sets, and competition for resources. Musil (2009) articulated several cognitive civic learning outcomes within the Civic Learning Spiral, including adeptness at critical thinking, understanding that knowledge is socially constructed and dynamic, awareness of historical struggles in the pursuit of democracy, and capacity to describe diverse civic traditions expressed by different cultural groups. Researchers also suggested that these intellectual capabilities are based on the acquisition and meaning-making of the nature, structure, and process of government and community. The complexity and currency of this knowledge may also be impacted by levels of interest in current affairs, trust in government, and optimism in the future of the community, nation, or world. Therefore, we defined civic-related cognitive capability (e.g., skills and potential abilities) as the capability to apply critical thinking and problem-solving skills to community, national, or global issues; make meaning of a complex and diverse global community; and recognize multiple diverse perspectives related to civic issues.

Cognitive Capability of Thinking Critically
The ability to use critical thinking and problem-solving skills (Joseph et al. 2007; Moely et al. 2002) emphasizes students' capability to apply credible information to make "critical decisions about communal life" (Anderson et al. 2003, p. 87). Anderson et al. extended the contemporary citizenship of communal life within a global context. The authors emphasized that knowledge and interest in politics include an increased sense of global awareness, an important component of civic-related capabilities because knowledge and awareness confined to local and national politics and issues are no longer sufficient in today's global knowledge-based economy. Obtaining information about political and community issues in the local and global context suggests perspective-taking, another aspect of cognitive civic outcomes.

Cognitive Capability of Making Meaning of the World
Civic knowledge has political and nonpolitical dimensions and much of the research on the political knowledge dimension encompasses undergraduates' understanding of political processes and government structures as an essential component of civic capability (Beaumont et al. 2006; Bernstein 2008; Bogard et al. 2008). In the political engagement project of the Carnegie Foundation for the Advancement of Teaching, foundational political knowledge was defined as knowledge of political theories, institutions, and organizations and knowledge of current events was defined as knowledge of current political and economic issues at the local, state, national, and international levels (Beaumont et al. 2006). Beaumont et al. operationally defined the scale of foundational knowledge as the understanding and functioning of political institutions, political and democratic theory, and organizations that work on social and political problems. Steinberg et al. (2011) also noted that multidimensionality of

civic knowledge, including understanding ways to contribute to society, understanding that academic disciplinary skills are vital to addressing societal issues, and understanding current events and the complexity of local, national, and global issues. The commitment to influence political structures is part of the humanitarian and civic value scale used by Pascarella et al. (1986) and others (Lott 2013), which will be discussed in the intrapersonal section.

Several studies examine the importance of keeping up-to-date in current events as an indicator of cognitive civic capability (Ball 2005; Bernstein 2007; Bogard et al. 2008; Johnson and Lollar 2002; Moely et al. 2002; Schamber and Mahoney 2008). The frequency of obtaining news, following elections, and discussing politics serves as the operational definition of political interest and political participation (Johnson and Lollar 2002). Sax (2004) also utilized the frequency of obtaining or discussing news and politics as a proxy for political or civic interest. Possessing interest in political processes, such as local, state, and federal elections, is necessary for pledging time and effort to remain knowledgeable about local, national, and global current events (Bernstein 2005; Lay and Smarick 2006). Studies of the acquisition of political information are combined with the relevance and accuracy of the information obtained. If seeking information related to political campaigns is considered an integral cognitive civic capability associated with increasing political knowledge and interest (Bernstein 2005), then obtaining relevant, credible information supports a strong foundation of political knowledge and participation in the political process (Bogard et al. 2008).

Civic literacy has been described as the ability to obtain and manage accurate information in addition to the knowledge and capacity to make sense of the political world (Bogard et al. 2008; Milner 2002). This capability consists of the use of effective information literacy, media literacy, and critical-thinking skills to evaluate the sources and credibility of political information (Bernstein 2007; Bogard et al. 2008; Huntemann 2008; Wells and Dudash 2007). Bernstein (2008) defined civic competence in part by referring to an individual's skills and ability to "make sense of vast amounts of political information" (p. 5). Students must be able to manage political information, a skill described by Bernstein (2008) as the ability to evaluate the sources of political information, measure the value of political propositions, and explain their own political positions.

Cognitive Capability of Perspective Taking

Several studies have examined the cognitive skill of perspective-taking (Antonaros et al. 2008; Gurin et al. 2002; Hurtado et al. 2002; Mayhew and Fernández 2007; Taylor and Trepanier-Street 2007). The "ability to see multiple perspectives" (Hurtado et al. 2002, p. 169) allows an individual to become better informed about different thoughts and opinions regarding a particular concept or issue. A globally aware civically engaged individual may also seek out information and "perspectives not often presented through the U.S. media," and incorporate an understanding of "how the U.S. might be perceived around the world" (Anderson et al. 2003, p. 97). Perspective-taking complements civic outcomes of effective information literacy and critical-thinking skills.

Evaluating political information, while possessing the ability and willingness to appreciate other perspectives, can support the capability to understand community issues from diverse viewpoints (Einfeld and Collins 2008). Knowledge and interest in politics culminate in increased attentiveness to community issues (Corbett and Kendall 1999; Joseph et al. 2007; Wilson et al. 2007). Corbett and Kendall (1999) defined citizenship as "an awareness of community problems, a sense of personal responsibility toward the community, and interest in solving community problems" (p. 70). Interest in solving community problems necessitates the ability to deal with conflict and difference (Keen and Hall 2009); indeed, prevailing forms of democratic thought advocate the importance of civil disagreement in political expression (Bernstein 2008). In Prentice and Robinson's (2007) conceptualization of civic engagement, awareness of issues and problems leads to a call for action, which has been studied in conjunction with students' levels of cynicism, trust, and optimism.

In an extension of the relationship between civic involvement and students' perceptions of the credibility of political information, several studies have examined students' level of cynicism and their perceptions of the trustworthiness and effectiveness of politicians themselves (Bernstein 2008; Bernstein and Meizlish 2003; Blackhurst and Foster 2003; Lay and Smarick 2006; McKinney and Chattopadhyay 2007). Feelings of apathy, optimism, and cynicism indicate how an individual perceives political and civic organizations and structures. Blackhurst and Foster's (2003) cynicism scale examined whether students had a "respect for and trust in politicians and the political process or, alternatively, exhibited a critical, mistrustful posture toward politicians and their ability to represent the interests of average citizens" (p. 159). Related to cynicism is the level of apathy, which the authors described as the extent to which individuals care about political processes and demonstrate a willingness to invest effort to involve themselves in the processes (Blackhurst and Foster 2003).

Intrapersonal Dimension in Civic Engagement

The construct of intrapersonal dimensions, including the exploration and examination of personal values, espousal of democratic aspirations, and development of character and integrity, are noted as civic learning outcomes within the civic learning spiral (Musil 2009). An individual's sense of civic identity forms over time as the individual responds to developmental tasks and encounters challenges to beliefs and values (Baxter Magolda and King 2004; Knefelkamp 2008). Much as cognitive development progresses from externally derived knowledge to a more relativistic understanding of knowledge, intrapersonal development can progress from external absolute values and beliefs to an appreciation of a unique set of values that support personal integrity (Chickering and Reisser 1993; Pascarella and Terenzini 2005).

The intrapersonal domain of undergraduates' civic capabilities encompasses the student's lack of a firm identity, questioning self and others' beliefs, and ultimately reconciling sense of self with personally espoused values. Personal values and beliefs provide the foundation for these intrapersonal civic-related capabilities and levels of awareness of diversity and sociocultural and socioeconomic conditions, and community issues influence the developmental tasks that can propel students to achieve a more cohesive sense of self. Lack of awareness of the broader community can limit the development of civic values and responsibilities. Intrapersonal civic capabilities reflect a student's ability to develop and acknowledge values in the context of an interdependent complex world, recognize responsibilities to the broader community, and enhance efficacy for individual and community involvement.

Intrapersonal Capability of Acknowledging Values and Commitments

Intrapersonal civic capabilities are based upon the values, beliefs, and commitments of individual members of the local, national, or global community. Intrapersonally skilled civic individuals "situate their own lives within the broad social-political context of an increasingly global world" (Anderson et al. 2003, p. 90). The ability to situate one's life within a community requires open-mindedness and a willingness to reevaluate personal values (Anderson et al. 2003). Active membership in a diverse community is supported by participants able to value diverse perspectives (Cress et al. 2001; Gurin et al. 2002; Keen and Hall 2009; Moely et al. 2002; Spiezio et al. 2005; Steinberg et al. 2011) and engage in healthy conflict to promote a better democratic community (Hurtado et al. 2002).

Situating one's life implies a community orientation or perspective (Cress et al. 2001; Spiezio et al. 2005) that values a vital, healthy community. Pascarella et al. (1986) developed a construct of civic and humanitarian values that includes environmental causes, concern for others, community action, and the importance of influencing political institutions and social values. The construct has been used and adapted to investigate undergraduates' civic dispositions (Astin and Sax 1998; Astin et al. 1999; Ball 2005; Cress et al. 2001; Engberg 2004; Engberg and Mayhew 2007; Giles and Eyler 1994; Gurin et al. 2002; Rios-Aguilar and Mars 2011; Sax 2004), while other researchers have narrowed their focus of civic values to an altruistic concern for others (Astin 1993; Rhoads 1998). A commitment to helping others (Ball 2005; Einfeld and Collins 2008; Giles and Eyler 1994; Lott 2013) and helping the community at large (Einfeld and Collins 2008; Huerta and Jozwiak 2008; Lott 2013) are considered essential components of civic values. More commonly found in the literature are the civic values of the importance of political participation, community involvement, and social action engagement (Elder et al. 2007; Hunter and Brisbin 2000; Hurtado et al. 2002; Rowan-Kenyon et al. 2008).

Definitions of civic values refer to democratic ideals of civility, difference, and equality, including promoting racial understanding (Angelique et al. 2002; Corbett and Kendall 1999; Einfeld and Collins 2008; Lott 2013). These democratic ideals support social justice, an outcome sometimes intertwined with civic engagement and described as an advanced level of civic engagement (Einfeld and Collins 2008; Engberg and Mayhew 2007; Mayhew and Fernández 2007; Prentice 2007). A social justice-oriented civic value manifests itself in a realization of the importance institutions have on individual realities (Moely et al. 2002; Schamber and Mahoney 2008). Some researchers describe a social justice-oriented perspective as a sophisticated, personally relevant, and actualized concern for societal problems (Corbett and Kendall 1999; Peters and Stearns 2003). This complex conceptualization provides a continuum of intrapersonal manifestations, from a community orientation, acknowledging responsibility to others to improving the community, ultimately resulting in interpersonal actions (Prentice 2007).

Intrapersonal Capability of Recognizing Civic Responsibilities
Recognizing and embracing one's responsibilities to the community expands upon the notion of situating one's life. Acknowledging the world at large and incorporating diverse perspectives into one's worldview establishes the foundation of civic values; Keen and Hall (2009) stressed that students who engaged in community service had encounters with *others* that expanded their notions of the external "they" toward a newly reframed sense of "we" (p. 62). A distinction between values and responsibilities within the interpersonal civic capabilities is evident in the civic engagement literature and, in this sense, *valuing* others does not necessarily mean a sense of *responsibility* to others. Described as civic responsibility, a civically minded individual will extend personal values into a sense of accountability to others (Mabry 1998) and the broader community (Corbett and Kendall 1999; Rowan-Kenyon et al. 2008). We are our brother's keeper and this sense of responsibility supports a conscientiousness to help solve community problems (Corbett and Kendall 1999; Mabry 1998; Peters and Stearns 2003). Peters and Stearns (2003) contended that providing students an opportunity to bear witness to real social problems ripe with complexity reinforces students' sense of responsibility to be active, concerned citizens.

Intrapersonal Capability of Believing in Self and Community (Efficacy)
An undergraduate's "personal sense of political power" (Hunter and Brisbin 2000, p. 625) is vital to actualizing civic values and responsibilities. One's perceived belief of personal knowledge and competence to effectively contribute to the community appears in several studies of undergraduate student civic engagement (Angelique et al. 2002; Bernstein 2008; Hunter and Brisbin 2000; Lott 2008; Malaney and Berger 2005; McKinney and Chattopadhyay 2007; Spiezio et al. 2005; Steinberg et al. 2011). Lack of self-esteem or confidence can hamper self-efficacy and potentially affect the level of civic participation; for example, Reeb (2006) suggested that individuals' lack of confidence in their ability to make a significant contribution to their community—a construct known as community service self-efficacy—affects interest in service, level of effort, and perseverance in service. Civic agency, or belief that one can make a difference, involves the capacity for individuals to engage in collective social change (Bernstein 2007; Bogard et al. 2008; Giles and Eyler 1994; Mabry 1998; Rowan-Kenyon et al. 2008; Sax 2004; Spiezio et al. 2005). One can demonstrate a willingness to make a difference,

despite lack of self-efficacy or civic agency. This readiness or willingness to make a difference has been termed social action engagement (Cress et al. 2001; Hurtado et al. 2002; Jensen and Hunt 2007; Malaney and Berger 2005). Although the social action engagement constructs utilized by Hurtado et al. and Malaney and Berger are not identical, both encompass students' willingness to raise awareness and work on race, poverty, and other social issues. To foster recurring motivation for civic involvement, Fall (2006) studied undergraduates' belief that their civic involvement will benefit the community. An additional manner of analyzing self-efficacy of civic engagement is to understand the level of community efficacy students possess (Hunter and Brisbin 2000; Hutchinson 2005; Keen and Hall 2009; Lott 2008).

Interpersonal Dimensions of Civic Engagement

Students' capability to constructively interact with diverse others is an integral component of their civic-related capabilities. These outcomes—including an understanding, ability, and commitment to live in communal contexts; understanding that self is always embedded in relationships; appreciating the resources and wisdom of diverse communities; and understanding of the complex (and sometimes problematic and oppressive) legacies of communities—are important features of civic learning outcomes developed within the civic learning spiral (Musil 2009).

Interpersonal civic capability extends to interactions and associations with individuals, organizations, and institutions, such as local or state government. Dresner and Blatner (2006) defined civic engagement as active participation in real-world events that requires an investment of time, energy, and emotion in the political process (Blackhurst and Foster 2003).

Interpersonal Capability of Expressing Political Voice

The interpersonal domain of undergraduates' civic capabilities pertains to a student's acting upon the basis of cognitive and intrapersonal civic capabilities. More complex civic knowledge and understanding, accompanied by firm values and determined sense of self-efficacy, may lead to an increased investment in community involvement. Interpersonal civic capabilities reflect a student's expression of political voice, influencing of the political process, involvement in nonpolitical community activities, and ability to work in teams.

Beaumont et al. (2006) emphasized the importance of exercising one's political voice and expressing one's political opinions as fundamental components of interpersonal civic capabilities. This expression can take the form of traditional electoral activities, such as registering to vote or voting (Bernstein and Meizlish 2003; Blackhurst and Foster 2003; Bogard et al. 2008; Hunter and Brisbin 2000; Persell and Wenglinsky 2004); giving money to political campaigns (Ball 2005; Beaumont et al. 2006; González 2008; Persell and Wenglinsky 2004); active forms of involvement including taking part in protests, marches, or demonstrations, going door-to-door to campaign for a political cause, or running for political office (Beaumont et al. 2006; Colby et al. 2007); and contacting newspapers to write opinion editorials, calling in to radio stations to express opinions, signing or writing petitions, writing political blogs, or writing letters to public officials or newspapers (Beaumont et al. 2006; Persell and Wenglinsky 2004; Vogelgesang and Astin 2005). Involvement in these local, state, and national political events is the common indicator of political civic engagement; however, active participation in campus governance, student newspaper, debate clubs, and other student organizations can be a more relevant marker of undergraduates' civic engagement (Johnson and Lollar 2002; Klofstad 2007). Campus politics can also serve as a training ground to hone interpersonal civic capabilities.

Interpersonal Capability of Influencing the Political Process
Campaigning for political candidates and parties is traditional but active method of influencing the political process (Bernstein and Meizlish 2003; Persell and Wenglinsky 2004). Involvement in political groups and participation in public meetings is frequently found in the civic engagement literature (Ball 2005; Beaumont et al. 2006; González 2008; Hunter and Brisbin 2000; Jensen and Hunt 2007; Klofstad 2007; Persell and Wenglinsky 2004; Zuniga et al. 2005). Joining a political organization affirms cognitive and intrapersonal capabilities of civic engagement by fostering interactions with individuals of similar beliefs and goals. The purpose of the group may be to advocate for a specific issue, platform, or candidate. Membership and participation in such groups can take the form of in-person or Internet-mediated interactions. Participation in public meetings draws upon cognitive, intrapersonal, and interpersonal capabilities as individuals interact with others of diverse views and platforms.

Influencing the political process extends beyond traditional political engagement to a more active role. Individuals utilize their interpersonal civic capabilities to attempt to change the status quo and remedy societal inequities (Prentice 2007). These actions take the form of signing petitions (Beaumont et al. 2006; Blackhurst and Foster 2003) and participating in demonstrations, boycotts, and marches (Angelique et al. 2002; Beaumont et al. 2006). Expressing political voice and influencing the political process reflect the political element of interpersonal civic capabilities, as defined in the extant educational research literature.

Interpersonal Capability of Helping the Community
Definitions of undergraduates' civic engagement include community involvement in a general, nonpolitical sense (Angelique et al. 2002) and may be measured by the level of participation in or the number of organizations the student has joined (Ball 2005; Klofstad 2007). Participation in volunteer and community service organizations serve as a foundation for students' civic involvement (Astin and Sax 1998; Klofstad 2007), and service-learning, volunteering, and community service are predominant in the civic engagement literature (Astin and Sax 1998; Ball 2005; Blackhurst and Foster 2003; Einfeld and Collins 2008; González 2008; Persell and Wenglinsky 2004; Rowan-Kenyon et al. 2008; Sax 2004; Vogelgesang and Astin 2005; Zuniga et al. 2005).

Interpersonal Capability of Working in Teams
Bernstein (2008) suggested that civically competent citizens possess the capability of effectively working with others to achieve civic and political goals. Given the democratic composition of our society, it is not possible to effect significant social change alone (Bernstein 2008), and some definitions of civic agency include the capability of individuals to work collectively and collaboratively across differences (Boyte 2005, 2008). Possessing the capacity to work well with others, create consensus and build accord around controversial social issues, and develop relationships across multiple differences have emerged as prominent themes in several conceptual frameworks and studies examining students' civic-mindedness and civic learning, responsibility, and engagement (Bringle and Steinberg 2010; Einfeld and Collins 2008; Kirlin 2003; Musil 2009; Steinberg et al. 2011).

A Conceptual Framework of the Multidimensional Model of Civic-Related Capabilities

We present a conceptual model based on Baxter Magolda and King's (2004) model that describes how students develop their civic-related capabilities in each of the aforementioned developmental domains (Table 6.1).

Table 6.1   Developmental model of students' civic-related capabilities

Developmental domain	Early civic-related capabilities	Transitional civic-related capabilities	Advanced civic-related capabilities
Cognitive	Unequivocal thinking about civic issues and an unawareness of multiple perspectives	Evolving understanding of civic issues and an emerging awareness of multiple perspectives	A cogent understanding of civic issues and multiple perspectives
Intrapersonal	Limited understanding of own civic beliefs, values, and self-efficacy	Discernment of their own civic beliefs, values, and self-efficacy	A formed civic identity and ability to articulate civic beliefs, values, and self-efficacy
Interpersonal	Minimal exposure to and interactions with diverse others. Lack of or hesitant engagement in civic affairs	Openness to interaction with diverse others and infrequent and casual engagement in civic affairs	Meaningful interactions with diverse others and active participation in civic affairs

In order to advance the discourse of the civic engagement construct beyond the current research literature, we propose a model that examines civic-related capabilities. As mentioned earlier, we specifically use the term *civic-related capabilities* to reflect a student's capability, skill, or ability instead of the limited construct of civic engagement. Similar to Baxter-Magolda and King's intercultural model, this model examines the development of civic-related capabilities from early, transitional, and advanced perspectives across the cognitive, intrapersonal, and interpersonal domains. Please note that the development across these three domains is not linear, simultaneous, or only bound by experiences while students are enrolled in higher education.

Early Civic-Related Capabilities

Students within this developmental area possess a rudimentary capability across the three domains. For example, in the cognitive domain, students may have an unequivocal understanding of civic issues and concepts. This type of dualistic thinking about civic issues hinders students' capacity to appreciate multiple perspectives and, at this initial perspective, the intrapersonal domain suggests that students have limited understanding of their own civic beliefs, values, and self-efficacy. This type of limited civic-related capability does not allow students to understand their own civic-mindedness. Finally, in the interpersonal domain, students are less likely to engage with diverse others or lack the desire to engage in civic affairs (e.g., by voting, engaging in the political discourse, or engaging in the community).

Transitional Civic-Related Capabilities

These next columns of the model highlight how students have developed across the domains. At the cognitive domain, students are more likely to have an evolving understanding of civic issues that embraces different perspectives beyond their own, suggesting that they have an appreciation of the complex nature of civic-related issues and positions. Next, at the intrapersonal domain, students are beginning to discern their own civic-related beliefs and values (e.g., vocalizing their own position on civic-related views). Finally, at the interpersonal level, students are more likely to initiate civic affairs engagement with others from diverse backgrounds. Students within this domain are now likely to exercise their right to vote or attend a civic-related function (e.g., protest or rally).

Advanced Civic-Related Capabilities

Students in this area have developed an advanced perspective across all three domains but they may not arrive at this perspective for all three domains simultaneously. Students in the cognitive domain have developed a cogent understanding of complex civic issues, have an appreciation of multiple perspectives, and possess increased information literacy about civic issues and topics. Next, at the intrapersonal domain, students have formed a civic identity and are able to articulate and defend their personal civic beliefs and values (e.g., political affiliation or positions on civic matters). Students are also more likely to have developed self-efficacy to express these positions. Finally, in the interpersonal domain, students have the capability to have meaningful interactions with others from diverse backgrounds and actively participate in civic-related affairs. In this area, students are more likely to engage in their local communities, the broader state, and national political process, and become significantly more involved in other tangible civic-related behaviors.

CONCLUSION

This chapter provided a new framework to bring more clarity to the ubiquitous term "civic engagement." The nuanced model of civic engagement can be utilized by practitioners, researchers, and policymakers to better understand student development of civic-related capabilities. This chapter provides a critical framework to guide future discussions—a framework that can advance the scholarly work conducted at research universities to better understand the varied developmental trajectories of students who are engaged in community service, service-learning, volunteerism, social justice, political activism, and social change. We propose that such a model can enhance our understanding of the various ways in which students are engaged in their communities; however, further research is needed to validate the conceptual model to advance our discourse of undergraduates' civic-related development across cognitive, interpersonal, and intrapersonal domains. Applications of this model—especially in the context of research universities with their often decentralized models of operation—may prove useful as a means of collecting data associated with the varying levels of undergraduates' engagement in their communities.

REFERENCES

Anderson, J. L., Levis-Fitzgerald, M. R., & Rhoads, R. A. (2003). Democratic learning and global citizenship: The contribution of one-unit seminars. *JGE: The Journal of General Education, 52*(2), 84–107.

Angelique, H. L., Reischl, T. M., & Davidson, W. S. (2002). Promoting political empowerment: Evaluation of an intervention with university students. *American Journal of Community Psychology, 30*(6), 815–833.

Antonaros, M., Barnhardt, C., Holsapple, M., Moronski, K., & Vergoth, V. (2008). *Should colleges focus more on personal and social responsibility? Initial findings from campus surveys conducted for the Association of American Colleges and Universities as part of its initiative, core commitments: Educating students for personal and social responsibility.* Washington, DC: Association of American Colleges and Universities.

Astin, A. W. (1993). *What happens in college? Four critical years revisited.* San Francisco, CA: Jossey-Bass.

Astin, A. W., & Sax, L. J. (1998). How undergraduates are affected by service participation. *Journal of College Student Development, 39*(3), 251–263.

Astin, A. W., Sax, L. J., & Avalos, J. (1999). Long term effects of volunteerism during the undergraduate years. *The Review of Higher Education, 22*(2), 187–202.

Ball, W. J. (2005). From community engagement to political engagement. *PS, Political Science & Politics, 38*(2), 287–291.

Baxter Magolda, M. B. (2001). *Making their own way: Narratives for transforming higher education to promote self-development.* Sterling, VA: Stylus.

Baxter Magolda, M. B., & King, P. M. (2004). *Learning partnerships: A resource book for service-learning faculty in all disciplines.* Sterling, VA: Stylus.

Beaumont, E. (2005). The challenge of assessing civic engagement: What we know and what we still need to learn about civic education in college. *Journal of Public Affairs Education, 11*(4), 287–303.

Beaumont, E., Colby, A., Ehrlich, T., & Torney-Purta, J. (2006). Promoting political competence and engagement in college students: An empirical study. *Journal of Political Science Education, 2*(3), 249–270.

Bernstein, A. (2005). Gendered characteristics of political engagement in college students. *Sex Roles, 52*(5/6), 299–310.

Bernstein, J. L. (2007). Simulations and the dynamics of racial and gender gaps in civic competence. *New Directions for Teaching and Learning, 111,* 89–96.

Bernstein, J. L. (2008). Cultivating civic competence: Simulations and skill-building in an introductory government class. *Journal of Political Science Education, 4*(1), 1–20.

Bernstein, J. L., & Meizlish, D. S. (2003). Becoming congress: A longitudinal study of the civic engagement implications of a classroom simulation. *Simulation & Gaming, 34*(2), 198–219.

Blackhurst, A. E., & Foster, J. (2003). College students and citizenship: A comparison of civic attitudes and involvement in 1996 and 2000. *NASPA Journal, 40*(3), 153–174.

Bogard, C. J., Sheinheit, I., & Clarke, R. P. (2008). Information they can trust: Increasing youth voter turnout at the university. *Political Science & Politics, 41*(3), 541–546.

Boyte, H. C. (2005). Reframing democracy: Governance, civic agency, and politics. *Public Administration Review, 65*(5), 518–528.

Boyte, H. C. (2008). Against the current: Developing the civic agency of students. *Change: The Magazine of Higher Learning, 40*(3), 8–15.

Boyte, H., & Hollander, E. (1999). Wingspread declaration on renewing the civic mission of the American research university. Campus Compact [online].

Bringle, R. G., & Steinberg, K. S. (2010). Educating for informed community involvement. *American Journal of Community Psychology, 46,* 428–441.

Campus Compact. (2012). *Presidents' declaration on the civic responsibility of higher education.* Boston, MA: Campus Compact.

Chickering, A. W., & Reisser, L. (1993). *Education and identity* (2nd ed.). San Francisco, CA: Jossey-Bass.

Colby, A., Beaumont, E., Ehrlich, T., & Corngold, J. (2007). *Educating for democracy: Preparing undergraduates for responsible political engagement.* San Francisco, CA: Jossey-Bass.

Corbett, J. B., & Kendall, A. R. (1999). Evaluating service learning in the communication discipline. *Journalism & Mass Communication Educator, 53*(4), 66–76.

Cress, C. M., Astin, H. S., Zimmerman-Oster, K., & Burkhardt, J. C. (2001). Developmental outcomes of college students' involvement in leadership activities. *Journal of College Student Development, 42*(1), 15–27.

Dey, E. L., Barnhardt, C. L., Antonaros, M., Ott, C. M., & Holsapple, M. A. (2009). *Civic responsibility: What is the campus climate for learning?* Washington, DC: Association of American Colleges & Universities.

Dresner, M., & Blatner, J. S. (2006). Approaching civic responsibility using guided controversies about environmental issues. *College Teaching, 54*(2), 213–219.

Ehrlich, T. (Ed.). (2000). *Civic responsibility and higher education.* Phoenix, AZ: Oryx Press.

Einfeld, A., & Collins, D. (2008). The relationships between service-learning, social justice, multicultural competence, and civic engagement. *Journal of College Student Development, 49*(2), 95–109.

Elder, L., Seligsohn, A., & Hofrenning, D. (2007). Experiencing New Hampshire: The effects of an experiential learning course on civic engagement. *Journal of Political Science Education, 3*(2), 191–216.

Engberg, M. E. (2004). Improving intergroup relations in higher education: A critical examination of the influence of educational interventions on racial bias. *Review of Educational Research, 74*(4), 473–524.

Engberg, M. E., & Mayhew, M. J. (2007). The influence of first-year success courses on student learning and democratic outcomes. *Journal of College Student Development, 48*(3), 241–258.

Fall, L. (2006). Value of engagement: Factors influencing how students perceive their community contribution to public relations internships. *Public Relations Review, 32*(4), 407–415.

Giles, D. E., Jr., & Eyler, J. (1994). The impact of a college community service laboratory on students' personal, social and cognitive. *Journal of Adolescence, 17*(4), 327.

Gilligan, C. (1982). *In a different voice: Psychological theory and women's development.* Cambridge, MA: Harvard University Press.

González, R. G. (2008). College student civic development and engagement at a Hispanic serving institution. *Journal of Hispanic Higher Education, 7*(4), 287–300.

Gurin, P., Dey, E. L., Hurtado, S., & Gurin, G. (2002). Diversity and higher education: Theory and impact on educational outcomes. *Harvard Educational Review, 72*(3), 330.

Huerta, J. C., & Jozwiak, J. (2008). Developing civic engagement in general education political science. *Journal of Political Science Education, 4*(1), 42–60.

Huntemann, N. B. (2008). Seminar for freshman: Media literacy. In M. J. LaBare (Ed.), *Civic engagement in the first year of college* (pp. 91–92). New York, NY:

The New York Times Knowledge Network and the National Resource Center for the First-Year Experience and Students in Transition.

Hunter, S., & Brisbin, R. A. (2000). The impact of service learning on democratic and civic values. *PS, Political Science & Politics, 33*(3), 623–626.

Hurtado, S., Engberg, M. E., Ponjuan, L., & Landreman, L. (2002). Students' precollege preparation for participation in a diverse democracy. *Research in Higher Education, 43*(2), 163–186.

Hutchinson, M. (2005). Living the rhetoric: Service learning and increased value of social responsibility. *Pedagogy, 5*(3), 427–444.

Jensen, J. M., & Hunt, L. L. (2007). College in the state capital: Does it increase the civic engagement of political science undergraduate majors? *Political Science & Politics, 40*(3), 563–569.

Johnson, S. M., & Lollar, X. L. (2002). Diversity policy in higher education: The impact of college students' exposure to diversity on cultural awareness and political participation. *Journal of Education Policy, 17*(3), 305–320.

Joseph, M., Stone, G. W., Grantham, K., Harmancioglu, N., & Ibrahim, E. (2007). An exploratory study on the value of service learning projects and their impact on community service involvement and critical thinking. *Quality Assurance in Education: An International Perspective, 15*(3), 318–333.

Keen, C., & Hall, K. (2009). Engaging with difference matters: Longitudinal student outcomes of co-curricular service-learning programs. *Journal of Higher Education, 80*(1), 59–79.

Kegan, R. (1994). *In over our heads: The mental demands of modern life.* Cambridge, MA: President and Fellows of Harvard College, Harvard University Press.

King, P. M., & Baxter Magolda, M. B. (2005). A developmental model of intercultural maturity. *Journal of College Student Development, 46*(6), 571–592.

King, P. M., & Kitchener, K. S. (1994). *Developing reflective judgment: Understanding and promoting intellectual growth and critical thinking in adolescents and adults.* San Francisco, CA: Jossey-Bass.

King, P. M., & Kitchener, K. S. (2004). Reflective judgment: Theory and research on the development of epistemic assumptions through adulthood. *Educational Psychologist, 39*(1), 5–18.

Kirlin, M. (2003). *The role of civic skills in fostering civic engagement.* College Park, MD: University of Maryland. CIRCLE working paper 6. The Center for Information and Research on Civic Learning &Engagement.

Kirlin, M. (2005). Understanding the relationship between civic skills and civic participation: Educating future public managers. *Journal of Public Affairs Education, 11*(4), 305–314.

Klofstad, C. A. (2007). Talk leads to recruitment: How discussions about politics and current events increase civic participation. *Political Research Quarterly, 60*(2), 180–191.

Knefelkamp, L. (2008). Civic identity: Locating self in community. *Diversity and Democracy: Civic Learning for Shared Futures, 11*(2), 1–3.

Kuh, G. D., Kinzie, J., Schuh, J. H., & Whitt, E. J. (2010). *Student success in college: Creating conditions that matter.* San Francisco, CA: Jossey-Bass.

Lay, J., & Smarick, K. (2006). Simulating a senate office: The impact on student knowledge and attitudes. *Journal of Political Science Education, 2*(2), 131–146.

Lott, J. L., II. (2008). Racial identity and black students' perceptions of community outreach: Implications for bonding social capital. *Journal of Negro Education, 77*(1), 3–14.

Lott, J. L., II. (2013). Predictors of civic values: Understanding student-level and institutional-level effects. *Journal of College Student Development, 54*(1), 1–16.

Mabry, J. B. (1998). Pedagogical variations in service-learning and student outcomes: How time, contact, and reflection matter. *Michigan Journal of Community Service Learning, 5*, 32–47.

Macedo, S., Alex-Assensoh, Y., Berry, J. M., Campbell, D. E., Fraga, L. R., Fung, A., et al. (2005). *Democracy at risk: How political choices undermine citizen participation and what we can do about it.* Washington, DC: The Brookings Institution.

Malaney, G. D., & Berger, J. B. (2005). Assessing how diversity affects students' interest in social change. *Journal of College Student Retention: Research, Theory & Practice, 6*(4), 443–460.

Mayhew, M. J., & Fernández, S. D. (2007). Pedagogical practices that contribute to social justice outcomes. *Review of Higher Education, 31*(1), 55–80.

McKinney, M. S., & Chattopadhyay, S. (2007). Political engagement through debates: Young citizens' reactions to the 2004 presidential debates. *The American Behavioral Scientist, 50*(9), 1169.

Milner, H. (2002). *Civic literacy: How informed citizens make democracy work.* Medford, MA: Tufts University Press.

Moely, B. E., McFarland, M., Miron, D., Mercer, S., & Ilustre, V. (2002). Changes in college students' attitudes and intentions for civic involvement as a function of service-learning experiences. *Michigan Journal of Community Service Learning, 9*(1), 18–26.

Morse, R. S., Dudley, L. S., & Armstrong, J. P. (2005). Learning and teaching about deliberative democracy: On campus and in the field. *Journal of Public Affairs Education, 11*(4), 325–336.

Musil, C. M. (2009). Educating students for personal and social responsibility: The civic learning spiral. In B. Jacoby (Ed.), *Civic engagement in higher education* (pp. 49–68). San Francisco, CA: Jossey-Bass.

Pascarella, E. T., Ethington, C. A., & Smart, J. C. (1988). The influence of college on humanitarian/civic involvement values. *Journal of Higher Education, 59*(4), 412–437.

Pascarella, E. T., Smart, J. C., & Braxton, J. M. (1986). Postsecondary educational attainment and humanitarian and civic values. *Journal of College Student Personnel, 27*, 418–425.

Pascarella, E. T., & Terenzini, P. T. (2005). *How college affects students: A third decade of research* (Vol. 2). San Francisco, CA: Jossey-Bass.

Perry, W. G., Jr. (1970). *Forms of intellectual and ethical development in the college years: A scheme.* New York, NY: Holt, Rinehart, & Winston.

Persell, C. H., & Wenglinsky, H. (2004). For-profit post-secondary education and civic engagement. *Higher Education, 47*(3), 337–359.

Peters, J. R., & Stearns, D. E. (2003). Bringing educational relevancy to the first-year college experience by bearing witness to social problems. *Journal of Experiential Education, 25*(3), 332–342.

Prentice, M. (2007). Social justice through service learning: Community colleges as ground zero. *Equity & Excellence in Education, 40*(3), 266–273.

Prentice, M., & Robinson, G. (2007). *Linking service learning and civic engagement in community college students.* American Association of Community Colleges. One Dupont Circle NW Suite 410, Washington, DC.

Reeb, R. N. (2006). The community service self-efficacy scale. *Journal of Prevention and Intervention in the Community, 32*(1–2), 97–113.

Rhoads, R. A. (1998). In the service of citizenship: A study of student involvement in community service. *The Journal of Higher Education, 69*(3), 277–297.

Rios-Aguilar, C., & Mars, M. M. (2011). Integration or fragmentation? College student citizenship in the global society. *Education, Knowledge, and Economy, 5*(1–2), 29–44.

Rowan-Kenyon, H., Soldner, M., & Inkelas, K. K. (2008). The contributions of living-learning programs on developing sense of civic engagement in undergraduate students. *NASPA Journal, 44*(4), 750–778.

Sax, L. J. (2004). Citizenship development and the American college student. *New Directions for Institutional Research, 2004*(122), 65–80.

Schamber, J. F., & Mahoney, S. L. (2008). The development of political awareness and social justice citizenship through community-based learning in a first-year general education seminar. *The Journal of General Education, 57*(2), 75–99.

Schneider, C. G. (2006). Diversity, democracy, and goals for student learning. *Liberal Education, 92*(1), 1–2.

Spiezio, K. E., Baker, K. Q., & Boland, K. (2005). General education and civic engagement: An empirical analysis of pedagogical possibilities. *JGE: The Journal of General Education, 54*(4), 273–292.

Steinberg, K. S., Hatcher, J. A., & Bringle, R. G. (2011). Civic-minded graduate: A North Star. *Michigan Journal of Community Service Learning, 18*(1), 19–33.

Taylor, J. A., & Trepanier-Street, M. (2007). Civic education in multicultural contexts: New findings from a national study. *Social Studies, 98*(1), 14–18.

The National Task Force on Civic Learning and Democratic Engagement. (2012). *A crucible moment: College learning and democracy's future.* Washington, DC: Association of American Colleges and Universities.

Toossi, M. (2012). Labor force projections to 2020: A more slowly growing workforce. *Monthly Labor Review, 135*(1), 43–64.

U.S. Department of Education, Office of the Under Secretary and Office of Postsecondary Education. (2012). *Advancing civic learning and engagement in democracy: A road map and call to action.* Washington, DC: U.S. Department of Education.

Vogelgesang, L. J., & Astin, A. W. (2005). *Post-college civic engagement among graduates. HERI research report number 2.* Los Angeles, CA: Higher Education Research Institute, University of California.

Wells, S. D., & Dudash, E. A. (2007). Wha'd'ya know? Examining young voters' political information and efficacy in the 2004 election. *The American Behavioral Scientist, 50*(9), 1280.

Wilson, N. E., Diaz, A., O'Leary, L. S., & Terkla, D. G. (2007). Civic engagement: A study of changes in college. *Academic Exchange Quarterly, 11*(2), 141–147.

Zuniga, X., Williams, E. A., & Berger, J. B. (2005). Action-oriented democratic outcomes: The impact of student involvement with campus diversity. *Journal of College Student Development, 46*(6), 660–678.

PART II

Undergraduates' Participation in Community Service and Service-Learning: Involvement and Outcomes

CHAPTER 7

Civic Attitudes and the Undergraduate Experience

Gary R. Kirk and Jacob Grohs

A consistent assertion throughout the history of American higher education is that colleges and universities have a responsibility to serve the public good (Chambers 2005). This claim has been interpreted in a variety of ways by observers, scholars, and public policymakers, and, in recent decades, the explication of higher education's social contract received renewed attention as modern research universities attempted to meet the increasing number of demands and expectations placed on them by diverse stakeholder interests. In 2000, the Presidents' of dozens of American colleges and universities signed the Presidents' Declaration on the Civic Responsibilities of Higher Education (Campus Compact 2012). Among other things, this document stated:

> This country cannot afford to educate a generation that acquires knowledge without ever understanding how that knowledge can benefit society or how to influence democratic decision-making. We must teach the skills and values of democracy, creating innumerable opportunities for our students to practice and reap the real, hard work of citizenship. (p. 1)

To date, nearly 500 institutions have signed the declaration, including community colleges, liberal arts colleges, and major research universities.

Similarly, in 2005, the Talloires Declaration on the Civic Roles and Social Responsibilities of Higher Education signaled an *international* awareness of the need to invest in civic education initiatives (Taillores

© The Editor(s) (if applicable) and The Author(s) 2016
K.M. Soria, T.D. Mitchell (eds.), *Civic Engagement and Community Service at Research Universities*,
DOI 10.1057/978-1-137-55312-6_7

Network 2005). Ultimately signed by over 300 institutional leaders, Talloires was more direct in its call for change. In many ways, Talloires echoed the 2000 Declaration, stating, "Universities have the responsibility to foster...a sense of social responsibility and a commitment to the social good, which, we believe, is central to the success of a democratic and just society" (Taillores Network 2005, p. 1); however, it also contained a much more explicit list of required actions to achieve the changes sought by attendees. These actions included embedding social responsibility in university policies and practices and raising the rigor of community engagement activities to be on par with other forms of scholarship.

These national and international acknowledgments of the civic purposes of postsecondary education seemed to portend a shift in the way that colleges and universities prepared graduates to lead meaningful change responsive to the needs of communities. Champions of community engagement saw support from institutional leaders as a sign that their scholarship and pedagogy would gain increased legitimacy and garner new resources; yet, tensions remained within the network of engagement scholars and practitioners who were divided by the prospect of aligning service-learning practices with disciplinary expectations or using service-learning as an instrument for profound student and community change (Hartley 2009).

Perhaps burdened by these tensions, the engagement movement fueled in part by the Presidents' Declaration (Campus Compact 2012) and Taillores Network (2005) lost steam. As Saltmarsh and Hartley (2011) declared, the engagement movement had a very limited effect on curriculum at most institutions, and the number of schools that took their commitment to civic engagement beyond rhetoric was quite small. The failure of the movement to transform higher education was furthered by declines in support from foundations and federal budget cuts in 2011 to the Corporation for National and Community Service, a significant funder of service-learning initiatives (Saltmarsh and Hartley 2011).

As many postsecondary educational institutions face increasing external pressure to focus on economic goals for students such as job marketability (American Association of State Colleges and Universities 2014; Rawlings 2013), the civic and social missions of universities often are relegated to symbolic rhetoric (Saltmarsh and Hartley 2011). While most universities continue to proclaim a commitment to the moral development of their students (Einfeld and Collins 2008), political and financial realities often favor allocation of resources to revenue-generating research activities and academic disciplines with high starting salaries for graduates. To be clear, research and economic outcomes are not explicitly in conflict with civic missions, but in the highly political and competitive, limited-resource environment faced by most higher education institutions, prioritizing economic goals often leads to deprioritizing civic goals.

Parallel to these moves away from the civic goals at many higher education institutions, there is a growing recognition that society needs well-prepared, active citizens in order to address the short- and long-term issues that persist in communities throughout the world. Globalization, economic instability, new and evolving cultural unrest, political polarization, and rapid technological change have all contributed to a set of public issues that are more complex and interrelated than ever before. Prior to the new millennium, Paul (1993) posited that "[g]overnmental, economic, social, and environmental problems will become increasingly complex and interdependent ... The forces to be understood and controlled will be corporate, national, trans-national, cultural, religious, economic, and environmental, all intricately intertwined" (p. 13). Despite technological advances and multiple policy interventions, the persistence of long-standing issues, like food insecurity and health disparities, seems to confirm Paul's assertions two decades later.

In a society struggling with complex problems and deteriorating political dialogue, it is more important than ever for undergraduate students to graduate with the critical thinking and collaboration skills necessary for meaningful engagement in community (Hurtado and DeAngelo 2012). Graduates who are guided by a public ethic and sense of civic responsibility are clearly needed to take leadership roles as society considers its most pressing social problems. Recent thought leaders and scholars have called for the restructuring of higher education to advance the development of civic-minded graduates who have "the capacity and desire to work with others to achieve the common good" (Steinberg et al. 2011, p. 20). The imperative for higher education leaders, then, is to balance the competing demands to produce graduates who are both economically viable and civically minded by explicitly programming for both across diverse academic disciplines (Boyer 1996; Steinberg et al. 2011).

There are two broad approaches to achieving civic outcomes for undergraduate students. The first is to purposefully and strategically integrate, via institution-level planning and investment, content knowledge and pedagogies that advance civic outcomes into the undergraduate experience through academic curriculum and/or co-curricular programming.

This active approach is uncommon, especially at large research-focused universities, but it has been successfully implemented at a few schools (e.g., Tulane University). The second approach is to expect civic outcomes as a by-product of the overall undergraduate experience, an approach that relies upon decentralized faculty-led service-learning, co-curricular community service and volunteering, and other campus programs to contribute to civic learning without institutional coordination, targeted resources, or shared goals. This more passive approach, taken by many institutions, is supported by scholarly evidence demonstrating the efficacy of individual programs and pedagogies (e.g., Astin and Sax 1998).

In fact, a number of practices have been promoted as effective in advancing civic education for undergraduates, and many of them overlap with the "educationally purposeful practices" known to be effective in increasing student engagement and academic performance (Kuh 2009, p. 684). Formal course-based service-learning, co-curricular community service and volunteering, and living-learning communities have all been linked to enhanced civic attitudes and behaviors. Service-learning in particular has received significant attention for its potential to engage students with civic issues and communities while also contributing to mastery and retention of disciplinary knowledge (Bringle and Steinberg 2010; Eyler and Giles 1999; Jameson et al. 2013; Mitchell 2013; Zlotkowski and Duffy 2010). In fact, Chisholm (2005) asserted that service-learning is the primary mode by which most universities can "infuse the notion of social responsibility" into the higher education experience (p. 97). Peacock (2005) agreed that service-learning gives students "the competence and confidence" to address emerging social needs in a global economy (p. 114).

In studies of the student learning associated with participation in service-learning, researchers have found a variety of significant gains compared to students taught via other pedagogies. Antonio et al. (2000) found that service-learning was positively associated with several outcomes that have relevance to civic agency, including leadership skills, racial understanding, subject-matter knowledge, allocation of concepts to new situations, strengthened critical-thinking skills, civic responsibility (i.e., commitment to serving community), interest in influencing political structure, and engagement with future volunteer work. Other researchers found similar results related to appreciation of ethical issues that affect the world of practice: a better sense of self (i.e., personal values and motives), increased self-confidence, a clearer understanding of how to make a difference in communities, and a better understanding of communities and the problems they face (Beere et al. 2011). Einfeld and Collins (2008) found evidence that service-learning experiences have the potential to influence students' development of multicultural competence.

Like most educational interventions, the approach to—and quality of— service-learning can vary widely depending on the institution, the faculty member, the course content, and the community partner. Mabry (1998) found that specific attributes of the pedagogy had significant influence on student outcomes. Particularly, increased contact between students and community and intentional reflection, were found to be important predictors of civic and academic outcomes. Butin (2010) outlined a variety of different perspectives through which service-learning can be viewed by institutions and individual faculty, ranging from a technical perspective, which is concerned with the efficacy of the pedagogy in terms of student learning, to the anti-foundational perspective, whereby service-learning is viewed as an opportunity to challenge assumptions and to realize that "truths are local, contingent, and intersubjective" (p. 13). Clearly, if service-learning is not well-designed and well-implemented, or is employed without civic outcomes in mind, then it is difficult to expect it to be the magic bullet for civic education. Zlotkowski and Duffy (2010) observed:

> ...faculty increasingly recognize the importance of civic development within the overall frame of undergraduate education. Some are even willing to concede their own responsibility for contributing to this development. Nevertheless, the civic remains by and large one of the least well developed features of service-learning programs and community-based work. (p. 40)

Co-curricular practices and programs might also hold potential in developing students' civic outcomes. Two practices that stand out as having relevance for civic education are volunteer community service and participation in a living-learning community. Despite the lack of an academic context or formal opportunities for reflection, volunteering during higher education has been linked to positive civic outcomes (Sax et al. 1999; Steinberg et al. 2011). Living-learning communities have also been suggested as possible mechanisms to enhance civic outcomes (Adams et al. 2014; Jessup-Anger et al. 2012; Levine 2006; Soria and Mitchell 2015). While not all living-learning communities focus on civic outcomes for their residents, there are growing numbers of communities that do so nationally. Furthermore, living-learning communities often embrace practices consistent with service-learning, like reflection, community engagement, and diversity programming.

INSTITUTIONAL CONTEXT

The work that is described herein documents an attempt to understand how civic outcomes are being achieved at Virginia Tech, a large public research institution that has operated without coordinated university-level efforts to achieve civic learning outcomes for students. The university has programs and initiatives related to service-learning, community service, and living-learning communities. In addition, the student affairs division has named community service as one of its aspirational goals for students and is now working to link co-curricular programs to that goal. These efforts have had limited visibility in the university community, especially among academic faculty, and participation by students in the formal programs has been limited to date.

MEASUREMENT

Three constructs were selected for inclusion in a pilot effort to measure civic outcomes for students: social justice awareness, diversity attitudes, and community orientation. Additional areas that were identified for measurement but were not included in the initial pilot include: community service self-efficacy (Reeb et al. 2010), service motivation (Clary et al. 1998), and community systems thinking, which is a multifaceted concept that characterizes an individual's approach to problem-solving in a community context. The first two dimensions, social justice attitudes and diversity attitudes, were modified from the Civic Attitudes and Skills Questionnaire (CASQ) which was originally developed for evaluation of service-learning students (Moely et al. 2002). These two brief instruments, including eight and five items respectively, were extracted from a larger questionnaire and are self-reported on a five-point Likert-type scale. Previous research found acceptable levels of internal consistency ($\alpha = 0.70$, 0.70), and responses were only slightly affected by social desirability of responses (Moely et al. 2002). The original version of the CASQ included four additional dimensions, civic action, interpersonal and problem-solving skills, political awareness, and leadership skills; these items were excluded from the pilot.

After the initial pilot year, factor analysis suggested that in this institutional context, the CASQ social justice attitudes construct was actually two separate constructs. The first, which included four questions pertaining to the role of individual responsibility and the root causes of poverty, is referred to as "social justice-individual." The second construct, "social justice-systems," included three questions focused more on the systemic and institutional barriers to eliminating poverty. A single question that did not load with either of these two constructs was dropped for future measurement efforts.

Since no existing survey-based scales were identified for measurement of community orientation, a new twelve-item questionnaire (five-point response) was designed. The concept of community orientation included two main components: (1) the relative level of thoughtfulness about commitment to local, regional, national, and global communities, and (2) the ways in which that orientation is manifested, either as a propensity to volunteer or to make donations in support of community needs. Initial piloting of the new instrument, named Measures of Community Orientation (MoCO), and subsequent data-reduction efforts led to modifications implemented in 2015. The new instrument dropped efforts to differentiate four separate geopolitical scales, opting instead to focus on local and global orientations; this decision was based on the extremely high degree of collinearity between community levels. For the purposes of this study, two independent questions are used to represent community orientation at the local and global levels; they ask respondents to agree or disagree with the statements, "I often think about my role in my local community" and "I often think about my role in my global community."

Using these measurement tools, this study seeks to identify associations between participation in undergraduate experiences with potential civic outcomes and student civic attitudes. To that end, three research questions framed this study: (1) Is student participation in a living-learning community positively associated with civic outcomes, including social justice attitudes, diversity attitudes, and orientation to local or global communities? (2) Is student participation in co-curricular volunteerism positively associated with these civic outcomes? And, (3) Is student participation in course-based service-learning positively associated with the same civic outcomes?

METHODS

This study presents early results from an effort to implement institution-level assessment of civic attitudes for all undergraduate students at Virginia Tech, a public land-grant university classified as a very high research university by the Carnegie Foundation (n.d.). The effort was initiated by VT Engage, an administrative unit responsible for advancing curricular and co-curricular community engagement and service-learning. VT Engage partnered with the university's Office of Assessment and Evaluation to administer the assessment scales as part of two broader initiatives—the Survey of Incoming Freshmen and the Senior Survey.

Integrating the civic outcomes assessment in centrally administered pre-existing surveys addressed concerns about student-survey fatigue and added legitimacy to the efforts. The Survey of Incoming Freshmen was administered in the summer to all students who had been offered admission for the subsequent fall semester (and accepted that offer), and the Senior Survey was administered to all graduating seniors in the semester in which they declared their intent to graduate.

Piloting of the civic outcomes assessment began in fall 2012 with a subset of the scales selected to measure civic outcomes. In subsequent administrations, the specific scales have changed and, in the most recent administrations, have moved to a protocol that assigns respondents to a subset of scales based on birth month to address survey dropout rates by reducing overall survey length. This approach tied individuals to a specific set of assessment competencies across time without the need to make the connect based on personally identifying information. Consistent over all administrations are the social justice attitudes and diversity attitudes scales plus two key questions designed to understand community orientation, which formed the basis of the discussion in this chapter. Data presented in this report contain first-year student data collected prior to fall semester in 2013 and 2014 and senior survey data collected in fall and spring semesters during academic years 2012–2013 and 2013–2014.

Both the first-year and senior surveys were administered using online survey software to all students in each respective group. In recent years, response rates varied between 42 and 48 %. In addition to measuring the identified civic outcomes, these surveys also gather various demographic, academic, and community engagement data for each respondent. Information was collected about anticipated (first year) and actual (senior) participation in several course-based service-learning, general volunteering, living-learning communities, and other campus programs and activities.

The sample of first-year students and seniors had characteristics that roughly approximate the undergraduate population at Virginia Tech. The sample appears to include a lower proportion of female and White students than the overall undergraduate population, but substantial numbers of students chose not to answer or disclose various demographic characteristics. Those respondents are included in Table 7.1 in the "Other" category, which also includes categories with 10 or fewer respondents.

Table 7.1   Descriptive statistics for sample by status

	Entering first-year		Graduating senior	
	n	*%*	*n*	*%*
Gender				
Female	1990	46.00	1429	41.40
Male	2051	47.40	1363	39.50
Other (incl. "prefer not to answer")	286	6.60	661	19.10
Race				
White	2986	69.00	2278	66.00
Black/African American	113	2.60	66	1.90
Native American	11	0.30	4	0.10
Asian/Pacific Islander	460	10.60	173	5.00
Hispanic/Latino	158	3.70	81	2.30
Other (incl. "prefer not to answer")	599	13.80	851	24.70
GPA	*High school*		*Undergraduate*	
≤2.5	–	–	179	5.10
2.51–3.0	11	0.20	561	16.20
3.01–3.5	266	6.10	1117	32.30
3.51–4.0	1863	43.10	948	27.50
>4.0	1900	43.90	–	–
Did not answer	287	6.60	648	18.80
Undergraduate experiences	*Intent to participate*		*Self-reported participation*	
Course-based community service	3615	83.50	881	25.50
Volunteer work	3512	81.20	2236	64.80
Living-learning community	2044	47.20	420	12.20

In order to answer the research questions, independent samples *t*-tests were performed to compare senior students who participated in three experiences, with potential to influence civic outcomes—living-learning communities, co-curricular volunteerism, and course-based service-learning.

RESULTS

Table 7.1 reveals an exceptionally large gap between the proportion of incoming students who indicate a desire to participate in living-learning communities (47.2 %) and course-based service-learning (83.5 %) and the proportion of seniors who reported actually participating (12.2 and 25.5 %, respectively). A gap also exists for co-curricular volunteering, but it is considerably smaller (81.2 % first-year students' intent, 64.6 % senior participation). Assuming these proportions have remained relatively constant over time, this result could indicate a failure of the institution to provide adequate opportunities for interested students. It could also reflect the reality that many students face in trying to prioritize their participation in the overwhelming number of programs, activities, and experiences available at a large university.

While the intention of this study was not to make comparisons of changes in civic attitudes over time, the data in Table 7.2 indicate that average scores are higher for seniors than first-year students on the social justice-individual scale and the social justice-systems scale. Of equal interest, but perhaps greater concern, are the lower average scores for seniors on diversity attitudes and the local and global community orientation measures.

Table 7.3 shows results for the independent samples t-tests for senior-level students based on their self-reported participation in the three undergraduate experiences. Living-learning community participation was associated with statistically higher scores on the social justice-systems scale ($p < 0.05$) and local community orientation ($p < 0.001$). Despite the statistical significance of these findings, the effect size, reported as Cohen's d, was small in both cases. There was no significant difference detected for the other three civic outcomes.

For co-curricular volunteering, significant differences were observed for all five of the civic outcomes. The statistical significance is interpreted in the context of low effect sizes on all of the civic outcomes, with only local community orientation approaching a medium-sized effect. Finally, the results for course-based service-learning indicate a statistically significant relationship between participation and social justice-systems and the local and global measures of community orientation.

Table 7.2 Means of civic outcomes by status

	Entering first-year			Graduating senior		
	n	m	SD	n	m	SD
Civic outcome						
Social justice-individual	2812	3.51	0.71	2906	3.65	0.76
Social justice-systems	2800	3.55	0.62	2894	3.60	0.66
Diversity attitudes	2862	3.85	0.58	2890	3.84	0.61
Local orientation	2908	3.75	0.83	2601	3.52	0.97
Global orientation	2902	3.85	0.92	2586	3.60	1.00

Table 7.3 Independent samples t-test

	Participated			Did not participate				
	n	m	s	n	m	s	d	t
Living-learning community								
Social justice-individual	412	3.70	0.77	2494	3.65	0.76	0.08	−1.44
Social justice-systems	410	3.67	0.70	2484	3.59	0.65	0.12	−2.33*
Diversity attitudes	411	3.87	0.61	2479	3.83	0.61	0.06	−1.21
Local orientation	388	3.69	1.00	2213	3.49	0.96	0.20	−3.73***
Global orientation	388	3.67	1.04	2198	3.59	0.99	0.08	−1.45
Co-curricular volunteering								
Social justice-individual	2190	3.68	0.73	716	3.58	0.82	0.13	−3.21***
Social justice-systems	2179	3.62	0.65	715	3.55	0.68	0.11	−2.54*
Diversity attitudes	2176	3.87	0.60	714	3.75	0.63	0.19	−4.58***
Local orientation	1991	3.61	0.94	610	3.23	1.00	0.39	−8.56***
Global orientation	1978	3.65	0.99	608	3.44	1.03	0.21	−4.50***
Course-based community service (service learning)								
Social justice-individual	859	3.68	0.77	2047	3.64	0.75	0.04	−1.06
Social justice-systems	855	3.64	0.67	2039	3.59	0.65	0.08	−1.99*
Diversity attitudes	854	3.87	0.61	2036	3.83	0.61	0.06	−1.54
Local orientation	775	3.69	0.93	1826	3.44	0.97	0.26	−5.95***
Global orientation	775	3.66	0.98	1811	3.57	1.01	0.09	−2.16*

Note: $*p < 0.05$, $**p < 0.01$, $***p < 0.001$

DISCUSSION

The results of this study suggest that civic outcomes are positively influenced by student participation in three different types of programs available to many undergraduate students at research universities; however, the magnitude of the effects is small. The results indicate that participation in living-learning communities, co-curricular volunteering, and course-based service-learning, all positively influenced systemic social justice attitudes and local community orientation. Co-curricular volunteering was also positively associated with attitudes related to individual responsibility in social justice, diversity attitudes, and global community orientation. Course-based service-learning was associated with more positive attitudes toward global community orientation. The low effect size for all of these relationships may be an artifact of a variety of uncontrolled factors, such as participation in other, unmeasured programs and the depth of engagement with the programs. As well, a longitudinal, repeated measures design may allow for greater sensitivity to individual dispositions that exist prior to the undergraduate experience.

At the root of this study is the need to strike a manageable balance between (1) moving beyond traditional civic output measures (e.g., number of volunteer hours) to more rigorously quantify and qualify civic outcomes and (2) more comprehensively exploring civic outcomes institution-wide. Because this work is early in its lifecycle (i.e., reporting on 2 years of data that was designed as a within-subjects longitudinal study) and in order to balance these two demanding needs, significant conclusions drawn are directly associated with accompanying limitations. These conclusions, framed primarily as suggestions for further research and implications for practice, are as follows: understanding the demand for and availability of undergraduate civic learning experiences, intentionally designing curriculum and co-curriculum to emphasize and assess complex civic outcomes, developing more robust measures of civic outcomes, and informing and grounding institutional conversations about the civic outcomes of higher education.

Understanding Demand and Availability

Sizable differences between intent to participate in undergraduate experiences associated with civic learning and the self-reported actual participation from Table 7.1 are startling. Even after considering that intent to participate is hardly a reliable predictor of actual participation, the difference is meaningfully large and unexplained. Clearly, there is a need for additional efforts by administrators and researchers to better understand the barriers associated with participation in civic engagement activities. Building high-quality programs and designing effective learning outcomes and assessment strategies are insufficient strategies for civic learning if systemic barriers prevent students from participating. Administrators responsible for civic learning programs cannot assume that low turnout is due to weak advertising or the day/time programs are offered. Efforts to promote the value of the programs, their linkages to a variety of academic disciplines, and their potential impact on the individual and society may be necessary to change the culture at many institutions. Rather than focusing solely on students, these efforts may need to focus on convincing faculty, academic advisors, and academic administrators, who appear to be participating in authentic engagement work at low rates, of the relevance and value of civic engagement activities (Demb and Wade 2012).

Curriculum and Co-curriculum Design for Civic Outcomes

It was argued earlier that civic engagement work in higher education, particularly at large research institutions, remains at the margins of the curriculum and that student civic outcomes are often assumed to follow from the sum of their undergraduate experience. This study provided preliminary evidence that this approach can lead to inconsistent results related to civic outcomes. While students who chose to participate in living-learning communities, community service, or service-learning appeared to have more developed civic attitudes, in general, graduating seniors scored lower relative to incoming first-year students on several civic constructs. At an institution like Virginia Tech, where a large proportion of students study in science, technology, engineering, and math (STEM) disciplines, civic outcomes may be more difficult to achieve due to lower civic dispositions upon entering higher education, narrower socialization in the academic department, and lower likelihood of participation in relevant programs during higher education (Garibay 2015). While these data provide initial evidence to support future institutional investment in practices with evidence-based linkages to civic outcomes, it is clear that many students are not having these important experiences and that departmental cultures and student characteristics may present barriers to broader participation.

In light of those findings, we believe that a more strategic approach to civic education would include setting institutional civic learning outcomes and designing integrated curricular and co-curricular learning programs to advance students' civic development. Simply taking inventory of existing programs is not enough if efforts are uncoordinated and lack a shared purpose. If institutions expect their students to achieve specific civic outcomes, then the strategic approach includes explicitly stating these objectives, investing resources in programs designed to influence relevant student learning, and measuring student outcomes. In the modern higher education environment, articulating civic learning outcomes and measuring student mastery of those outcomes is aligned with expectations for documenting disciplinary academic learning outcomes.

Better Measures for Civic Outcomes

The tools available for measurement of civic outcomes are growing in number, and there is substantial research and scholarship to support the use of various instruments and scales. As with many constructs in the social and human sciences, civic attitudes and learning outcomes often are very complex. Many of the available measurement scales have been tested in limited environments (e.g., specific disciplines, specific pedagogies) and limited time frames (e.g., pre- and post-semester). As the field becomes more concerned with long-term civic outcomes and the effect that civic learning has on civic behaviors and community impact, there is a need to develop more robust measures, applicable in a variety of contexts, and a need to specify the sensitivity of the instruments available. This can be accomplished through continued work, like that presented in this volume, and through mixed-methods research that operationalizes and clarifies variations in quantitative measures. By building a suite of powerful measures related to civic outcomes, researchers empower administrators to better assess the efficacy of the programs on their campuses and the civic competencies of their graduates. In addition to informing programmatic continuous improvement, more robust evidence of civic learning gains also allows administrators to construct an evidence-based narrative to explain the value of investments in civic engagement programs.

Informing Institutional Conversations About Civic Outcomes of Higher Education

Though not directly linked to a reported result, a fundamental limitation resulting from embedding these instruments in an institutional survey is the inability to know how individuals interpret specific survey language. For example, course-based community service is not the specific language used in the service-learning scholarly community, and it may or may not evoke in the minds of students and faculty the specific set of characteristics that the service-learning community would indicate as essential. While a simple improvement in the future could involve qualitative studies to better understand interpretation, it also highlights a much broader issue within institutional practice. While identifying a universally acceptable definition of service-learning might be impossible, a fundamental reason that such work remains on the margins could be that too many individuals define it differently. From our experience, we know that "course-based community service" lumps together incredibly thoughtful community-engaged learning experiences and haphazard community experiences without strong connections to course content, reflection, or assessment efforts. Since, at least at our institution, the designation of a course as a service-learning course is decentralized, the range of student experiences in service-learning varies widely in quality and outcome. Clearly, the essential elements of these educationally purposeful practices must remain intact in order to expect high quality learning outcomes, civic or otherwise.

References

Adams, A. N., Brock, R. J., Gordon, K. A., Grohs, J. R., & Kirk, G. R. (2014). Service, dialogue, and reflection as foundational elements in a living learning community. *Journal of College and Character, 15*(3), 179–188.

American Association of State Colleges & Universities (2014). *AASCU's position on the Obama administration's proposed Postsecondary Institutions Ratings System (PIRS)*. http://www.aascu.org/policy/federal-policy/outreach/PIRStestimony09122014.pdf.

Antonio, A. L., Astin, H. S., & Cress, C. (2000). Community service in higher education: A look at the faculty. *The Review of Higher Education, 23*(4), 373–398.

Astin, A. W., & Sax, L. J. (1998). How undergraduates are affected by service participation. *Journal of College Student Development, 39*(3), 251–263.

Beere, C. A., Votruba, J. C., & Wells, G. W. (2011). *Becoming an engaged campus: A practical guide to institutionalizing public engagement*. San Francisco, CA: Jossey-Bass.

Boyer, E. L. (1996). The scholarship of engagement. *Journal of Public Service and Outreach, 1*(1), 11–20.

Bringle, R. G., & Steinberg, K. (2010). Educating for informed community involvement. *American Journal of Community Psychology, 46*(3–4), 428–441.

Butin, D. W. (2010). *Service-learning in theory and practice: The future of community engagement in higher education*. New York, NY: Palgrave Macmillan.

Campus Compact (2012). Presidents' declaration on the civic responsibilities of higher education. http://www.compact.org/wp-content/uploads/2009/02/Presidents-Declaration.pdf.

Carnegie Classification of Institutions of Higher Education (n.d.). *About Carnegie Classification*. http://carnegieclassifications.iu.edu/.

Chambers, T. C. (2005). The special role of higher education in society: As a public good for the public good. In A. J. Kezar, T. C. Chambers, & J. C. Burkhardt (Eds.), *Higher education for the public good: Emerging voices from a national movement* (pp. 3–22). San Francisco, CA: Jossey-Bass.

Chisholm, L. (2005). Committing to the world community. In L. Chisholm (Ed.), *Knowing and doing: The theory and practice of service-learning* (pp. 95–108). New York, NY: International Partnership for Service-Learning and Leadership.

Clary, E. G., Snyder, M., Ridge, R. D., Copeland, J., Stukas, A. A., Haugen, J., et al. (1998). Understanding and assessing the motivations of volunteers: A functional approach. *Journal of Personality and Social Psychology, 74*(6), 1516–1530.

Demb, A., & Wade, A. (2012). Reality check: Faculty involvement in outreach & engagement. *The Journal of Higher Education, 83*(3), 337–366.

Einfeld, A., & Collins, D. (2008). The relationship between service learning, social justice, multicultural competence, and civic engagement. *Journal of College Student Development, 49*(2), 95–109.

Eyler, J. S., & Giles, D. E. (1999). *Where's the learning in service learning?* San Francisco, CA: Jossey-Bass.

Garibay, J. C. (2015). STEM students' social agency and views on working for social change: Are STEM disciplines developing socially and civically responsible students? *Journal of Research in Science Teaching, 52*(5), 610–632.

Hartley, M. (2009). Reclaiming the democratic purposes of American higher education: Tracing the trajectory of the civic engagement movement. *Learning and Teaching, 2*(3), 11–30.

Hurtado, S., & DeAngelo, L. (2012). Linking diversity and civic-minded practices with student outcomes: New evidence from national surveys. *Liberal Education, 98*(2), 14–23.

Jameson, J. K., Clayton, P. H., & Ash, S. L. (2013). Conceptualizing, assessing, and investigating academic learning in service learning. In P. Clayton, R. Bringle, & J. Hatcher (Eds.), *Research on service learning* (Vol. 2A, pp. 85–110). Sterling, VA: Stylus.

Jessup-Anger, J. E., Dowdy, R. P., & Janz, M. (2012). Social justice begins at home: The challenges and successes of a social justice living learning community. *Journal of College and Character, 13*(4). doi:10.1515/jcc-2012-1936.

Kuh, G. D. (2009). What student affairs professionals need to know about student engagement. *Journal of College Student Development, 50*(6), 683–706.

Levine, P. (Ed.). (2006). *Higher education: Civic mission & civic effects*. Stanford, CA: The Carnegie Foundation for the Advancement of Teaching and the Center for Information and Research on Civic Learning and Engagement.

Mabry, J. B. (1998). Pedagogical variations in service-learning and student outcomes: How time, contact, and reflection matter. *Michigan Journal of Community Service Learning, 5*, 32–47.

Mitchell, T. D. (2013). Critical service-learning as a philosophy for community engagement. In A. Hoy & M. Johnson (Eds.), *Deepening community engagement in higher education: Forging new pathways* (pp. 263–272). New York, NY: Palgrave-MacMillan.

Moely, B. E., Mercer, S. H., Ilustre, V., Miron, D., & McFarland, M. (2002). Psychometric properties and correlates of the civic attitudes and skills questionnaire (CASQ): A measure of students' attitudes related to service learning. *Michigan Journal of Community Service Learning, 8*(2), 15–26.

Paul, R. (1993). The logic of creative and critical thinking. In J. Wilsen & A. J. A. Binker (Eds.), *Critical thinking: How to prepare students for a rapidly changing world* (pp. 195–215). Santa Rosa, CA: Foundation for Critical Thinking.

Peacock, D. (2005). Developing human values. In L. Chisholm (Ed.), *Knowing and doing: The theory and practice of service-learning* (pp. 109–116). New York, NY: International Partnership for Service-Learning and Leadership.

Rawlings, H. (2013). Letter to Jamie Studley, Deputy under Secretary, Department of Education on behalf of the Association of American Universities (AAU). http://www.aau.edu/WorkArea/DownloadAsset.aspx?id=14835.

Reeb, R. N., Folger, S. F., Langsner, S., Ryan, C., & Crouse, J. (2010). Self-efficacy in service-learning community action research: Theory, research, and practice. *American Journal of Community Psychology, 46*(3), 459–471.

Saltmarsh, J., & Hartley, M. (2011). Introduction. In J. Saltmarsh & M. Hartley (Eds.), *"To serve a larger purpose": Engagement for democracy and the transformation of higher education* (pp. 1–13). Philadelphia, PA: Temple University Press.

Sax, L. J., Astin, A. W., & Avalos, J. (1999). Long-term effects of volunteerism during the undergraduate years. *The Review of Higher Education, 22*(2), 187–202.

Soria, K. M., & Mitchell, T. D. (2015). Learning communities: Foundations for first-year students' development of pluralistic outcomes. *Learning Communities Research and Practice, 3*(2).

Steinberg, K., Hatcher, J., & Bringle, R. (2011). Civic-minded graduate: A north star. *Michigan Journal of Community Service Learning, 18*(1), 19–33.

Taillores Network (2005). Declaration on the civic roles and social responsibilities of higher education. http://talloiresnetwork.tufts.edu/who-we-ar/talloires-declaration/.

Zlotkowski, E., & Duffy, D. (2010). Two decades of community-based learning. *New Directions for Teaching and Learning, 123*, 33–43.

CHAPTER 8

Modeling the Influence of Service-Learning on Academic and Sociocultural Gains: Findings from a Multi-institutional Study

Andrew Furco, Daniel Jones-White, Ronald Huesman Jr., and Laura Segrue Gorny

Over the past 20 years, there has been a national movement to encourage higher education institutions to deepen students' community involvement and civic development. The passage of the *National and Community Service Trust Act* in 1993 established the Learn and Serve America program, which set into motion a national agenda to integrate civic- and community-engaged service initiatives into the academic curriculum of the country's primary, secondary, and higher education institutions. The federally sponsored funding, support, and visibility for this work catalyzed the development of a strong community of service-learning practitioners as well as the formation of campus-wide service-learning and civic engagement centers and units. While many colleges and universities enthusiastically embraced this agenda, research universities generally took a more critical stance, casting service-learning and the broader national service agenda as just another educational fad. At the time, Ward (1996) wrote: "For service-learning to transcend its critics' cynicism as merely another fad for educational reform, then it must be integrated into campus cultures and become central to organizational mission. Institutionalization is essential

© The Editor(s) (if applicable) and The Author(s) 2016   143
K.M. Soria, T.D. Mitchell (eds.), *Civic Engagement and Community Service at Research Universities*,
DOI 10.1057/978-1-137-55312-6_8

if service-learning is to survive on college campuses" (p. 3). Although several prominent research universities did embrace service-learning and the furthering of student civic development, the deepest programming and institutionalization of student civic engagement efforts were found in non-research intensive universities (Furco 2001).

As student service-learning programming continued to expand and flourish throughout the 1990s and 2000s, as the call for more university civic involvement strengthened following several national tragedies (e.g., 9/11, Hurricane Katrina), and as empirical evidence of the potential power and impact of these experiences on students' civic development began to emerge, more research universities adopted community engagement agendas and made greater investments in programs focused on enhancing student community involvement and civic development. Indeed, during the 2000s, service-learning and other academically connected community-based learning strategies had finally found their place as recognized, legitimate, and valued pedagogical approaches to fostering students' civic development across all types of higher education institutions (Kuh 2008). Grounded in experiential and authentic learning theories, these community-engaged approaches also began to be linked to enhancements in students' academic learning and social development (Kolb et al. 2000; Kuh 2008; Slavkin 2004).

Over the last 30 years, more than 600 published studies have examined issues concerning undergraduate students' involvement in various types of community-engaged learning experiences. With the rise of the federal national service agenda during this time, most of these studies have focused on the practice of service-learning and its impact on students (Eyler et al. 2003). Overall, the findings from studies of service-learning can be categorized as having potentially positive student impacts in six areas: *academic* learning and educational success; *personal* development (e.g., self-esteem, empowerment); *civic* development (e.g., citizenship, civic capacity); *social* development (e.g., sociocultural development, interpersonal development); *ethical/moral* development; and *career* awareness and preparation. The majority of service-learning studies point to generally positive findings within and across these outcome domains.

Because service-learning engages students in community service experiences that both are situated in diverse community contexts and are integrated with students' academic work, the call for more evidence that supports the impact of service-learning on students' academic achievement, civic behaviors (Sherrod et al. 2010), and sociocultural development has been especially strong (Celio et al. 2011; Simons and Cleary 2006; Steinke and Buresh 2002; Yorio and Ye 2012). In regard to academic outcomes, findings from several studies reveal that students' participation in service-learning can promote higher outcomes in students' course-content knowledge (Mpofu 2007), cognitive skills (Eyler and Giles 1999; Steinke and Buresh 2002), grade point averages (Astin et al. 2000), and re-enrollment and retention (Bringle et al. 2010; Gallini and Moely 2003).

However, when comparing service-learning students to students in control and comparison groups, the findings regarding the academic benefits of service-learning for participating students have been generally mixed. Even among the studies that have shown a positive relationship between service-learning and academic achievement, the effect sizes are generally small. Similarly, service-learning studies that have explored outcomes in the areas of civic (or citizenship) development, career development, and ethical (or moral) development have also revealed mixed results (Conway et al. 2009).

However, the most positive and consistent findings of service-learning participation across different types of educational settings, student populations, and community settings are found primarily in the personal and social development domains. These service-learning studies reveal the largest effect sizes when compared to findings in the other domains. The personal development outcomes most correlated with service-learning are enhanced student sense of empowerment (McBride and Sherraden 2007; Morgan and Streb 2003), sense of belonging (Kezar 1998; Litke 2002), self-authorship (Jones and Abes 2004), self-esteem (Blyth et al. 1997; Furco 2006; Miller and Neese 1997), personal insight (Yorio and Ye 2012), motivation for learning (Covitt 2006; Steinke and Buresh 2002), and engagement in tasks (Feldman et al. 2006; Morgan and Streb 2003; Mpofu 2007). In the social development domain, the most consistent positive outcomes appear to be in the areas of enhancing students' appreciation of diversity (Boyle-Baise 2002), interactions and relationships with peers and mentors (Gallini and Moely 2003), capacity for social responsibility (Batchelder and Root 1994; Celio et al. 2011; Eccles and Gootman 2002; Eyler and Giles 1999), and intercultural interactions (Borden 2007).

An enhanced understanding of the role that service-learning and related community-based learning practices play in advancing educational outcomes is important, given the current rise of community-engaged pedagogies in higher education (Butin 2010). While the extant literature on community-engaged pedagogies suggests that students' involvement in service-learning experiences can have positive impacts on a variety of student development areas, persistent limitations in the research call for more advanced and multi-site analyses (Howard 2003; Waterman 2003).

Most service-learning studies have focused on assessing the *direct* relationship between students' participation in service-learning and outcomes across the various aforementioned domains. Critiques of the research on service-learning have pointed to the need for more studies that include larger sample sizes, multi-site investigations, and more comprehensive designs that incorporate multi-level and multi-variate analyses (Waterman 2003). Findings from several recent studies have revealed how more advanced design models can help explain the ways in which intermediary, moderating, and mediating variables influence the outcomes students experience from service-learning participation (Bringle et al. 2010; Conway et al. 2009; Lester et al. 2005).

For our investigation, we sought to use the robust data from the Student Experience in the Research University (SERU) survey to hypothesize and test structural equation models that would examine more fully the direct and indirect impacts of service-learning on a set of key student outcome variables. We constructed the model by first identifying constructs from the survey that might best match and are most relevant to the outcome domains cited in the service-learning literature. Through this process, we selected items from four categories:

1. *Service-learning participation and involvement:* Composed of three items, this variable assesses the extent of students' service-learning participation, such as number of times students enrolled in a service-learning course, average number of hours students engaged in service-learning, and so on.
2. *Citizenship/civic behaviors:* Composed of six items, this variable assesses students' perceptions of their capacity to interact with others who hold different points of view to deal with controversial issues and to reflect on and implement solutions to address challenges and societal issues. In service-learning, students engage in both classroom-based and community-based civic-oriented experiences; therefore, we assessed students' perceptions of their operationalization of citizenship behaviors both in-class and out-of-class.
3. *Academic gains:* Composed of three items, this variable assesses students' perceptions of gains in their analytical and critical thinking, writing effectiveness, and comprehension of academic materials.

4. *Sociocultural gains:* Composed of three items, this variable assesses students' perceptions of gains in their capacity and ability to understand racial and ethnic diversity, to appreciate cultural and global diversity, and to understand the importance of personal social responsibility.

We applied these constructs to two structural equation models to examine whether participation in service-learning opportunities contributes directly to students' civic/citizenship development and either directly or indirectly to improving students' academic and sociocultural gains. Through these models, we sought to assess if students' civic capacity is an intermediary outcome, which, when achieved, promotes students' academic and/or sociocultural gains.

CONCEPTUAL MODEL

Through the two latent variable structural equation models, we posit that students' perceptions of their academic and/or sociocultural gains in higher education are a direct function of their academic background (*parent education, ACT score, year in school*), experiences in higher education (*faculty interaction, critical thinking, service-learning*), and in-class and out-of-class civic-focused or citizenship-oriented experiences. Our models also examine the importance of the respondents' campus environment in affecting their perceptions of academic and sociocultural gains. In addition to these direct relationships, we also hypothesize two relevant indirect relationships. The first is associated with curriculum-based (or *in-class*) opportunities to engage in civic-focused and citizenship-oriented behaviors; the second is associated with students' propensity to engage in civic-focused and citizenship-oriented behaviors *outside of the classroom*. Based on previous service-learning studies, it is our hypothesis that both of these are likely to influence students' gains in academic and sociocultural development (Knapp et al. 2010; Parker-Gwin and Mabry 1998).

In developing our models to assess gains over time, we considered and adapted Astin's (1993) Input-Environment-Outcome (I-E-O) framework, which focuses on *inputs* (e.g., student background characteristics) at the start of higher education, the *environment* (e.g., the programs, people, and/or educational experiences encountered while in higher education), and *outcomes* (e.g., state of student characteristics upon leaving higher education). Figure 8.1 maps our hypothesized model to the I-E-O framework.

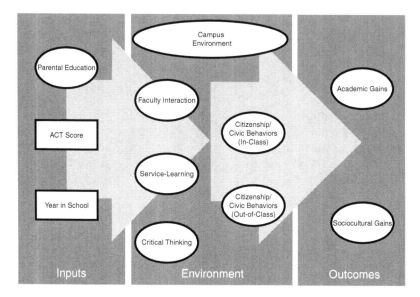

Fig. 8.1 Conceptual model

Utilizing results from the SERU survey plus central records, we secured the necessary data elements needed to build the structural equation models using the I-E-O conceptual framework.

Methods Instrument and Sample

We used data collected from the 2010 annual administration of the SERU survey. The SERU survey was administered at 12 large public research universities during this administration year. We analyzed the selected items from the community and civic engagement (CCE) module of the survey, which is randomly assigned to approximately 10–30 % of the respondents at participating institutions.

We used the data for all students who responded to the CCE module *and* who responded in the affirmative to the module's introductory question: "During this academic year, have you done community service either on or off campus?" The SERU survey asks all students who respond affirmatively to this introductory question to then respond to a series of additional items that explore the nature of students' service-learning and other community engagement experience(s). Among the questions asked are: "During this academic year, how many times have you enrolled in a course that had a service-learning component?" and "What was the average number of total service hours for the service-learning courses you took?" Through the questions in this module, we were able to create an indicator of the number of semesters over the past academic year each student enrolled in service-learning courses. We assumed that the students who responded affirmatively to the introductory question about community-service involvement and who responded to the follow-up items participated in some form of community engagement, and therefore their SERU data were eligible for inclusion in our study.

Our study sample included undergraduate students at the 12 public research universities that administer the CCE module. Individual institutional response rates for overall SERU survey (all modules) varied from 24 to 55 %, with an overall response survey response rate approximately 35 % ($n = 114,124$). The CCE module of the SERU survey produced a sample size of 20,426 (17.89 % of all SERU respondents).

The large-scale nature of the SERU survey provides methodological flexibility. For the analyses of our structural equation models, we used listwise deletion to handle missing data, and then we divided the study population into random halves prior to data analysis (Maruyama 1997). The first random half sample ($n = 5746$) was used for exploratory analysis and model refinement, and the second random sample ($n = 5793$) was used to cross-validate our perceived findings.

Measures

In total, we applied 37 items from CCE module to assess the direct and indirect effects of service-learning on students' perceived academic and sociocultural gains. These items produced eight latent variables and two manifest variables. We also selected four items from another module of the 2010 SERU survey (academic module), which formed the exogenous portion of our model.

The exogenous portion included one latent variable (*parental education*) and two manifest variables (*ACT score* and *year in school*) that controlled for possible individual differences in students' educational backgrounds. The latent variable (*parental education*) included two survey items that assessed the highest level of education for both the respondents' mother and father based on an ordinal scale ranging from "no formal education" to PhD completion. The respondents' *ACT score* approximated students' educational ability. We converted students' SAT scores to ACT scores when ACT scores were not present. To control for the life-cycle effects associated with the different stages of undergraduate education, we classified respondents on an interval scale (1–4) as freshman, sophomore, junior, or senior (*year in school*).

Table 8.1 provides the means, standard deviations, and standardized factor loadings associated with each of our latent constructs across random half samples as well as the associated internal consistency of the proposed latent constructs for the endogenous part of our structural equation model. As mentioned previously, we used 11 items from the survey to construct three latent variables to assess students' academic experiences on campus during the year measuring the amount of *faculty interaction, critical thinking*, and *service-learning* that the student may have encountered during the academic year. We applied a set of seven items to create each of two latent variables (*out-of-class civic/citizenship behaviors* and *in-class civic/citizenship behaviors*) that measure students' experience in operationalizing civic-oriented behaviors inside or outside the classroom (Table 8.1).

Students' campus environment influences and contributes to student learning (Astin 1993); therefore, we incorporated into our model a latent variable (*campus* environment) composed of seven survey items that ask about students' perceptions of the respect they are proffered regardless of their economic or social class, gender, race or ethnicity, religious beliefs, sexual orientation, or disabilities. The final two latent variables are outcome variables (*academic gains* and *sociocultural gains*), which are composed of six survey items that measure students' self-perceptions of their academic and sociocultural skills at the time of arrival at their institution and at present.

Analysis

To assess the potential relationship between service-learning and academic and sociocultural gains, we utilized LISREL 8.80, which allowed us to apply our theoretical model to observed data (Hahs-Vaughn 2004; Joreskog and Sorbom 2007). Specifically, the latent variable structural equation model allowed us to confirm the proposed factor analytic model (or measurement model) as well as to assess our hypotheses about the potential direct and indirect effects of service-learning on students' perceptions of gains in their academic and sociocultural development (or structural model).

Table 8.1   Means, standard deviations, and standardized factor loadings of latent constructs—random half samples

	Mean	Standard deviation	Factor loading	Mean	Standard deviation	Factor loading
Faculty interaction			$\alpha 1 = 0.808$			$\alpha 2 = 0.808$
Communicated with faculty member by e-mail/in person	3.83	1.29	0.71	3.79	1.31	0.77
Talked with the instructor outside of class about class issues	2.79	1.4	0.82	2.76	1.41	0.83
Interacted with faculty during lecture class sessions	3.01	1.44	0.69	2.98	1.42	0.69
Critical thinking			$\alpha 1 = 0.861$			$\alpha 2 = 0.886$
Judge the value of information…based on the soundness of sources	4.4	1.31	0.71	4.41	1.31	0.71
Create or generate new ideas, products, or ways of understanding	4.17	1.38	0.7	4.14	1.39	0.69
Incorporated ideas…from different courses when completing assignments	4.39	1.26	0.74	4.4	1.25	0.72
Examined how others gathered and interpreted data and assessed their conclusions	4.06	1.33	0.83	4.05	1.35	0.82
Reconsidered your own position on a topic after assessing the arguments of others	4.06	1.29	0.74	4.08	1.28	0.76
Service-learning			$\alpha 1 = 0.820$			$\alpha 2 = 0.842$
How many times have you enrolled in a course that had a service-learning component?	0.1	0.41	0.93	0.1	0.4	0.88
Average number of hours for the service-learning courses you took	0.16	0.63	0.89	0.17	0.65	0.93
Course-based service-learning	0.09	0.35	0.71	0.09	0.33	0.66
Campus environment			$\alpha 1 = 0.913$			$\alpha 2 = 0.915$
Students are respected here regardless of their economic or social class	4.59	1.08	0.77	4.59	1.09	0.77

(continued)

Table 8.1   (continued)

	Mean	Standard deviation	Factor loading	Mean	Standard deviation	Factor loading
Students are respected here regardless of their gender	4.91	0.95	0.78	4.9	0.96	0.78
Students are respected here regardless of their race or ethnicity	4.63	1.09	0.83	4.61	1.09	0.84
Students are respected here regardless of their religious beliefs	4.62	1.05	0.8	4.6	1.09	0.8
Students are respected here regardless of their political beliefs	4.51	1.14	0.7	4.53	1.12	0.7
Students are respected here regardless of their sexual orientation	4.68	1.03	0.76	4.66	1.04	0.77
Students are respected here regardless of their disabilities	4.76	0.98	0.74	4.74	0.99	0.74
Citizenship/civic behaviors (in class)			$\alpha 1 = 0.921$			$\alpha 2 = 0.923$
Interact with someone with views that are different from your own	4.23	1.26	0.73	4.19	1.28	0.73
Discuss and navigate controversial issues	3.91	1.32	0.84	3.89	1.33	0.84
Define an issue or challenge and identify possible solutions	3.99	1.31	0.91	3.99	1.31	0.91
Implement a solution to an issue or challenge	3.72	1.38	0.85	3.72	1.38	0.84
Reflect upon the solution of an issue or challenge	3.88	1.32	0.92	3.88	1.31	0.91
Reflect on your responsibility for community or social issues	3.61	1.38	0.82	3.59	1.38	0.8
Citizenship/civic behaviors (out of class)			$\alpha 1 = 0.934$			$\alpha 2 = 0.934$
Interact with someone with views that are different from your own	4.59	1.15	0.66	4.58	1.17	0.37
Discuss and navigate controversial issues	4.14	1.23	0.84	4.14	1.24	0.84

(continued)

Table 8.1   (continued)

	Mean	Standard deviation	Factor loading	Mean	Standard deviation	Factor loading
Define an issue or challenge and identify possible solutions	4.08	1.26	0.93	4.08	1.26	0.93
Implement a solution to an issue or challenge	3.84	1.35	0.85	3.85	1.34	0.84
Reflect upon the solution of an issue or challenge	4.04	1.28	0.92	4.03	1.28	0.91
Reflect on your individual responsibility for community or social issues	3.98	1.32	0.81	3.96	1.33	0.81
Perceived academic gains			$\alpha1 = 0.767$			$\alpha2 = 0.781$
Gains in analytical and critical thinking	0.73	0.81	0.77	0.72	0.81	0.77
Gains in clear and effective writing	0.68	0.89	0.7	0.66	0.9	0.69
Gains in reading and comprehending academic material	0.72	0.87	0.72	0.72	0.86	0.68
Perceived sociocultural gains			$\alpha1 = 0.771$			$\alpha2 = 0.784$
Gains in ability to appreciate, tolerate, and understand racial and ethnic diversity	0.48	0.89	0.74	0.48	0.87	0.73
Gains in ability to appreciate cultural and global diversity	0.5	0.82	0.87	0.5	0.81	0.83
Gains in understanding the importance of personal social responsibility	0.6	0.88	0.63	0.6	0.89	0.61

We discuss each of these associated pieces separately, as they provide different information about the relationship between our hypothesized models to the underlying data.

The construct validity of our hypothesized model is presented in Table 8.2, which lists the absolute and comparative fit indicators from maximum likelihood confirmatory factor analysis of the full measurement model. We evaluated the following fit indicators for the associated measurement models using Schreiber et al.'s (2006) associated cutoffs including a ratio of chi-square to degrees of freedom ≤ 3, a SRMR ≤ 0.08, CFI ≥ 0.95, TLI ≥ 0.95, RMSEA ≤ 0.06–0.08.

Table 8.2   Model fit statistics

Model	χ^2	df	χ^2/df	SRMR	CFI	TLI	RMSEA
Measurement model: 1st half	14585.68	734	19.87	0.11	0.95	0.95	0.057
Measurement model: 2nd half	15016.84	734	20.45	0.11	0.95	0.95	0.058
Structural model: 1st half	11120.58	692	16.07	0.03	0.97	0.96	0.051
Structural model: 2nd half	11812.93	692	17.07	0.04	0.96	0.96	0.05

The information in Table 8.2 generally confirms that our theoretical constructs fit the observed data; however, the ratio of chi-squared to degrees (χ^2/df) and the standardized root mean square residual (SRMR) exceed the suggested thresholds. This value inflation may be due to the large sample size of the study (Bryant et al. 2012).

RESULTS

Given our interest in examining the impact of service-learning activities on the students' perceptions of academic and sociocultural gains, while in higher education, we evaluated the following absolute and relative fit indicators for these latent variables to determine the fit of the hypothesized structural model. Specifically, we assessed the ratio of chi-squared to degrees of freedom (χ^2/df), standardized root mean squared residual (SRMR), comparative fit index (CFI), the Tucker-Lewis index (TLI), and the root mean square error of approximation (RMSEA). Given that all of the fit indicators fall outside the cutoff criteria (except, once again the χ^2/df), we concluded that the proposed structural models fit the underlying data reasonably well.

Academic Gains

Figure 8.2 provides a partial representation of the full structural equation model illustrating the direct and indirect paths associated with self-reported academic gains and service-learning. While other latent variables were estimated, their effects are omitted from this graphical display to allow for greater focus on the outcome variables and to reduce confusion for the reader.

Across the two random half samples, the hypothesized model explains just less than one-fifth of the variance associated with students' self-reported gains in academic skills. In terms of direct relationships, the standardized parameter estimates provided in Fig. 8.2 illustrate that our latent construct

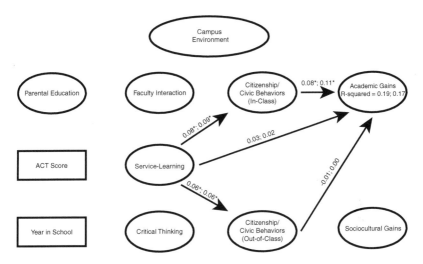

Fig. 8.2 Representation of the direct and indirect pathways of service-learning on academic gains from the proposed structural equation model

of service-learning has a small positive, but *statistically insignificant*, effect on students' self-reported gains in academic skills. This suggests that there is no evidence of a direct causal relationship between service-learning participation and students' perception of academic skills gains. This finding is consistent with other service-learning research, which suggests that academic outcomes from service-learning participation are mixed, and that perhaps they are mediated and/or moderated by variables such as students' citizenship capacity and civic behaviors (Sherrod et al. 2010), sense of self-efficacy (Knapp et al. 2010), and motivation for learning (Covitt 2006; Steinke and Buresh 2002).

We did find, however, that service-learning is positively associated with students' capacity to operationalize citizenship/civic behaviors, both in- and out-of-class ($p < 0.05$). Additionally, the evidence from Fig. 8.2 suggests that civic-oriented in-class behavior is also positively associated with students' perceptions of academic gains ($p < 0.05$), while civic-oriented out-of-class behavior is unrelated to academic gains. In line with findings from Levine (2011), Sherrod et al. (2010), and others, we conclude that in-class civic-oriented behavior plays a significant, albeit small, role in mediating the relationship between service-learning and students' perceptions of academic gains.

Sociocultural Gains

Figure 8.3 highlights the standardized path coefficients of service-learning as it directly and indirectly affects students' self-reported sociocultural gains. Across both samples, the hypothesized model explains less than one-tenth of the variance associated with self-reported sociocultural gains. This suggests that a significant amount of variation associated with gains in cultural competencies remains unexplained by our model. In contrast to the findings related to perceived academic gains, Fig. 8.3 provides evidence of a positive direct relationship between service-learning and student perceptions of sociocultural gains as well as with students' civic-oriented behaviors both inside and outside the classroom ($p < 0.05$). Additionally, as Fig. 8.3 illustrates, there are also positive direct relationships between civic-oriented behaviors inside and outside the classroom and students' perceptions of sociocultural gains ($p < 0.05$), suggesting that both the in-class and out-of-class *citizenship/ civic behaviors* latent variables play a mediating role between service-learning and sociocultural outcomes. This finding reveals that in addition to the observed direct gains in sociocultural outcomes associated

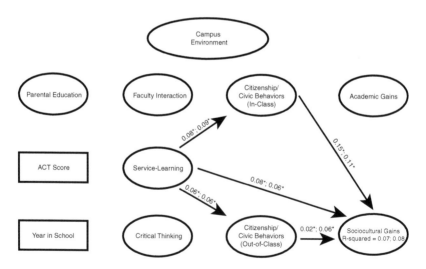

Fig. 8.3 Representation of the direct and indirect pathways of service-learning on sociocultural gains from the proposed structural equation model

with service-learning, students' sociocultural gains can benefit from opportunities to operationalize civic-focused and citizenship-oriented behaviors in and out of the classroom.

LIMITATIONS

Limitations of our study include those associated with many survey-based research studies: non-response bias, student self-reporting, and potential measurement error associated with items in the survey. Of these limitations, we conclude that issues related to measurement error were the most problematic to our research plans. Not all of the items in the SERU survey (a standardized measure) are as clearly worded or phrased as we would have liked.

Another limitation relates to the small effects sizes associated with this study. Although the large sample size of the SERU provides sufficient power to identify small effects, the consistency of the small effect sizes in this study raises questions about utilizing difference scores constructed from the self-assessment of skills items in the SERU survey. The average difference (across both samples) on the items used to construct our latent variable for academic gains ranged from 0.64 (SD = 0.89) to 0.74 (SD = 0.82). For the items used to construct the latent variable for sociocultural gains, the differences across both samples ranged from 0.47 (SD = 0.81) to 0.61 (SD = 0.89). Put another way, the average reported gain on any of these items is statistically insignificant from zero. Consequently, this makes it extremely difficult for statistical models to pick up any significant relationships or correlation between variables. A final limitation concerns the nominalistic fallacy. We sought to take great care, both in theory and in measurement, to identify appropriate latent constructs for our hypothesized model. However, as Cliff (1983) has suggested, naming something does not necessarily mean one fully understands it.

DISCUSSION

While our study found direct, positive relationships between service-learning and the civic/citizenship in-class behaviors, as well as between in-class civic-oriented behavior and students' perceptions of academic gains, no direct, statistically significant relationship was found between service-learning and students' perceptions of academic gains. However, a statistically significant, positive direct relationship was found between service-learning and students' perceptions of sociocultural gains. The findings also revealed direct, positive relationships between service-learning and their civic-oriented behaviors (both inside and outside the classroom) as well as between civic-oriented behaviors (both inside and outside the classroom) and students' perceptions of sociocultural gains. These findings suggest that both the in-class and out-of-class *citizenship/civic behaviors* latent variables serve as mediators between service-learning and sociocultural outcomes.

Through our analyses, we found that the direct effect of service-learning on self-reported academic gains represented the smallest of students' gains. Such findings are not completely unexpected, as the extant literature on service-learning has pointed to mixed effects in this outcome area (Celio et al. 2011; Eyler et al. 2003). While our research did not confirm a positive direct effect between service-learning and students' perceptions of academic gains, we did find that participation in service-learning enhanced civic-oriented and citizenship behaviors operationalized both inside and outside of the classroom, and that these enhanced behaviors have the potential to lead to greater academic and sociocultural gains (Kuh and Schneider 2008).

The SERU is administered at large public research universities that are funded, in part, by their states. One of the goals of state-funded education is to produce graduates who will take what they learned in school and put it to use for the betterment of society. Our measures of civic-oriented and citizenship behaviors reflect this goal: through this study, we were able to assess students' ability to interact with diverse individuals, navigate controversy, and identify and implement solutions to problems. Also in this domain are the civic-oriented and citizenship behaviors of acting upon community and societal issues as well as reflecting on personal responsibility for addressing them.

One of the most interesting findings of this study is the direct effect we observed between service-learning and students' perceptions of sociocultural gains. We included measures that tapped students' perceptions of their cultural understanding, such as their ability to appreciate, tolerate, and understand racial, ethnic, cultural, and global diversity, and their understanding of the importance of personal social responsibility. Many colleges and universities have indicated a need for graduates who can effectively interact within a diverse, multi-cultural global society—especially amid a widespread perception by employers that recent college graduates lack global knowledge (Hovland 2009).

Additionally, the workforce literature has repeatedly emphasized the need for graduates who not only possess skills related to doing their jobs, but who also possess well-developed social skills. Given the increasing diversity in the workforce, the ability to interact with individuals from different ethnic backgrounds and cultures is of vital importance. Referring to some survey work conducted by Peter D. Hart Research Associates, Inc (2007), 76 % of business leaders indicate that they want higher education institutions to emphasize "intercultural competence" and "teamwork skills in diverse groups" (p. 3). It is worth noting that the direct effect of service-learning on sociocultural gains was larger than any of the other latent constructs of academic experiences utilized in our model.

Overall, the findings from this study help extend our understanding of some of the factors that contribute to key outcomes of service-learning. In particular, through analyses of both direct and indirect effects, this research furthers understanding of the relationship among student participation in service-learning, citizenship/civic behaviors, and perceived academic and sociocultural gains. Additional investigations that explore the direct and indirect effects of service-learning and community engagement should seek to apply more extended models of direct and indirect impacts, and should aim to use data that incorporate more defined constructs in order to ascertain the full effects of service-learning and other community-based learning pedagogies on student learning and development.

CONCLUSION

Through our study, we hoped to contribute to the service-learning literature by extending and deepening our understanding of the ways that particular factors contribute to key outcomes of service-learning. We proposed and tested a structural equation model to provide a deeper examination of both the potential direct and indirect effects of service-learning on students' academic and sociocultural development. Consistent with findings from previous studies, our investigation found no direct causal relationship between service-learning and students' perception of academic skills gains. However, the study did find service-learning to have a direct, positive, and statistically significant impact on students' capacity to operationalize citizenship/civic behaviors, both in- and out-of-class. While *in-class* civic-oriented behavior was found to be positively associated with students' perceptions of academic gains, *out-of-class* civic-oriented behavior was not. The study also found a direct, statistically significant, positive relationship between service-learning and students' perceptions of socio-cultural gains, as well as between service-learning and their civic-oriented behaviors, both inside and outside the classroom. The study also revealed direct, statistically significant, positive relationships between civic-oriented behaviors (both in- and out-of-class) and students' perceptions of socio-cultural gains, suggesting that both the in-class and out-of-class *citizenship/civic behaviors* play a mediating role between service-learning and sociocultural outcomes. In this regard, students' sociocultural gains can benefit from opportunities to operationalize civic-focused and citizenship-oriented behaviors in and out of the classroom.

REFERENCES

Astin, A. (1993). *Assessment for excellence: The philosophy and practice of assessment and evaluation in higher education.* Phoenix, AZ: Oryx Press.

Astin, A., Vogelgesang, L., Ikeda, E., & Yee, J. (2000). *How service learning affects students (executive summary).* Los Angeles, CA: University of California Los Angeles, Higher Education Research Institute.

Batchelder, T., & Root, S. (1994). Effects of an undergraduate program to integrate academic learning and service: Cognitive, prosocial cognitive, and identity outcomes. *Journal of Adolescence, 17*(4), 341–355.

Blyth, S. R., Saito, D. A., & Berkas, T. (1997). A quantitative study of the impact of service-learning programs. In A. Waterman (Ed.), *Service-learning: Applications for the research* (pp. 39–56). Mahwah, NJ: Lawrence Erlbaum.

Borden, A. W. (2007). The impact of service-learning on ethnocentrism in an intercultural communication course. *Journal of Experiential Education, 30*(2), 171–183.

Boyle-Baise, M. (2002). *Multicultural service-learning: Educating teachers in diverse communities.* New York, NY: Teachers College Press.

Bringle, R. G., Hatcher, J. A., & Muthiah, R. (2010). The role of service-learning on retention of first-year students to second year. *Michigan Journal of Community Service Learning, 16*(2), 38–49.

Bryant, A., Gayles, J., & Davis, H. (2012). The relationship between civic behavior and civic values: A conceptual model. *Research in Higher Education, 53*(1), 76–93.

Butin, D. (2010). Can I major in service-learning? An empirical analysis of certificates, minors, and majors. *Journal of College and Character, 11*(2), 1–19.

Celio, C. I., Durlak, J., & Dymnicki, A. (2011). A meta-analysis of the impact of service-learning on students. *Journal of Experiential Education, 34*(2), 164–181.

Cliff, N. (1983). Some cautions concerning the application of causal modeling methods. *Multivariate Behavioral Research, 18*(1), 115–126.

Conway, J. M., Amel, E. L., & Gerwien, D. P. (2009). Teaching and learning in the social context: A meta-analysis of service learning's effects on academic, personal, social, and citizenship outcomes. *Teaching of Psychology, 36*(4), 233–245.

Covitt, B. (2006). Self-determination and student perceptions in environmental service-learning. *Applied Environmental Education & Communication, 5*(3), 171–181.

Eccles, J., & Gootman, J. (2002). *Community programs to promote youth development.* Washington, DC: National Academy Press.

Eyler, J., & Giles, D. (1999). *Where's the learning in service-learning?* San Francisco, CA: Jossey-Bass.

Eyler, J., Giles, D. E., Jr., Stenson, C. M., & Gray, C. J. (2003). *At a glance: What we know about the effects of service-learning on college students, faculty, institutions and communities, 1993–2003.* Nashville, TN: Vanderbilt University.

Feldman, M., Khademian, A., Ingram, H., & Schneider, A. (2006). Ways of knowing and inclusive management practices. *Public Administration Review, 66*(s1), 89–99.

Furco, A. (2001). Advancing service-learning at research universities. In M. Canada & B. Speck (Eds.), Service learning: Practical advice and models. *New Directions in Higher Education Series 114,* 67–78.

Furco, A. (2006). Is service-learning really better than community service? In A. Sliwka, M. Diedrich, & M. Hofer (Eds.), *Citizenship education* (pp. 155–181). Berlin: Waxmann.

Gallini, S., & Moely, B. (2003). Service-learning and engagement, academic challenge, and retention. *Michigan Journal of Community Service Learning, 10*(1), 5–14.

Hahs-Vaughn, D. (2004). The impact of parents' education level on college students: An analysis using the beginning post-secondary students longitudinal study 1990-92/94. *Journal of College Student Development, 45*(5), 483–500.

Hovland, K. (2009). Global learning: What is it? Who is responsible for it? *Peer Review, 11*(4), 4–7.

Howard, J. (2003). Service-learning research: Foundational issues. In A. Waterman & S. Billig (Eds.), *Studying service-learning: Innovations in education research methodology* (pp. 1–12). Mahwah, NJ: Lawrence Erlbaum.

Jones, S. R., & Abes, E. S. (2004). Enduring influences of service-learning on college students' identity development. *Journal of College Student Development, 45*(2), 149–166.

Joreskog, K., & Sorbom, D. (2007). Lisrel 8.8. Scientific Software.

Kezar, A. (1998). Community service-learning movement. In J. A. Craig (Ed.), *Advances in education research* (Vol. 3, pp. 1–5). Washington, DC: The National Library of Education.

Knapp, T., Fisher, B., & Levesque-Bristol, C. (2010). Service-learning's impact on college students' commitment to future civic engagement, self-efficacy, and social empowerment. *Journal of Community Practice, 18*(2–3), 233–251.

Kolb, D. A., Boyatzis, R. E., & Mainemelis, C. (2000). Experiential learning theory: Previous research and new directions. In R. J. Sternberg & L. F. Zhang (Eds.), *Perspectives on cognitive, learning, and thinking styles*. Mahwah, NJ: Lawrence Erlbaum.

Kuh, G. (2008). *High-impact educational practices: What they are, who has access to them, and why they matter*. Washington, DC: Association of American Colleges and Universities.

Lester, S. W., Tomkovick, C., Wells, T., Flunker, L., & Kickul, J. (2005). Does service-learning add value? Examining the perspectives of multiple stakeholders. *Academy of Management Learning & Education, 4*(3), 278–294.

Levine, P. (2011). What do we know about civic engagement? *Liberal Education, 97*(2), 12–19.

Litke, R. A. (2002). Do all students "get it?": Comparing students' reflections to course performance. *Michigan Journal of Community Service Learning, 8*(2), 27–34.

Maruyama, G. (1997). *Basics of structural equation modeling*. Thousand Oaks, CA: Sage Publications, Inc.

McBride, A., & Sherraden, M. (2007). *Civic service worldwide: Impacts and inquiry*. Armonk, NY: M.E. Sharpe.

Miller, G., & Neese, L. (1997). Self-esteem and reaching out: Implications for service learning. *Professional School Counseling, 1*(2), 29–32.

Morgan, W., & Streb, M. (2003). First, do no harm: Student ownership and service-learning. *Metropolitan Universities, 14*(3), 36–52.

Mpofu, E. (2007). Service-learning effects on the academic learning of rehabilitation services students. *Michigan Journal of Community Service Learning, 14*(1), 37–49.

Parker-Gwin, R., & Mabry, J. B. (1998). Service learning as pedagogy and civic education: Comparing outcomes for three models. *Teaching Sociology, 26*(4), 276–291.

Peter D. Hart Research Associates, Inc. (2007). *How should colleges prepare students to succeed in today's global economy?* Washington, DC: Peter D. Hart Research Associates, Inc.

Schreiber, J., Nora, A., Stage, F., Barlow, E., & King, J. (2006). Reporting structural equation modeling and confirmatory factor analysis results: A review. *The Journal of Educational Research, 99*(6), 323–338.

Sherrod, L. R., Torney-Purta, J., & Flanagan, C. A. (2010). *Handbook of research on civic engagement in youth* (p. 2010). Hoboken, NJ: Wiley.

Simons, L., & Cleary, B. (2006). The influence of service learning on students' personal and social development. *College Teaching, 54*(4), 307–319.

Slavkin, M. L. (2004). *Authentic learning: How learning about the brain can shape the development of students*. Lanham, MD: Roman & Littlefield Education.

Steinke, P., & Buresh, S. (2002). Cognitive outcomes of service-learning: Reviewing the past and glimpsing the future. *Michigan Journal of Community Service Learning, 8*(2), 5–14.

Ward, K. (1996). *Service-learning and student volunteerism: Reflections on institutional commitment.* Paper presented at the annual meeting of the American Educational Research Association, New York, NY.

Waterman, A. (2003). Issues regarding the selection of variables for study in the context of the diversity of possible student outcomes of service-learning. In A. Waterman & S. Billig (Eds.), *Studying service-learning: Innovations in education research methodology* (pp. 72–90). Mahwah, NJ: Lawrence Erlbaum.

Yorio, P. L., & Ye, F. (2012). A meta-analysis on the effects of service-learning on the social, personal, and cognitive outcomes of learning. *Academy of Management Learning & Education, 11*(1), 9–27.

CHAPTER 9

Pluralistic Outcomes Associated with Undergraduates' Citizenship Development

Krista M. Soria, Matthew Johnson, and Tania D. Mitchell

One of the most challenging and yet imperative goals of higher education is to prepare undergraduates to face future leadership challenges and address the most pressing societal demands of the twenty-first century (Colby et al. 2007; Jacoby and Associates 2009; Komives 2011; Soria et al. 2015). As the USA continues to become more diverse, it is increasingly paramount for higher education institutions to develop effective citizens and leaders who promote inclusion, social justice, and equity in a diverse democracy (Colby et al. 2007; Hurtado 2007). Research-intensive higher education institutions are ideal settings in which to develop social change agents who can affect permanent change in our diverse society, as these institutions can connect students with people from diverse backgrounds, invite students to learn about diverse perspectives through formal and informal interactions, and develop students' multicultural and intercultural competence (Astin and Astin 2000; Gurin et al. 2002; Soria and Troisi 2014).

Yet, amid the growing body of literature related to undergraduates' citizenship, researchers have called for more scholarship to discover whether institutional efforts to promote students' citizenship can have extended effects on students' development of outcomes critical to our nation (Bowman 2011; Hurtado 2007); therefore, the goal of this chapter is to investigate the relationships between institutional contributions to students' development of citizenship and two important outcomes: leadership skills and multicultural competence. As prior researchers examining the relationships between

© The Editor(s) (if applicable) and The Author(s) 2016
K.M. Soria, T.D. Mitchell (eds.), *Civic Engagement and Community Service at Research Universities*,
DOI 10.1057/978-1-137-55312-6_9

students' multicultural competence, leadership, and citizenship have focused on the outcomes of programmatic efforts such as courses or extracurricular activities (Bowman 2011; Hurtado 2007), the present study is unique in that it examines broader institutional contributions to citizenship rather than specific programmatic or pedagogical interventions.

CREATING CONDITIONS TO ELEVATE STUDENTS' LEADERSHIP AND MULTICULTURAL COMPETENCE

Higher education institutions are well positioned to create environments to deepen students' commitment to civic life and magnify their leadership skills—and many of these opportunities can intersect with initiatives to enhance students' multicultural competence. While reviews of prior research have suggested that the very act of attending higher education engenders positive changes in openness toward others (Pascarella and Terenzini 2005), practitioners also play a vital role in providing structured opportunities for students to participate in diversity initiatives spanning extracurricular and curricular programs (Bowman 2011; Hurtado 2007). Scholars have discovered positive relationships between students' participation in diversity initiatives and students' openness to diversity (Gurin et al. 2002); acceptance of diversity, leadership development, and multicultural awareness (Hurtado 2001); intellectual engagement, racial/cultural engagement, citizenship engagement, and active learning (Gurin et al. 2002); and socially responsible leadership (Parker and Pascarella 2013). Students who enrolled in diversity courses or participated in diversity-related extracurricular activities were more likely to vote in elections, possess higher leadership skills, and hold higher democratic sensibilities including concern for the public good, beliefs in social equality, and beliefs that making a civic contribution was important (Hurtado 2007).

Apart from formal diversity initiatives, diverse educational environments are positively associated with students' leadership development, including the ability to work effectively with others (Hurtado 2001). Results from additional studies have suggested positive relationships between the frequency in which students have participated in conversations about and across differences with their peers and elements of socially responsible leadership (Dugan and Komives 2007; Soria et al. 2013b). Students' interactions with diverse peers can also enhance their multicultural awareness and citizenship; for example, students who reported positive and informal interactions with diverse peers had higher multicultural awareness, perspective-taking skills (defined as the ability to see the world from someone else's perspective), pluralistic orientation, interest in poverty issues, and concern for the public good (Hurtado 2007). Peer conversations across a wide array of differences (e.g., lifestyles, political ideologies) can provide a platform for clarification of personal values and social perspective-taking, both of which were shown to be positive predictors of socially responsible leadership development (Dugan and Komives 2010).

While those studies suggest important links between diversity, leadership, and civic outcomes, among all of the studies that have been published in these areas, little is known about the more holistic effects of students' development of citizenship and the corresponding benefits to students' multicultural competence and leadership development. Given the critical need for future citizens who can work on diverse teams, understand the perspectives of others, seek to reconcile social injustices, and participate effectively in democratic processes, the present study was designed to determine whether students' citizenship development is associated with their capacities to effectively engage as leaders in a multicultural democracy.

CONCEPTUAL FRAMEWORK

The conceptual framework for this study is built upon Astin's (1993) well-established Input-Environment-Output model, which hypothesizes that the background characteristics of undergraduate students (inputs) and relevant aspects of the undergraduate experience (environment) influence outcomes. Adhering to this model, controls for inputs (i.e., gender, parental education, racial/ethnic identity), additional undergraduate experiences (i.e., grade point average, campus climate, and students' satisfaction with social activities), and academic major were included as separate blocks in the models predicting students' multicultural competence and leadership development so as to isolate their contributions from the focal independent variable—students' growth in citizenship.

Bowman's (2011) conceptual framework representing the relationship between diversity experiences and civic outcomes also informs this study. Bowman (2010) suggested that students who engage in diversity experiences may become more aware of issues of difference, inequality, or discrimination, which leads students to place greater personal interest in civic action. Bowman also posited that students who have diverse peer groups and engage in diversity-related activities—and in turn develop cultural awareness and intergroup empathy—also develop acceptance and tolerance of diverse others and perspective-taking skills, thereby fostering leadership skills development.

The primary independent variable in the present study is students' perception of their growth in citizenship. This more general framework in capturing institutions' contributions is unique in higher education impact research examining the relationships between diversity, leadership development, and development of citizenship; yet, research in this area is important in providing evidence for the potential benefits of institutions' efforts to cultivate students' multicultural competence and leadership.

METHODS

Instrument

Survey data were collected from the ACT College Outcomes Survey, which was administered to seniors at 14 public higher education institutions from 2000 to 2011. All of the institutions offered master's and doctoral degrees, suggesting these institutions are more research-intensive in scope. Whereas the preponderance of researchers have utilized surveys asking students to rate the frequency of their interations with diverse peers or their engagement in diversity initiatives, the ACT College Outcomes Survey was selected because it offers a unique measure of students' perception of their institutions' more holistic contributions to their multicultural competence. The instrument is comprehensive and asks students questions about their satisfaction with a variety of aspects of their institutions (e.g., student health/wellness services), their institutions' contributions to a variety of outcomes (e.g., interacting well with people from cultures other than their own), and students' personal growth in a variety of outcomes (e.g., learning to be adaptable, tolerant, and willing to negotiate), among many other areas.

Sample

At each of the 14 institutions in the sample, the entire population of undergraduate seniors were administered the survey, whether electronically, in class, via campus mail, by individual interviews, by US mail, or by a combination of those means. The entire student population (first year through senior) for the participating institutions ranged from 3560 to 24,530. The majority of institutions in the sample granted master's degrees as the highest degree (76.8 %), with the remaining 23.2 % granting doctoral degrees. Each of the institutions administered the survey during one of the sample years (2000–2011), so no institution is represented more than once in the sample. We selected these 14 institutions from among a greater list of 305 higher education institutions that administered the ACT College Outcomes Survey from 1993 to 2011 by first selecting those administering the survey in the most recent decade. Next, we selected public institutions granting master's and doctoral-level programs as they constituted the majority of the overall sample and held the most potential for generalizability to other research-intensive public institutions in the USA.

The institutional response rates varied, ranging from 15 % to 100 %, although the average response rate for enrolled seniors across all institutions was 64.4 % ($n=5922$). The sample was 59.5 % female ($n=3331$), 2.3 % American Indian or Alaska Native ($n=135$), 6.1 % Hispanic or Latino ($n=359$), 3.9 % Asian or Pacific Islander ($n=228$), 4.9 % Black ($n=290$), 83.0 % White ($n=4917$), 2.7 % multiracial ($n=158$), and 2.1 % other or unknown race ($n=125$). We selected undergraduate seniors for this analysis because they were most likely to have experienced several full years enrolled at their respective institutions.

Measures

Dependent Variables

This study contained two dependent variables: students' self-reported leadership development and multicultural competence. The first variable—students' leadership development—was constructed from six survey items that asked students to rate their personal growth on a scale from one (none) to five (very much) in the following areas: developing leadership skills; becoming an effective team or group member; learning to be adaptable, tolerant, and willing to negotiate; developing self-confidence; improving their ability to stay with projects until they are finished; and becoming more willing to consider opposing points of view.

The second dependent variable—institutions' contributions to students' multicultural competence—was a variable constructed from eight survey items that asked students to rate the extent of their institutions' contribution to their personal growth in several areas. Students were asked to rate their institutions' contributions to their ability to interact well with people from cultures other than their own, deal fairly with a wide range of people, improve their ability to relate to others, become a more effective member in a multicultural society, develop productive working relationships with both men and women, understand religious values different from their own, overall social growth, and overall personal growth. These items were measured on a scale from one (none) to five (very great). Questions in this scale refer to students' awareness, knowledge, and skills related to multiculturalism (Pope and Reynolds 1997).

Independent Variable
The primary independent variable of interest—students' growth in civic responsibility—was constructed from four survey items that asked students to rate their personal growth on a scale from one (none) to five (very much) in the following areas: becoming more aware of local and national political and social issues; recognizing their rights, responsibilities, and privileges as a citizen; preparing themselves to participate effectively in the electoral process; and, becoming sensitive to moral injustices and finding ways of avoiding or correcting them.

Block One
This block included students' pre-college demographic characteristics, including sex, race/ethnicity, and status as a first-generation student (students who are the first in their families to earn a baccalaureate degree). All of these variables were self-reported by students. Sex was dummy-coded (female = 1, male = 0) and all of the race/ethnicity categories were dummy-coded with White students as the referent. Students listed their mothers' and fathers' education levels, which we used to create the first-generation variable.

Block Two
This block included variables associated with students' experiences in higher education, including their cumulative grade point average (scaled 1–6, "1.00–1.49" to "3.50–4.00" in increments), academic major, the contributions of their non-major courses to their personal development, campus climate, and students' satisfaction with social and recreational opportunities on campus. We hypothesized that these variables may be important in predicting student outcomes; for example, campus climate is associated with students' intellectual and personal growth (Pascarella

and Terenzini 2005). Given previous association between involvement on campus and students' development of civic and leadership skills (Astin and Sax 1998; Dugan 2006; Dugan and Komives 2010; Soria et al. 2013a), students dissatisfied with the opportunities for involvement may have received fewer opportunities to develop their leadership or civic skills compared to their peers. Due to the wide variety of academic majors, academic majors were recoded according to larger categories provided by ACT. For each of the larger major categories, there were anywhere from 10 to 20 different majors included.

In addition to those items, students were asked to indicate their agreement about whether their required courses outside of their major helped them develop as a whole person, develop as an independent and self-directed learner, organize their learning, and broaden their awareness of diversity. Those items were measured using a scale of one (strongly disagree) to five (strongly agree). Students' satisfaction with social and involvement opportunities were measured in three items with a scale from one (very dissatisfied) to five (very satisfied). Finally, three items assessing campus climate for diversity—represented by whether students perceived the institution to be equally supportive of women and men and all racial/ethnic groups and whether the institution welcomed/used feedback from students—were included. The campus climate items were measured on a scale from one (strongly disagree) to five (strongly agree).

Data Analysis

All analyses were conducted using SPSS 21.0. We first conducted a factor analysis using 28 items with oblique rotation (promax). The final analysis retained the following factors: institutions' contributions to students' multicultural competence (multicultural competence), students' leadership development (leadership development), students' development of citizenship (citizenship), the impact of courses on students' development (course impact), students' satisfaction with the availability of social activities (social satisfaction), and perceptions of campus climate for diversity (campus climate). Table 9.1 shows the factor loadings after rotation in a pattern matrix. We selected loadings greater than 0.40 given that they explain approximately 16 % of the variance in the factors (Stevens 2002). Each component had high internal consistency: multicultural competence ($\alpha = 0.90$), leadership development ($\alpha = 0.86$), ($\alpha = 0.85$), social satisfaction ($\alpha = 0.85$), civic responsibility ($\alpha = 0.87$), and campus climate ($\alpha = 0.75$).

Table 9.1 Summary of factor analysis results for the ACT College Outcomes Survey ($n = 5922$)

Item	Multicultural competence	Leadership development	Course impacts	Citizenship	Social satisfaction	Campus climate
Interacting well with people from cultures other than my own	0.823					
Dealing fairly with a wide range of people	0.815					
Improving my ability to relate to others	0.790					
Becoming a more effective member in a multicultural society	0.785					
Developing productive work relationships with both men and women	0.746					
Understanding religious values that differ from my own	0.708					
Overall contribution to social growth (understanding others and their views, adapting successfully to a variety of social situations)	0.659					
Overall contribution to personal growth (developing self-understanding, self-discipline, and mature attitudes, values, and goals)	0.653					
Developing leadership skills		0.831				
Becoming an effective team or group member		0.829				
Developing self-confidence		0.733				
Improving my ability to stay with projects until they are finished		0.676				
Becoming more willing to consider opposing points of view		0.653				
Learning to be adaptable, tolerant, and willing to negotiate		0.611				
Required courses outside my major area of specialization helped me develop as a whole person			0.855			

Item	Multicultural competence	Leadership development	Course impacts	Citizenship	Social satisfaction	Campus climate
Required courses outside my major area of specialization helped me become a more independent and self-directed learner			0.854			
Required courses outside my major area of specialization helped me build a framework to organize my learning within and across areas of study			0.852			
Required courses outside my major area of specialization helped me broaden my awareness of diversity among people, their values, and cultures			0.782			
Preparing myself to participate effectively in the electoral process				0.909		
Becoming more aware of local and national and political and social issues				0.880		
Recognizing my rights, responsibilities, and privileges as a citizen				0.696		
Becoming sensitive to moral injustices and finding ways of avoiding or correcting them				0.598		
Opportunities for involvement in campus activities					0.910	
College social activities					0.867	
Recreational and intramural programs					0.839	
This college is equally supportive of all racial/ethnic groups						0.913
This college is equally supportive of women and men						0.893
This college welcomes and uses feedback from students to improve the college						0.566
Range	−3.57 to 2.00	−4.68 to 2.15	−3.57 to 1.72	−3.44 to 2.19	−3.84 to 2.19	−4.04 to 1.58

The factor scores were computed using the regression method and saved as standardized scores with a mean of zero and a standard deviation of one.

In accordance with the conceptual framework of this study, hierarchical multiple regression was employed and the independent and control variables were entered in the equation using forced entry of three blocks: (1) pre-college demographic indicators; (2) undergraduate experiences, academic major, cumulative grade point average, campus climate, and social satisfaction; and, (3) institutional contributions to students' citizenship (the focal independent variable). We examined assumptions of multicollinearity, homoscedasticity, linearity, and independent/normal errors, and the results of the analyses suggested assumptions were not violated in our models.

LIMITATIONS

Students may have developed citizenship through interpersonal interactions with peers, diversity-themed courses, participation in diversity or cultural awareness activities, or in other critical areas; however, these measures were not included in the current study, presenting a limitation with regards to the interpretation of institutions' contributions to students' development. Additionally, the sample was derived from a 10-year time frame in which opportunities for students to develop outcomes like multicultural competence may have changed due to internal or external motivations, pressures, shifts, or challenges. The demographic shifts in higher education during this time frame include increased enrollment by women, people of color, and those above age 24 (Hussar and Bailey 2013). For example, the number of international students enrolled in USA higher education institutions rose by 32 % in the last decade (Institute of International Education 2011), and the number of internationalization at home initiatives on campuses have increased over time, serving to promote students' development of intercultural competencies in the absence of study abroad (Soria and Troisi 2014).

The data used in this study also relied upon students' self-reported personal growth in multicultural competence and leadership, and we did not utilize pre-tests. Bowman (2011) noted that students' self-reported gains tend to show a greater relationship between diversity and civic growth than their longitudinal gains, a fact attributable to the bias of students' self-reports. Amid these limitations, we suggest that researchers continue to examine the many ways in which colleges and universities contribute to students' citizenship and the ways in which those contributions may positively relate to students' leadership development and multicultural competence.

Results

Results from the hierarchical regression analyses predicting students' leadership development suggested that students' pre-college demographic characteristics explained 1.6 % of the variance in students' leadership development. The second block—which included students' grade point average, academic major, satisfaction with social aspects of campus, campus climate, and non-major courses' contribution to their development—explained 18.8 % of the variance in leadership development. Finally, the third block containing students' growth in citizenship explained 17.5 % of the variance in students' leadership development—a significant amount of variance ($p < 0.001$) above and beyond that explained by the variables entered in the first two blocks.

There are several significant relationships observed among the demographic variables; specifically, females ($\beta = 0.060$, $p < 0.001$), Hispanic ($\beta = 0.030$, $p < 0.05$), and Black students ($\beta = 0.043$, $p < 0.001$) reported higher personal growth in their leadership development compared to their peers. Among the collegiate variables, course contributions to overall development ($\beta = 0.170$, $p < 0.001$), campus climate for diversity ($\beta = 0.110$, $p < 0.001$), and students' satisfaction with social and recreational opportunities on campus ($\beta = 0.088$, $p < 0.001$) were positively associated with students' leadership development. Students pursuing computer and information science majors ($\beta = -0.028$, $p < 0.001$), cross-disciplinary majors ($\beta = -0.028$, $p < 0.001$), social science majors ($\beta = -0.046$, $p < 0.001$), agriculture ($\beta = -0.029$, $p < 0.001$), engineering and architecture ($\beta = -0.030$, $p < 0.001$), and community/personnel majors ($\beta = -0.051$, $p < 0.001$) reported significantly less personal growth in leadership development compared to their peers.

Finally, students' growth in citizenship was positively associated with their growth in leadership development. Examinations of the standardized coefficients suggest that this variable was the most important predictor in the model ($\beta = 0.453$, $p < 0.001$) followed by the contributions of general education courses to students' development ($\beta = 0.139$, $p < 0.001$).

Results from the hierarchical regression analyses predicting students' development of multicultural competence showed similar results to the model predicting students' leadership development. Pre-college demographic characteristics explained 1.9 % of the variance in students' multicultural competence, while the second block of undergraduate experiences explained 37.6 % of the variance in multicultural competence. The third block containing students' growth in citizenship explained 6.9 % of the variance in students' multicultural competence—a significant amount of variance ($p < 0.001$) above and beyond that explained in the first two blocks.

There are several significant relationships observed among the demographic variables; specifically, females ($\beta = 0.031$, $p < 0.01$) and first-generation students ($\beta = 0.028$, $p < 0.01$) reported significantly higher personal growth in multicultural competence compared to males and non-first-generation students. Asian students ($\beta = 0.046$, $p < 0.001$), and Black students ($\beta = 0.034$, $p < 0.001$) reported significantly higher multicultural competence. Multiracial students ($\beta = -0.029$, $p < 0.05$) reported significantly lower multicultural competence compared to their peers. Among the collegiate variables, students' grade point average was negatively associated with their multicultural competence ($\beta = -0.031$, $p < 0.01$). Students' perception of campus climate ($\beta = 0.215$, $p < 0.001$), course contributions to development ($\beta = 0.259$, $p < 0.001$), and satisfaction with social and recreational opportunities on campus ($\beta = 0.214$, $p < 0.001$) were positively associated with multicultural competence. Agriculture majors were significantly less likely to report growth in multicultural competence compared to their peers ($\beta = -0.031$, $p < 0.01$), although communications majors ($\beta = 0.039$, $p < 0.01$) were significantly more likely to report multicultural competence development over their peers.

As in the first model predicting students' leadership development, institutions' contributions to students' citizenship were the most important predictor in the model ($\beta = 0.453$, $p < 0.001$) followed by the contributions of general education courses to students' development ($\beta = 0.170$, $p < 0.001$). Both models suggest students' demographic characteristics explain very little variance in their leadership development or multicultural competence, suggesting that other variables are more influential in contributing to those outcomes. Furthermore, students' undergraduate experiences—including their academic major, non-major course contributions to growth and development (which might include general education courses), satisfaction, and perceptions of campus climate—are important in predicting students' leadership and multicultural competence. Finally, the results of the model support the notion that research-intensive institutions that support the development of students' citizenship may be more likely to graduate students who possess higher leadership skills and multicultural competence.

Discussion

Overall, the results of the analyses suggest that institutional efforts to raise students' citizenship may be associated with students' personal growth in leadership and multicultural competence. This study suggests that colleges and universities that provide undergraduates with opportunities to develop citizenship—to become more aware of local and national political and social issues; recognize their rights, responsibilities, and privileges as a citizen; prepare themselves to participate effectively in the electoral process; and, become sensitive to moral injustices and ways of avoiding or correcting them—may also be working in tandem to develop leaders who possess the ability to effectively lead diverse teams and citizens who are prepared to participate in a diverse democracy. These results add to a burgeoning literature base that underscores the vital role of colleges and universities in fostering leadership development, multicultural competence, and citizenship (Astin and Astin 2000; Colby et al. 2007; Dugan and Komives 2007, 2010; Gurin et al. 2004; Jacoby et al. 2009; Soria et al. 2013a, b). While demographic characteristics are important contributors to students' leadership and multicultural competence, the vast majority of explained variance in this study is attributable to collegiate experiences, including a supportive campus climate.

The academic contributions to student leadership and multicultural competence are intriguing. The current study shows that required courses outside students' majors are important vehicles for both students' leadership and multicultural competence. These results bolster the claims of liberal education, which purport the importance of liberal education over strict vocational aims (National Leadership Council for Liberal Education and America's Promise 2007). Academic courses that help students develop as a whole person become more self-directed, help build frameworks to organize learning, and broaden their awareness of diverse populations and are positively associated with students' leadership and multicultural competence. At a time when business leaders continue to call on higher education to bolster the civic capacities of graduates (National Leadership Council for Liberal Education and America's Promise 2007; The National Task Force on Civic Learning and Democratic Engagement 2012), the importance of liberal education should not be overlooked. Graduates who demonstrate increased civic responsibility are highly sought after and vital for participation in a diverse democracy. The current study's results show that academic courses that help students develop their whole selves and provide exposure to diverse viewpoints help achieve these important higher education outcomes (Colby et al. 2007; Komives 2011).

In shifting the focus onto colleges and universities' unique roles in framing the contexts for students' citizenship, this study suggests that higher education institutions can adequately set the stage for undergraduates' leadership development and multicultural competence—and that one important way in which colleges and universities can foster the development of future leaders is through enhancing undergraduates' citizenship. Curricular and co-curricular opportunities that advance civic learning and citizenship education are varied (Musil 2015; The National Task Force on Civic Learning and Democratic Engagement 2012), but recent research shows that alumni from these experiences exercise their responsibilities as citizens, including voting and participation in community service (Mitchell et al. 2015). This study lends further credence to the opportunity colleges and universities have to prepare future citizens for leadership in a diverse democracy.

CONCLUSION

Higher education continues to face pressure to prepare civically engaged leaders from both institutional mission statements (Komives 2011) and the business community (National Leadership Council for Liberal Education and America's Promise 2007; The National Task Force on Civic Learning and Democratic Engagement 2012). Efforts to build students' capacities for leadership and multicultural competence are abundant, as evidenced by the groundswell of leadership, service-learning, immersion, and study-abroad programs that have emerged in the last two decades within higher education (Roberts 2007). The developmental power of these experiences, research illuminates, is in the opportunity to engage with diverse perspectives (Bowman 2011; Dugan and Komives 2010). The results suggest the strong and positive associations between students' growth of citizenship and their development of leadership and multicultural competence.

REFERENCES

Astin, A. W. (1993). *What matters in college? Four critical years revisited.* San Francisco, CA: Jossey-Bass.
Astin, A. W., & Sax, L. J. (1998). How undergraduates are affected by service participation. Journal of College Student Development, *39*(3), 251–263.

Astin, A. W., & Astin, H. S. (2000). *Leadership reconsidered: Engaging higher education in social change.* Battle Creek, MI: W. K. Kellogg Foundation.

Bowman, N. A. (2011). Promoting participation in a diverse democracy: A meta-analysis of college diversity experiences and civic engagement. *Review of Educational Research, 81*(1), 29–68.

Colby, A., Beaumont, E., Ehrlich, T., & Corngold, J. (2007). *Educating citizens: Preparing America's undergraduates for lives of moral and civic responsibility.* San Francisco, CA: Jossey-Bass.

Dugan, J. P. (2006). Explorations using the social change model: Leadership development among college men and women. *Journal of College Student Development, 47,* 217–225.

Dugan, J. P., & Komives, S. R. (2007). *Developing leadership capacity in college students: Findings from a national study* (A Report from the Multi-Institutional Study of Leadership). College Park, MD: National Clearinghouse for Leadership Programs.

Dugan, J. P., & Komives, S. R. (2010). Influences on college students' capacities for socially responsible leadership. *Journal of College Student Development, 51*(5), 525–549.

Gurin, P., Dey, E. L., Hurtado, S., & Gurin, G. (2002). Diversity and higher education: Theory and impact on educational outcomes. *Harvard Educational Review, 72*(3), 330–366.

Gurin, P., Nagda, B. A., & Lopez, G. (2004). The benefits of diversity in education for democratic citizenship. *Journal of Social Issues, 60*(1), 17–34.

Hurtado, S. (2001). Linking diversity and educational purpose: How diversity affects the classroom environment and student development. In G. Orfield (Ed.), *Diversity challenged: Evidence on the impact of affirmative action* (pp. 187–203). Cambridge, MA: Harvard Education Publishing Group and the Civil Rights Project at Harvard University.

Hurtado, S. (2007). Linking diversity with the educational and civic missions of higher education. *The Review of Higher Education, 30*(2), 185–196.

Hussar, W. J., & Bailey, T. M. (2013). *Projections of education statistics to 2021 (NCES 2013–008).* Washington, DC: U.S. Department of Education, National Center for Education Statistics.

Institute of International Education. (2011). *Open doors report.* http://www.iie.org/Research-and-Publications/Open-Doors.

Jacoby, B., et al. (Eds.). (2009). *Civic engagement in higher education: Concepts and practices.* San Francisco, CA: Jossey-Bass.

Komives, S. R. (2011). Advancing leadership education. In S. R. Komives, J. P. Dugan, J. E. Owen, C. Slack, W. Wagner, et al. (Eds.), *The handbook for student leadership development* (2nd ed., pp. 35–57). San Francisco, CA: Jossey-Bass.

Mitchell, T. D., Richard, F. D., Battistoni, R. M., Rost-Banik, C., Netz, R., & Zakoske, C. (2015). Reflection practice that persists: Connections between reflection in service-learning and reflection in current life. *Michigan Journal of Community Service Learning, 21*(2), 49–63.

Musil, C. M. (2015). *Civic prompts: Making civic learning routine across the disciplines.* Washington, DC: Association of American Colleges and Universities.

National Leadership Council for Liberal Education and America's Promise. (2007). *College learning for the new global century.* Washington, DC: Association of American Colleges and Universities.

Parker, E. T., III, & Pascarella, E. T. (2013). Effects of diversity experiences on socially responsible leadership over four years of college. *Journal of Diversity in Higher Education, 6*(4), 219–230.

Pascarella, E. T., & Terenzini, P. T. (2005). *How college affects students: Vol. 2. A third decade of research.* San Francisco, CA: Jossey-Bass.

Pope, R. L., & Reynolds, A. L. (1997). Student affairs core competencies: Integrating multicultural awareness, knowledge, and skills. *Journal of College Student Development, 38*, 266–277.

Roberts, D. C. (2007). *Deeper learning in leadership: Helping college students find the potential within.* San Francisco, CA: Jossey-Bass.

Soria, K. M., Fink, A., Lepkowski, C. C., & Snyder, L. (2013a). Undergraduate student leadership and social change. *Journal of College and Character, 14*(3), 241–252.

Soria, K. M., Nobbe, J., & Fink, A. (2013b). Examining the intersections between undergraduates' engagement in community service and development of socially responsible leadership. *Journal of Leadership Education, 12*(1), 117–140.

Soria, K. M., Snyder, S., & Reinhard, A. (2015). Strengthening college students' capacity for integrative leadership by building a foundation for civic engagement and multicultural competence. *Journal of Leadership Education, 14*(1), 55–71.

Soria, K. M., & Troisi, J. N. (2014). Internationalization at home alternatives to study abroad: Implications for students' development of global, international, and intercultural competencies. *Journal of Studies in International Education, 18*(3), 260–279.

Stevens, J. P. (2002). *Applied multivariate statistics for the social sciences* (4th ed.). Hillsdale, NJ: Erlbaum.

The National Task Force on Civic Learning and Democratic Engagement. (2012). *A crucible moment: College learning and democracy's future.* Washington, DC: Association of American Colleges and Universities.

CHAPTER 10

Belonging and Satisfaction of Service-Minded Students at American Research Universities

Teniell L. Trolian, Sarah SanGiovanni, and Wayne Jacobson

Since the 1980s, the public mission of higher education has attracted increasing attention from educators, policymakers, institutional administrators, and community members. This groundswell of interest has stemmed from many sources, including funding models that place increasing pressure on colleges and universities to justify their practices and relevance, concerns about students' levels of political apathy, critiques of higher education institutions' relationships to their surrounding communities, and desires to reinvigorate the civic commitments upon which many American colleges and universities were founded (Ehrlich 2000). Overwhelmingly, these interests have resulted in calls for colleges and universities to adopt teaching, research, and service practices that make positive contributions to society and produce graduates with the knowledge, skills, and values they need to sustain lifelong commitments to social responsibility. Notably, in 2012, the US Department of Education and the National Task Force on Civic Learning and Democratic Engagement produced the landmark report *A Crucible Moment* (2012), which represented a national call to action

© The Editor(s) (if applicable) and The Author(s) 2016
K.M. Soria, T.D. Mitchell (eds.), *Civic Engagement and Community Service at Research Universities*,
DOI 10.1057/978-1-137-55312-6_10

to "ensure that postsecondary study contributes significantly to undergraduates' students' preparation as informed, engaged, and globally knowledgeable citizens" (p. vii).

In response to this growing movement, several networks and programs dedicated to advancing the civic capacities of higher education have emerged. In 2012, the Association of American Colleges & Universities (AAC&U) formed the Civic Learning and Democratic Engagement Action Network to forward the agenda of *A Crucible Moment* (National Task Force on Civic Learning and Democratic Engagement 2012). The Campus Compact, a national coalition of colleges and universities dedicated to the public mission of higher education, has grown to include over 1100 members since its formation in 1985 (Campus Compact 2015). Colleges and universities are increasingly incorporating service into their curriculums: in 2014, a survey completed by Campus Compact found that 91 % of 434 responding institutions offered service-learning courses and nearly 100 % had a central office with the primary purpose of coordinating student volunteering (Campus Compact 2014). In 2006, the Carnegie Foundation began to distinguish such campuses through their community engagement classification, which recognizes colleges and universities that "prepare educated, engaged citizens; strengthen democratic values and civic responsibility; address critical societal issues; and contribute to the public good" (Carnegie Community Engagement Classification 2015, para. 15). As of 2010, 361 institutions were recognized with this classification (Carnegie Community Engagement Classification 2015).

As service activity in higher education institutions has grown, so too has a body of research, linking service participation to various beneficial outcomes for students, including educational, personal, professional, and social benefits. However, student satisfaction is relatively less well-studied as an outcome of service, particularly in the research university context. Research institutions educate large numbers of USA undergraduates and have a high potential for contributing to the growing civic engagement movement. There is also increasing attention to the importance of retaining students and increasing undergraduate success at these institutions. This research, therefore, addresses this gap by investigating the relationship between service participation and students' sense of belonging and satisfaction at public research universities in the USA.

The Benefits of Service and the Research University Context

The benefits of service participation on student success have been well-documented in the higher education literature. In a comprehensive review of over 100 studies, Eyler et al. (2001) found strong evidence for positive correlations between service-learning experiences and students' (1) personal development outcomes (e.g., moral development, sense of personal efficacy, leadership skills); (2) social engagement outcomes (e.g., citizenship skills, commitment to service); (3) learning outcomes (e.g., academic learning, real-world application); (4) career development outcomes; and (5) relationships with faculty in their higher education institutions and overall satisfaction with their experiences in higher education. More recent scholarship has confirmed these well-established relationships. Academically, service-learning shows positive relationships with deep learning (Bureau et al. 2014; Warren 2012) and enhanced development of discipline-specific skills (Kearney 2013; Lemons et al. 2011). In regard to social engagement outcomes, a review of 55 studies examining student diversity outcomes by Holsapple (2012) found that service-learning is linked to "tolerance of difference, stereotype confrontation, recognition of universality, interactions across difference, knowledge about the served population, and belief in the value of diversity" (p. 15). Outside of the classroom, volunteer experience has also been shown to result in many benefits for students, including engaging in community service after graduation, socializing with persons from different racial or ethnic groups, and developing a meaningful philosophy of life (Sax et al. 1999). Findings such as these have led Fenzel and Peyrot (2005) to the conclusion that "participating in either general community service or service-learning in college has long-term positive effects" for young adults (p. 29).

Although much evidence supports that service leads to a variety of positive outcomes for students, less is known about the relationship between service and student satisfaction with the higher education experience (Webber et al. 2013). This is particularly true for research universities, where the movement toward civic engagement has proceeded more quietly than in liberal arts colleges or state universities (Gibson 2006). An increased understanding of how service influences student satisfaction at research universities is important for several reasons. First, research shows a strong relationship between student satisfaction and persistence

184 T. L. TROLIAN ET AL.

(Bowman and Denson 2014; Fischer 2007; Hausmann et al. 2007), a goal that all universities strive toward for reasons that range from the ethical to the economic (Bringle et al. 2004). Second, student satisfaction is an important goal for university educators and administrators in its own right. Higher education is increasingly defining its quality in terms of the student experience, emphasizing the importance of meeting students' needs and expectations while helping them achieve success (Belcheir 2003; Elliott and Healy 2001).

SERVICE AS STUDENT INVOLVEMENT

Because opportunities to engage in service are embedded in students' undergraduate experiences, this research is situated in theories pertaining to the effect of the undergraduate environment on student change. Specifically, Astin's theory of involvement (Astin 1984) and Tinto's theory of student departure (Tinto 1975, 1987, 1993) are foundational to this work.

Astin's theory of involvement suggests that students achieve learning outcomes by becoming involved in their colleges and universities. Astin (1975) developed his theory based on a longitudinal study of college dropouts, in which he found that elements of the undergraduate environment likely to increase students' involvement were significantly related to student persistence, and aspects of the undergraduate environment likely to reduce students' involvement were associated with student departure (Astin 1984). Astin (1984) defined involvement as "the amount of physical and psychological energy that [students devote] to the academic experience" (p. 518), a definition that elevates the importance of students' *behavior* over their thoughts or feelings. His theory consists of five postulates, including his two main arguments that student learning is directly proportional to the quality and quantity of student involvement and that the effectiveness of academic programs rests on their ability to increase student involvement.

Like Astin's (1984) theory of involvement, Tinto's theory of student departure Tinto (1975) considers student success in relation to the undergraduate environment (Pascarella and Terenzini 2005); however, while Astin's model considers students' behavioral involvement in relation to learning outcomes, Tinto's model of student departure considered students' perceived social and academic integration in relation to persistence (Berger and Milem 1999). Tinto posited that student retention is a result of social and academic integration, or the "extent to which the individual shares the normative attitudes and values of peers and faculty in the institution and abides by the formal and informal structural requirements for membership in that community or in subgroups of it" (Pascarella and Terenzini 2005, p. 54).

The current study draws on both Astin (1984) and Tinto (1975, 1987, 1993) as conceptual frameworks to situate the research questions and analyses associated with students' involvement in service. Speaking of the benefits of students' involvement in higher education, Berger and Milem (1999) suggested, "Student involvement leads to greater integration in the social and academic systems of the college and promotes institutional commitment" (p. 644). Indeed, Berger and Milem (1999) found that students' involvement in their institutions had significant indirect effects on social and academic integration and later persistence. Sax et al. (1999) took a similar position on service as a form of involvement: the authors proposed that "participating in community service during the undergraduate years can be regarded as a form of student involvement" (p. 2) as community service, similar to involvement, requires students to devote substantial time and energy. According to this perspective, community service may be understood as a type of involvement that has the potential to academically and socially integrate students into their higher education institutions in ways that will likely lead to higher satisfaction with their undergraduate experiences.

SERVICE, STUDENTS' SATISFACTION, AND STUDENTS' SENSE OF BELONGING

Substantial research backs the claims of both Astin (1984) and Tinto (1975, 1987, 1993). In particular, the majority of studies confirm that satisfaction and sense of belonging are important outcomes of involvement and integration in higher education (Hausmann et al. 2007; Strapp and Farr 2009; Strayhorn 2015; Webber et al. 2013). However, few researchers have directly investigated the link between service as a type of student involvement and subsequent satisfaction with the higher education experience. In part, this may be symptomatic of a larger gap in knowledge concerning the differential benefits that may accrue to students who pursue different types of involvement. Several researchers have called for work that closes this gap by investigating if some types of involvement lead to higher benefits for students than others (Berger and Milem 1999; Fischer 2007; Strapp and Farr 2009).

Scholars who have examined the relationship between service and satisfaction have found positive results. For example, Berson and Younkin (1998) compared students in six community college courses that did and did not include service-learning components and discovered that students in the courses featuring service-learning reported significantly higher satisfaction with the course. Likewise, in a similar survey of students across courses that did and did not include service-learning components, students in the service-learning group had significantly higher course satisfaction (Gray et al. 1998). This trend also remains true for service outside the classroom: Soria et al. (2012) found that students who participated in community service were more likely than their peers to report a higher sense of belonging at their research universities. Astin and Sax (1998) discovered undergraduates who participate in service are more satisfied with their institution's leadership opportunities, relevance of coursework to everyday life, and preparations for future career. Webber et al. (2013) found that service participation also positively impacts students' overall rating of their educational experience as excellent.

This study seeks to add to the literature on service and student satisfaction by examining whether relationships exist between participation in several types of service and service-learning experiences during higher education and students' satisfaction with–and sense of belonging at–their institutions. The primary research question guiding this study is: Is there a positive relationship between participation in service and service-learning experiences and students' overall institutional satisfaction and sense of belonging?

METHODS

Data and Sample

Data used in this study are from the 2014 Student Experience in the Research University (SERU) survey, a cross-sectional, multi-institutional study of student experiences at research universities. The SERU survey was designed to "help improve the undergraduate experience and educational processes by generating new, longitudinal information on the undergraduate experience at research universities" (Center for Studies in Higher Education, n.d., para. 1). The SERU is administered annually to undergraduate students attending SERU consortium institutions. The consortium includes 23 research universities across the USA which participate in survey administration in varying years.

The SERU consortium institutions elect whether to participate in each year's SERU data collection, as well as which modules of the SERU survey students complete, and all data collection is completed using an online survey instrument. The 2014 wave of the SERU survey included more than 60,000 students. After narrowing the 2014 SERU sample to those who completed the modules of interest to this study and using list-wise deletion to handle missing data, this study used a sample of 5643 student participants from six SERU consortium universities.

Participants

The overall sample used in this study was 61 % female and 39 % male. The overall sample was 7 % Asian/Asian American/Pacific Islander, 4 % Black/African American, 7 % Latino/a/Hispanic, less than 1 % Native American, and 81 % White/Caucasian. The sample was 24 % first-generation students and 76 % were continuing-generation students. Within the sample, 76 % aspired to earn a master's or higher graduate/professional degree and 24 % aspired to earn a bachelor's degree or less. Fields of study represented were 16 % arts or humanities, 15 % engineering, 13 % business, 12 % social sciences, 10 % biological sciences, 5 % physical sciences, 3 % professional fields, 3 % technology-related fields, 2 % education, and 21 % undecided or "other" major.

Variables

The dependent variables of interest in this study included five self-reported measures of student satisfaction and belonging, including (1) satisfaction with the overall social experience at one's institution, (2) satisfaction with the overall academic experience at one's institution, (3) satisfaction with the value of one's education for the price paid, (4) sense of belonging at one's institution, and (5) an indication that one would still choose to enroll at their current institution. The variables were measured using a six-point continuous rating scale where students were asked to determine their level of satisfaction or agreement with the following prompts: "Please rate your level of satisfaction with: overall social experience, overall academic experience, value of your education for the price you are paying at [this institution]" and "Please state your level of agreement with: I feel that I belong at this institution, and knowing what I know now, I would still choose to enroll at [this institution]." Each of these outcome variables was considered separately, in order to determine whether a relationship existed between several types of service and service-learning experiences and each measure of student satisfaction and belonging.

The independent variables of interest in this study were four variables measuring students' self-reported participation in service and service-learning experiences during higher education, including (1) participation in a service-learning course, (2) participation in a community-based capstone experience, (3) participation in on-campus community service experiences during the current academic year, and (4) participation in off-campus community service experiences during the current academic year. Participation in a service-learning course was measured by asking students, "How many times have you enrolled in a course that had a service-learning component?" and response options included 0, 1, 2, 3, or 4 (recoded for analysis to Participated in a Service-Learning Course = 1, Did Not Participate in a Service-Learning Course = 0). Participation in a community-based capstone experience was measured by asking students, "To what extent have you been involved in the following community-focused experiences during this academic year—community-based capstone experience?" and response options included Not at All = 1, One Term or Less = 2, More than One Term = 3 (recoded for analysis to Participated in a Community-Based Capstone = 1, Did Not Participate in a Community-Based Capstone = 0).

Participation in on-campus community service experiences during the current academic year was measured by asking students, "During this academic year, have you participated in community service on campus?" and response options included Yes = 1, No = 0. Finally, participation in off-campus community service experiences during the current academic year was measured by asking students, "During this academic year, have you participated in community service off campus?" and response options included Yes = 1, No = 0. These varying service and service-learning experiences were considered separately within each model, in order to determine whether there were differences between course-based and non-course-based experiences and to determine whether there were differences between on- and off-campus service experiences in terms of their association with students' satisfaction and sense of belonging.

This study also utilized a number of control variables in all models in order to more appropriately estimate the relationship between students' service experiences during higher education and students' satisfaction and sense of belonging. Control variables included student background characteristics such as sex, race/ethnicity, social class, parental education, and whether the student was an in-state resident where they attended higher education. Control variables also included students' attitudes and undergraduate experiences such as their political views, religious denomination or sense of spirituality, educational aspirations, college GPA, undergraduate major, class standing/year in college, and how many hours students spent engaged in on- and off-campus employment during higher education. Additionally, all models also controlled for three scaled measures of students' experiences during higher education, including a scaled measure of student-faculty interaction (5 items; $\alpha = 0.78$), a scaled measure of students' involvement in co-curricular clubs and organizations (8 items; $\alpha = 0.88$), and a scaled measure of students' perceptions of the climate for diversity on campus (12 items; $\alpha = 0.58$).

Analyses

Analyses were performed using ordinary least-squares (OLS) regression in Stata. All models were examined for potential multicollinearity issues, and all models included a host of control variables to control for potential confounding factors. Models also utilized a clustering command to control for the nested nature of the data, where students are nested within institutions.

LIMITATIONS

This study and its findings are limited in a number of important ways. First, the SERU sample used in this study is largely female (61 %) and White (79 %). Additionally, some of the racial/ethnic groups included in the study are very small (e.g., Native American students comprise less than 1 % of the sample), and the findings of this study, therefore, are not necessarily representative of the racial/ethnic composition of all USA research universities. Moreover, while this study included data from six research universities, including six of the largest public universities in the USA, the small number of institutions represented in the sample further limits the generalizability of this study's results to all USA research universities.

This study is also limited by the cross-sectional nature of the SERU study, wherein student experiences and attitudes are captured at a single point in time, a factor that limits our ability to conclude that service and service-learning experiences have an *effect* on student satisfaction and sense of belonging, but rather that they seem to be positively associated.

Further research, using a longitudinal or experimental design, is needed to determine the extent to which service and service-learning experiences affect student satisfaction and sense of belonging. Additionally, this study is limited by use of a pre-existing dataset, where survey prompts and response options were pre-determined and where potential control variables were limited to items featured in the SERU study.

RESULTS

Table 10.1 presents sample statistics for reported participation in service and service-learning, where the percentage of students in each category who participated and did not participate in each service experience is noted. We found that students were, on average, most likely to participate in off-campus community service (63 % of females and 53 % of males), followed by on-campus service (49 % of females and 35 % of males), with smaller percentages of students participating in service-learning (21 % of

Table 10.1   Sample statistics: participation in service and service-learning

Variable	Service-learning		On-campus service		Off-campus service		Community-based capstone	
	Yes (%)	No (%)	Yes (%)	No (%)	Yes (%)	No (%)	Yes (%)	No (%)
Female	21	79	49	51	63	37	9	91
Male	14	86	35	65	53	47	6	94
African American/Black	23	77	51	49	52	48	12	88
Asian/Pacific Islander	19	81	44	56	52	48	11	89
Latina/o/Hispanic	19	81	54	46	67	33	13	87
Native American	19	81	52	48	75	25	9	91
White/Caucasian	18	82	43	57	59	41	7	93
Residency—In state	19	81	42	58	61	39	8	92
Residency—Out of state	18	82	48	52	54	46	8	92
Level—Freshman	11	89	48	52	55	45	6	94
Level—Sophomore	14	86	48	52	59	41	6	94
Level—Junior	19	81	43	57	60	40	5	95
Level—Senior	23	77	39	61	60	40	11	89
Social class—Low income	21	79	42	58	54	46	10	90
Social class—Working class	19	81	38	62	54	46	7	93
Social class—Middle class	19	81	43	57	59	41	8	92
Social class—Upper-middle class	17	83	46	54	62	38	7	93
Social class—Wealthy	14	86	48	52	64	36	9	91

females and 14 % of males) and community-based capstone experiences (9 % of females and 6 % of males). There were also differences in participation in each type of service or service-learning experience by students' race/ethnicity, residency status, level, and socioeconomic class. For example, African American students were most likely to report participation in service-learning (23 %), while Latina/o students were most likely to report participation in on-campus service (54 %). Similarly, senior students were most likely to report participation in service-learning (23 %), on-campus service (61 %), and off-campus service (60 %).

Table 10.2 presents regression estimates for the association between service and service-learning experiences during higher education and students' satisfaction and sense of belonging. In terms of students' overall satisfaction with their social experiences in higher education, results suggested a positive relationship with participation in on-campus service ($\beta = 0.19$, $p < 0.01$) and a positive relationship with participation in community-based capstone experiences ($\beta = 0.11$, $p < 0.05$).

In terms of students' overall satisfaction with their academic experiences in higher education, results suggested no positive associations with any of students' reported service or service-learning experiences. In terms of students' satisfaction with the value received for the price paid, results suggested a marginal, but positive relationship with participation in on-campus service ($\beta = 0.06$, $p < 0.10$) and a positive relationship with participation in off-campus service ($\beta = 0.07$, $p < 0.05$). In terms of students' sense of belonging, results suggested a positive relationship with participation in on-campus service ($\beta = 0.12$, $p < 0.01$). Finally, in terms of students' indication that they would choose to reenroll at their current institution, results suggested a positive relationship with participation in on-campus service ($\beta = 0.10$, $p < 0.05$) and a marginal, but positive relationship with participation in off-campus service ($\beta = 0.10$, $p < 0.10$).

DISCUSSION

First, it is noteworthy that service is not rare among research university students. In our study, 73 % of students reported participation in some form of service-learning, community service, or volunteering, slightly higher than the rate of participation across higher education institutions reported by Finley (2012). These findings suggest that research university students seek out and participate in these experiences at rates comparable to those of their peers at other types of colleges and universities.

Table 10.2 Regression estimates: the relationship between service and service-learning participation and students' satisfaction and sense of belonging

	Social experiences	Academic experiences	Value for price paid	Sense of belonging	Reenroll at same university
Sex: Male	0.00(0.02)	-0.08***(0.01)	-0.09*(0.02)	-0.04*(0.02)	-0.06*(0.02)
Race: African American/Black	-0.14****(0.06)	0.08(0.07)	0.26*(0.07)	-0.18*(0.07)	-0.13(0.09)
Race: Asian/Pacific Islander	-0.18**(0.03)	-0.20*(0.07)	-0.07(0.08)	-0.20**(0.02)	-0.18**(0.04)
Race: Latina/o/Hispanic	0.06(0.03)	0.17*(0.04)	0.17****(0.08)	0.11*(0.03)	0.13***(0.06)
Race: Native American	-0.24(0.14)	-0.21(0.20)	-0.03(0.17)	-0.22(0.17)	-0.07(0.14)
Residency: In state	-0.06(0.04)	0.03(0.02)	0.27**(0.05)	-0.01(0.04)	0.11*(0.04)
Level/class standing	0.05*(0.02)	0.06*(0.01)	0.02(0.02)	0.03***(0.00)	0.02(0.01)
Social class	0.07**(0.01)	0.04****(0.02)	0.08**(0.02)	0.04*(0.01)	0.02(0.01)
First-generation student	0.03(0.02)	0.03(0.03)	0.03(0.03)	0.06*(0.02)	0.04*(0.02)
Spirituality: Spiritual, no denomination	-0.02(0.04)	0.05(0.06)	0.01(0.08)	-0.02(0.04)	0.06(0.05)
Spirituality: Spiritual, denomination	0.14*(0.04)	0.10*(0.03)	0.10*(0.04)	0.21**(0.04)	0.20***(0.02)
Political views	0.04****(0.02)	0.03(0.02)	0.03****(0.01)	0.08*(0.02)	0.05*(0.02)
Cumulative college GPA	0.05*(0.02)	0.17**(0.03)	0.08****(0.03)	0.01(0.02)	0.01(0.03)
Educational aspirations: MA or higher	-0.04*(0.01)	0.04(0.03)	0.09*(0.02)	-0.01(0.03)	-0.01(0.03)
Work: On campus 1–10 h/week	0.07(0.04)	-0.04(0.05)	-0.05(0.05)	0.05(0.04)	0.02(0.06)
Work: On campus 11–20 h/week	0.02(0.05)	-0.06*(0.02)	-0.17**(0.04)	0.02(0.04)	-0.01(0.03)
Work: On campus 21+ h/week	0.07(0.08)	-0.06***(0.03)	-0.17*(0.06)	-0.01(0.06)	-0.08(0.09)
Work: Off campus 1–10 h/week	-0.13***(0.06)	-0.18***(0.02)	-0.24*(0.06)	-0.11**(0.02)	-0.10*(0.03)
Work: Off campus 11–20 h/week	0.06(0.03)	-0.02(0.04)	-0.15*(0.05)	-0.05(0.03)	-0.09*(0.03)
Work: Off campus 21+ h/week	-0.15(0.04)	-0.17*(0.04)	-0.24**(0.06)	-0.10(0.08)	-0.19****(0.08)
College involvement scale	0.05****(0.02)	-0.01(0.02)	0.01(0.02)	0.02(0.02)	0.01(0.02)
Faculty interaction scale	0.08**(0.01)	0.15**(0.03)	0.11***(0.01)	0.09**(0.02)	0.09**(0.02)
Diversity climate scale	0.27***(0.01)	0.25***(0.01)	0.23***(0.02)	0.33***(0.01)	0.28***(0.01)

	Social experiences	Academic experiences	Value for price paid	Sense of belonging	Reenroll at same university
Major: Professional	0.01(0.08)	0.08(0.07)	-0.12(0.11)	0.07(0.08)	0.05(0.09)
Major: Social science	0.03(0.05)	0.03(0.06)	0.01(0.05)	0.09(0.06)	0.07(0.07)
Major: Business	0.17*(0.06)	0.08(0.07)	0.11(0.08)	0.11(0.06)	0.09(0.05)
Major: Technology	-0.18(0.11)	-0.07*(0.03)	0.08(0.08)	-0.13(0.07)	0.00(0.09)
Major: Education	0.04(0.11)	0.04(0.07)	-0.24****(0.09)	-0.03(0.09)	-0.06(0.14)
Major: Engineering	0.06(0.03)	-0.10(0.06)	0.01(0.05)	0.11*(0.04)	0.09(0.05)
Major: Biological science	-0.06(0.05)	-0.07(0.07)	-0.02(0.05)	0.01(0.06)	0.00(0.06)
Major: Physical science	-0.01(0.07)	-0.02(0.06)	0.02(0.08)	0.05(0.08)	0.06(0.06)
Major: Other	0.09(0.05)	0.03(0.08)	-0.04(0.06)	0.09****(0.04)	0.05(0.07)
Service-learning	0.04(0.03)	-0.02(0.02)	0.01(0.05)	0.03(0.04)	0.01(0.04)
On-campus service	0.19*(0.03)	0.05(0.03)	0.06****(0.03)	0.12**(0.02)	0.10*(0.03)
Off-campus service	0.09(0.04)	0.03(0.04)	0.07*(0.03)	0.11(0.05)	0.10****(0.04)
Community-based capstone	0.11*(0.03)	0.03(0.04)	0.02(0.04)	0.04(0.02)	0.03(0.03)
R^2	0.17	0.16	0.14	0.20	0.15

Note. $*p<0.05$; $**p<0.01$; $***p<0.001$; $****p<0.10$; all continuous variables are standardized; reference group for Sex is Female; reference group for Race is White/Caucasian; reference group for Residency is Out of state; reference group for First-generation student is Continuing-generation student; reference group for Spirituality is Non-spiritual; reference group for Educational aspirations is Less than an MA degree; reference group for Work is 0 h/week; reference group for Major is Arts or Humanities

These results demonstrate that different forms of service are associated in varying degrees with student satisfaction, sense of belonging, perceived value for the price paid, and expectation of reenrolling at the same institution. This confirms the observations of the *Wingspread Declaration* (Boyte and Hollander 1999), Campus Compact (Gibson 2006), and the National Task Force on Civic Learning and Democratic Engagement (2012) that service, like other forms of student engagement, can make important contributions to students' overall experiences and their sense of connection with the university.

These findings also suggest that outcomes most strongly associated with service are not necessarily tied to particular curricular experiences. Other studies have observed that the benefits of service are associated with the larger campus experience and the visibility of campus efforts to cultivate a climate for civic engagement. Keen and Hall (2009) observed, for example, that student commitment to dialogue and social justice was more strongly associated with broader co-curricular experiences than to particular service-learning courses. Barnhardt et al. (2015) also found that campuses that publicly advocated for students to be active and involved citizens were more likely to graduate students who possessed long-term commitments to service.

Likewise, the findings of this study suggest that belonging and satisfaction are broadly associated with on-campus service, but are less apparent among service-learning courses. This result may be due, in part, to the fact that the number of students in academic service-learning experiences is relatively smaller, and it is therefore more difficult to identify measurable effects within our statistical models. Another possibility is that a single academic service-learning experience is tied to a specific period of time in one course, but these findings are based on students' broad reflection on their experience across all courses and also out-of-class experiences. The effects of a single course or experience might not be readily distinguishable using broader survey data.

These findings demonstrate that service intersects with the mission of research universities in multiple ways. Service by research university students often contributes to carrying out the public mission of the university, allowing universities to expand their reach as students contribute to surrounding communities. The high rate of student participation, combined with the fact that the majority of these experiences are co-curricular and voluntary, suggests that students are committed to service and are looking for opportunities to be involved. Associations between service and satisfaction, belonging, perceived value, and institutional commitment further suggest that service strengthens student ties to the institution once they are enrolled. These findings suggest that research universities with an interest in strengthening their contributions to surrounding communities, attracting engaged students, and deepening their students' ties to the institution will stand to benefit from making explicit institutional commitments to service and facilitating opportunities for their students to serve.

IMPLICATIONS FOR RESEARCH UNIVERSITIES AND OPPORTUNITIES FOR FUTURE RESEARCH

The findings of this study also suggest several questions for researchers and policymakers: How can research institutions convey the value of service to students? How can institutions create messages that will facilitate more students participating in service and benefiting from the outcomes associated with community engagement? What other measures might help demonstrate specific outcomes of particular experiences for individual students?

In addition to the immediate benefits of particular service projects and the gains students experience through their participation in service, universities benefit when student-service experiences strengthen student ties to the institution. For all these reasons, it is in the university's interest to intentionally facilitate and explicitly support these opportunities. Findings show that curricular service opportunities (service-learning and capstone courses) are less frequently experienced by students, and institutions would do much to communicate the value of these experiences by systematically integrating them into established curricula. Support for department-level curriculum transformation, faculty course design, and formation of community partnerships would provide important support for communicating to students that the university recognizes service as a learning experience that is important enough to be a part of the university's curriculum. Future research might be designed to examine the specific effects of particular curricular service experiences, in order to better understand their contributions to student satisfaction, sense of belonging, and other student outcomes.

Universities might also prioritize recognition of co-curricular experiences, where a vast amount of student service currently occurs, and communicate to students that service is more than simply one among many choices for how they use their discretionary time. Taking steps to show-case student service, providing infrastructure for recognizing or logging service hours, and ensuring that co-curricular organizations have suffi-cient resources to facilitate these experiences for students would all help communicate the university's commitment to civic engagement. Future research might also examine the extent to which co-curricular service experiences both shape and are shaped by students' academic experiences, in order to explore ways to connect service and service-learning experi-ences across campus.

The fact that we see a stronger influence for on-campus service, which includes programs that provide students with opportunities to engage in on-campus volunteering and service to campus or the campus commu-nity, suggests the possibility that service gives students a stronger sense of belonging to the community in which they serve, because they may feel a greater social responsibility in their institutional contexts (Soria et al. 2012; Soria et al. 2013a, b). More than any other form of service, on-campus service was consistently associated with student satisfaction, sense of belonging, perceived value for the price paid, and agreement that they would choose the same institution again. However, the current study does not let us examine the extent to which service off campus might similarly be associated with a greater sense of belonging to the larger community off campus, commitments to future civic participation beyond the cam-pus, and perception of ability to apply their learning in settings beyond the classroom. These potential outcomes of civic engagement may in fact be significant, long-term civic contributions of the university to surround-ing communities, and examining these outcomes offers another promising direction for future research.

Overall, this study points to the promising influence of service expe-riences in improving students' satisfaction and sense of belonging at research universities. Given the connections between students' satisfac-tion and sense of belonging and their persistence in higher education (Tinto 1975, 1987, 1993), research university professionals inter-ested in improving retention and feelings of institutional commitment ought to consider whether service experiences might hold promise for addressing these important issues. By fostering students' engagement in service experiences during higher education, research universities have the potential to not only fulfill promises of developing civically engaged students but also improve student satisfaction and belonging in the process.

References

Association of American Colleges & Universities. (2015). *Civic learning and democratic engagement (CLDE)*. http://aacu.org/clde.

Astin, A. W. (1975). *Preventing students from dropping out.* San Francisco, CA: Jossey-Bass.

Astin, A. W. (1984/1999). Student involvement: A developmental theory for higher education. *Journal of College Student Development, 40*(5), 518–529.

Astin, A. W., & Sax, L. J. (1998). How undergraduates are affected by service participation. *Journal of College Student Development, 39*(3), 251–263.

Barnhardt, C., Sheets, J., & Pasquesi, K. (2015). You expect what? Students' perceptions as resources in acquiring commitments and capacities for civic engagement. *Research in Higher Education, 56*(6), 622–624.

Belcheir, M. L. (2003). *The campus environment as viewed through the lens of the national survey of student engagement.* Research Report 2003-01. Boise, ID: Boise State University.

Berger, J. B., & Milem, J. F. (1999). The role of student involvement and perceptions of integration in a causal model of student persistence. *Research in Higher Education, 40*(6), 641–664.

Berson, J. S., & Younkin, W. F. (1998, November). *Doing well by doing good: A study of the effects of a service-learning experience on student success.* Paper presented at the American Society of Higher Education, Miami, FL.

Bowman, N. A., & Denson, N. (2014). A missing piece of the departure puzzle: Student–institution fit and intent to persist. *Research in Higher Education, 55*(2), 123–142.

Boyte, H., & Hollander, E. (1999). *Wingspread declaration on renewing the civic mission of the American Research University.* Providence, RI: Campus Compact.

Bringle, R. G., Philips, M. A., & Hudson, M. (2004). *The measure of service learning: Research scales to assess student experiences.* Washington, DC: American Psychological Association.

Bureau, D. A., Cole, J. S., & McCormick, A. C. (2014). Frequent participation in service learning: Examining institutional difference and individual benefits. *New Directions for Institutional Research, 162,* 17–27.

Campus Compact. (2014). Three decades of institutionalizing change: 2014 annual membership survey. http://kdp0l43vw6z2dlw631ififc5.wpengine.netdna-cdn.com/wp-content/uploads/2015/05/2014-CC-Member-Survey.pdf.

Carnegie Community Engagement Classification. (2015). How is "community engagement" defined? Boston, MA: University of Massachusetts Boston, New England Resource Center for Higher Education. http://nerche.org/index.php?option=com_content&view=article&id=341&Itemid=92#CE%20def.

Center for Studies in Higher Education, University of California Berkeley. (n.d.) *SERU mission.* http://www.cshe.berkeley.edu/SERU/seru-mission.

Campus Compact. (2015). Mission and vision. http://compact.org/who-we-are/mission-and-vision/.

Ehrlich, T. (Ed.). (2000). *Civic responsibility and higher education*. Phoenix, AZ: Oryx Press.

Elliott, K. M., & Healy, M. A. (2001). Key factors influencing student satisfaction related to recruitment and retention. *Journal of Marketing for Higher Education, 10*(4), 1–11.

Eyler, J., Giles, D. E. J., Stenson, C. M., & Gray, C. J. (2001). *At a glance: What we know about the effects of service learning on college students, faculty, institutions, and communities, 1993–2000: Third Edition*. Campus Compact. http://www.compact.org/wp-content/uploads/resources/downloads/aag.pdf.

Fenzel, L. M., & Peyrot, M. (2005). Comparing college community participation and future service behaviors and attitudes. *Michigan Journal of Community Service Learning, 12*(1), 23–31.

Finley, A. (2012). *A brief review of evidence on civic learning in higher education*. Washington, DC: Association of American Colleges and Universities.

Fischer, M. J. (2007). Settling into campus life: Differences by race/ethnicity in college involvement and outcomes. *Journal of Higher Education, 78*(2), 125–161.

Gibson, C. M. (2006). New times demand new scholarship: Research universities and civic engagement: A leadership agenda. http://www.compact.org/wp-content/uploads/initiatives/research_universities/conference_report.pdf.

Gray, M. J., Ondaatje, E. H., Fricker, R., Campbell, N., Rosenblatt, K., Kaganoff, T., et al. (1998). *Coupling service and learning in higher education: The final report of the evaluation of the Learn and Serve America, Higher Education Program*. The RAND Corporation.

Hausmann, L. M., Schofield, J., & Woods, R. (2007). Sense of belonging as a predictor of intentions to persist among African American and White first-year college students. *Research in Higher Education, 48*(7), 803–839.

Holsapple, M. A. (2012). Service-learning and student diversity outcomes: Existing evidence and directions for future research. *Michigan Journal of Community Service Learning, 18*(2), 5–18.

Kearney, K. R. (2013). Impact of a service-learning course on first-year pharmacy students' learning outcomes. *American Journal of Pharmaceutical Education, 77*(2), 1–7.

Keen, C., & Hall, K. (2009). Engaging with difference matters: Longitudinal student outcomes of co-curricular service-learning programs. *The Journal of Higher Education, 80*(1), 59–79.

Lemons, G., Carberry, A., Swan, C., & Jarvin, L. (2011). The effects of service-based learning on metacognitive strategies during an engineering design task. *International Journal of Service Learning, 6*(2), 1–18.

National Task Force on Civic Learning and Democratic Engagement. (2012). *A crucible moment: College learning and democracy's future*. Washington, DC: Association of American Colleges and Universities.

Pascarella, E. T., & Terenzini, P. T. (2005). *How college affects students: A third decade of research.* San Francisco, CA: Jossey-Bass.

Sax, L. J., Astin, A. W., & Avalos, J. (1999). Long-term effects of volunteerism during the undergraduate years. *The Review of Higher Education, 22*(2), 187–202.

Soria, K. M., Fink, A., Lepkowski, C. C., & Snyder, L. (2013a). Undergraduate student leadership and social change. *Journal of College and Character, 14*(3), 241–252.

Soria, K. M., Nobbe, J., & Fink, A. (2013b). Examining the intersections between undergraduates' engagement in community service and development of socially responsible leadership. *Journal of Leadership Education, 12*(1), 117–140.

Soria, K. M., Troisi, J. N., & Stebleton, M. J. (2012). Reaching out, connecting within: Community service and sense of belonging among college students. *Higher Education in Review, 9*, 65–85.

Strapp, C. M., & Farr, R. J. (2009). To get involved or not: The relation among extracurricular involvement, satisfaction, and academic achievement. *Teaching of Psychology, 37*(1), 50–54.

Strayhorn, T. L. (2015). *College students' sense of belonging: A key to educational success for all students.* Independence, KY: Routledge.

Tinto, V. (1975). Dropout from higher education: A theoretical synthesis of recent research. *Review of Educational Research, 45*, 89–125.

Tinto, V. (1987). *Leaving college: Rethinking the causes and cures of student attrition.* Chicago, IL: University of Chicago Press.

Tinto, V. (1993). *Leaving college: Rethinking the causes and cures of student attrition.* Chicago, IL: University of Chicago Press.

Warren, J. L. (2012). Does service-learning increase student learning? A meta-analysis. *Michigan Journal of Community Service Learning, 18*(2), 56–61.

Webber, K. L., Krylow, R. B., & Zhang, Q. (2013). Does involvement really matter? Indicators of college student success and satisfaction. *Journal of College Student Development, 54*(6), 591–611.

PART III

Engaging Undergraduates for Social Justice and Social Change: Critical Perspectives on Students' Civic Engagement

Realizing a Critical Framework for Service-Learning at an American Public Research University

Douglas Barrera, Keali'i Troy Kukahiko,
Lauren N. Willner, and Kathy O'Byrne

At a time when the social consciousness has been raised around issues of diversity and systems of oppression, public universities have an increasing responsibility to address what it means to live in a world where growing inequality is ever present. Though our communities are becoming more diverse, increased diversity has not translated into equality of opportunity for all. While *all* colleges and universities are grappling with how to meet the challenges that a more diverse world presents for their graduates, this issue is particularly relevant for *public* institutions, whose existence is predicated on serving a broader population than those directly connected to the school. From constituents within higher education to residents of our local communities, the belief exists that public institutions have a responsibility to address the social outcomes of this growing opportunity gap (Barrera 2015). As Smith (2009) suggested in discussing the relevance of diversity issues to higher education, "The issue today is fundamentally whether and how institutions are building the capacity to function in society in a way that is appropriate to their mission" (p. viii).

© The Editor(s) (if applicable) and The Author(s) 2016
K.M. Soria, T.D. Mitchell (eds.), *Civic Engagement
and Community Service at Research Universities,*
DOI 10.1057/978-1-137-55312-6_11

On many campuses across the country, discussions of diversity are as prevalent as ever. The University of California, Los Angeles (UCLA), for example, recently became the second-to-last University of California campus to pass a diversity learning course graduation requirement for the majority of its undergraduates. The passage of this requirement by the academic senate came after a series of public criticisms on the state of the campus climate for diversity for both students and faculty of color. Despite the fact that undergraduates within the College of Letters and Science will now be required to take a course that examines the intersections of multiple forms of identity, criticisms of the climate persist. A recent op-ed in the student newspaper chided the university's administration for failing to launch an official examination of racism on campus following racially based attacks of the Afrikan Student Union, and called for more substantive responses than what it charged as hollow responses to racial incidents across the country, including the killing of nine Black parishioners at a historic Black church in Charleston, South Carolina ("Charleston shooting" 2015).

What is particularly disturbing about the criticism in this case is the fact that UCLA is located in one of the most diverse urban centers in the world. In 2013, Los Angeles County was home to the largest number of minorities in the USA, with 4.8 million Latinos/as, 922,000 African-Americans, 1.5 million Asians, 401,000 Native Hawaiian and Pacific Island residents, and 150,000 Native Americans (U.S. Census Bureau 2013). Just by traveling a few miles off campus, students can immerse themselves in a demographically and culturally diverse array of communities, and, by doing so, be confronted in real time by the issues making headlines on a daily basis. This fact should be viewed as a rich educational opportunity, as it allows educators to tap into all the benefits that come with diversity (Page 2007; Smith 2009).

Recent events represent critical incidents, or crises, that when recurring over time, create public and political platforms for change by producing opportunities for interest convergence. Rather than simply responding, public research universities have a responsibility to act proactively, which they can do by investing in civic engagement programs. Such civic engagement programs can be effectively tied to the knowledge bases of academic disciplines that humanize marginalized groups and communities while developing understanding and empathy among students and faculty. Efforts like these can, in turn, improve the campus climate for students, staff, and faculty of underrepresented backgrounds. As our society's racial and cultural demographics continue to shift, the symptoms of intergroup intolerance will continue to manifest themselves on our campuses without such deliberate and purposeful intervention.

As practitioners of community-based learning, we believe that civic engagement initiatives like service-learning provide an ideal opportunity for students to acquire cognitive and affective learning about diversity in diverse environments. In particular, we believe in the potential of this pedagogical model to realize intellectual and moral outcomes to the degree that they stimulate critical consciousness development in undergraduates (Fitch et al. 2013; Jones and Hill 2001). And research confirms such outcomes associated with students' engagement in the community; for instance, Wang and Rodgers (2006) found that undergraduate students in service-learning courses demonstrated growth in complex thinking and reasoning abilities. However, if service-learning is going to meet its potential for teaching students about issues of diversity, the curricula of such courses, in all disciplines, must be crafted to include examinations of systemic-level issues like privilege and oppression. Furthermore, curricula should require students to articulate their perspectives on such issues based upon their own backgrounds and experiences. In other words, if the cognitive gains tied to diversity learning are to be fully realized, the curriculum must include a *social justice orientation* (Wang and Rodgers 2006).

We found such maxims to be true through our own research. After conducting an exploratory evaluation of service-learning on our campus, our findings confirmed that, although critical consciousness development may occur within these courses, the extent of developmental outcomes is inconsistent and arbitrary in the absence of intentionality toward a critical approach. One reason may be that traditional service-learning courses only provide surface exposure and opportunities for "cultural safaris." Whereas assigned reading and community experiences frequently elicit "a-ha!" moments for students through interactions with people and environments different from the typical campus settings, instructors often do not connect sociopolitical critique to specific developmental goals. This finding is particularly true with regards to students' identity development.

Thus, we propose here a pedagogical framework which we believe better situates service-learning to meet the developmental outcomes expected to emerge from diversity learning requirements. Building on previous frameworks for critical models of service-learning (Camacho 2004; Cipolle 2010; Iverson and James 2013; Mitchell 2007, 2008; Rosenberger 2000; Wang and Rodgers 2006), we suggest the incorporation of identity development as a necessary element in the curriculum if socially conscious habits of mind are to be developed. Based on existing theoretical frameworks, we provide a structure for faculty and practitioners who want to create purposeful critical service-learning curricula that align with their diversity and community engagement goals, specifying tenets within the framework to guide student development toward these intentions. We then briefly discuss the challenges and opportunities present within public research universities in implementing such a model.

A Conceptual Model of Critical Service-Learning

Although a culture of service is alive and well on many higher education campuses today, even the most dedicated efforts have the potential to reify hierarchical structures of inequality and power imbalance (Camacho 2004; Mitchell 2008). Rather than examining social structural conditions that lead to systemic racism, sexism, classism, and the like, traditional service-learning is typically focused on exposing individual students to diverse environments, asking them to consider what it means to participate, and assessing the skills they have acquired by going through the experience. Critical service-learning models, on the other hand, focus on helping students to gain a more nuanced and complex understanding of the root causes of inequality and oppression. Mitchell (2007) summarized these distinctions by noting "the distinction between service-learning and critical service-learning can be summarized in its attention to social change, its questioning of the distribution of power in society, and its focus on developing authentic relationships between higher education institutions and the community served" (p. 101). To achieve the goals of critical service-learning, practitioners and faculty must shift the service-learning experience from an emphasis on meeting individual needs to one that focuses on the underlying causes of the circumstances and issues that define those individuals' struggles (e.g., homelessness, poverty). Similarly, student-learning outcomes become less about surface exposure and the acquisition of specific skills and more about the development of a critical consciousness (Mitchell 2007, 2008; Nieto 2000; Rosenberger 2000).

Beyond these goals for social critique, we contend that a critical approach to service-learning also includes an emphasis on student identity awareness and development, particularly as it relates to course subject matter and the larger social issues that shape the experiences of members of the communities within which students are performing their service. Such an emphasis acknowledges the need for students to understand and internalize the multitude of identities they inhabit and how these distinct indicators of self affect how one exists within a social environment.

To help further illuminate what a more critical approach to service-learning looks like in practice, we have developed a conceptual model of critical service-learning that underscores the development of students' critical consciousness by way of identity awareness and development. Additionally, for faculty interested in employing a critical service-learning approach, we suggest a model of operationalization that rests upon the identified framework.

Critical Consciousness

The idea of a critical consciousness is most closely aligned with the work of Brazilian educator and social activist Paulo Freire, who defined his philosophy of education as a liberatory process. In this process of liberation, individuals become aware of the conditions that lead to oppression, and, by taking action against those conditions, are empowered to become agents of change (Freire 1970; Peet 2006). The development of a critical consciousness requires recognizing, intellectualizing, and acting upon this knowledge to become more aware of one's own personal earned and unearned privilege and how such benefits contribute to—and maintain or reinforce—systems of oppression (Freire 1970). Furthermore, a key component of developing a critical consciousness includes possessing a greater recognition of how systems of oppression—including racism, classism, sexism, homophobia, ableism, and other types of overt and systemic discrimination—preserve privilege for protected groups of people (viz., White, male, heterosexuals) (Rosenberger 2000).

Students' recognition of their own agency in the larger social and political context is an important marker in this type of sociopolitical development (Peet 2006); however, cultivating an awareness of systems of oppression, as well as one's place within the system is not a simple process because it requires students to reconceptualize (1) a world that is familiar to them, and (2) an epistemology that reifies those systems of oppression and the students' place of privilege as participants in higher education. Such a realization does not come without students' active participation in their own education: to question dominant narratives, to validate feelings and experiential knowledge as crucial components of their academic journey, and to contribute to the formation and production of knowledge through their own critical thought and ideologies.

Critical Consciousness and Identity Awareness

Critical consciousness development does not only include gaining an understanding of concepts such as power and privilege at the systemic level, but also requires individuals to understand and analyze how these notions shape their own personal existence. Thus, we propose that the development of a critical consciousness is part of a circuitous process whereby students must first become aware of, and acknowledge, the components of their own identity. As a critical consciousness is built, identity markers become increasingly understood as not isolated, but instead, situated in relation to social location. A more nuanced understanding of self in relation to others leads to greater identity development, which, in turn leads to a more complex awareness of one's identity, which further informs their consciousness (Fig. 11.1).

To illustrate this process, we provide the following example. At the start of a 10-week service-learning course, a student is asked to identify the factors contributing to how she understands her identity. She identifies as both White and female, but when pressed to consider how these markers impact her existence and that of others on a daily basis, she is not able

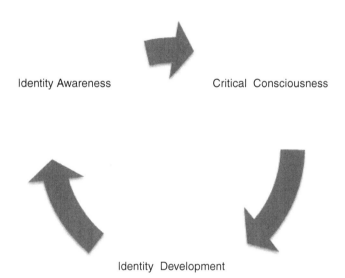

Identity Awareness   Critical Consciousness

Identity Development

Fig. 11.1 Conceptual model of critical consciousness development among service-learners

to specifically identify how her race and gender influence and define her social location in relation to others. By way of an intentional pedagogical process aimed at developing one's critical consciousness (described in detail in a subsequent section), over the course of 10 weeks, the student undergoes a process of identity development that helps her to become more aware of the larger implications of being both White and female. By the completion of the 10 weeks, her awareness of her personal identity is more acutely developed than it was when she began the course. We argue that any service-learning course rooted in a critical perspective should aim to encourage the development of students in this way.

OPERATIONALIZING A CRITICAL APPROACH

Building upon the conceptual framework of critical consciousness development outlined above, we offer a model for how faculty members seeking to employ a critical service-learning perspective might design a course that reflects the tenets and student-learning outcomes that are germane to the critical service-learning approach. We do not suggest specific assignments, activities, or course topics; instead, we propose an approach to course design and implementation that can be adapted to suit specific course subject matter and learning outcomes. The course design is based on three main ideas: (1) the use of a counter-hegemonic narrative that provides students with a critical lens through which they can examine course subject matter; (2) the intentional selection of service-learning sites based on the ability of organizations to help students understand issues of social injustice and oppression, and; (3) the interrogation of one's identity in relation to the course subject matter and the experiences of the people they engage within the community.

Counter-Hegemonic Narrative

The first component of employing a critical service-learning approach requires the active and intentional use of a "counter-hegemonic narrative." First introduced by the Italian Marxist theorist Antonio Gramsci, the term "hegemony" is understood to mean the manner by which dominant viewpoints and experiences come to be assumed and accepted as the norm (Gramsci 1995). Although Gramsci first introduced the concept of *counter-hegemony* as the process of developing an alternative to the dominant class capitalist values and norms with the goal of overthrowing the capitalist state (Carnoy 1989), researchers in the field of education have utilized this notion to espouse a philosophy of critical pedagogy aimed at helping to transform educational and other systems that sustain dominant ideologies and, in turn, support the maintenance of oppression (Giroux 2011; Kincheloe 2008; McLaren 2014).

Regardless of course topic, to truly employ a critical service-learning model, the concept of counter-hegemony must be actively employed in course design and implementation. Doing so requires faculty to consider how their course subject matter is informed and shaped by dominant ideology that may privilege one or more perspectives over another—and, as a result, provide benefits to one or more groups based on social location. These actions ask faculty to provide students with an alternative to the dominant, accepted perspective with the goal of helping students to explore the multidimensional nature of the course subject matter.

Intentionality in Service Site Selection

The utilization of a counter-hegemonic narrative to cultivate students' critical consciousness requires that faculty connect critical analyses of subject matter to the engagement with systemic inequality that students encounter while immersed in the community; however, in order for this to be realized, faculty must intentionally select locations that will lay bare for students the ways that oppression and social injustice exist within and impact historically marginalized communities on a daily basis. The opportunity that service-learning provides is for students to interrogate these concepts not just in theory, but specifically within the context of the communities in which oppression and social injustice are transformed into determinants of inequality. In this way, the conceptual material and the hands-on practice do not occupy separate spheres within the curriculum, but rather are interdependent factors in reaching the intended developmental goals.

We do not suggest that substantive learning cannot take place in wealthy or predominantly White locales. One can engage in social critique within the confines of privileged environments. In fact, most campuses, where most of the critical learning in higher education takes place, are intentionally set off from urban life to provide a buffer from the perils of "the real world" (i.e., "the ivory tower"); however, these same spaces can create a bubble, in which most students are cut off from confronting the daily impact of systems of oppression and their debilitating outcomes. This is not to say that oppression is absent within the ivory tower, but institutions of higher education may offer more resources and supports that lessen the burdens experienced by marginalized students. If we want students to garner a real sense of why it is important to develop socially conscious habits of mind, then, like with the counter-hegemonic approach, we must provide them with opportunities to witness the real implications of policies based on dominant ideologies.

Interrogation of Identity

As we have mentioned, interrogation of one's personal identity is a key component to this critical service-learning approach. This examination builds upon the practice of active reflection that is emblematic of service-learning methods of teaching and learning more generally (Jones and Hill 2001; Wang and Rodgers 2006). Throughout a critical service-learning course, students should be asked to engage in a range of assignments devised to help students consider the multitude of markers that make up their identity (e.g., race, class, gender, sexual orientation, nationality, ability, age, culture, religion) and how they have been affected by these indicators, particularly in relation to the course topic and the service-learning experiences in the community. Such a critical self-analysis should occur throughout the duration of the course and should be an intentional and integral aspect of the syllabus. Futhermore, this identity work should be explicitly linked with the specific counter-hegemonic narrative(s) being taught in the course.

MATH EDUCATION: AN EXAMPLE

To illustrate the implementation of this model, we use a math education course designed for undergraduate students in a teacher education program. This example was chosen specifically to highlight some of the complexities that might be inherent in implementing a critical model of service-learning in a course where the focus is on the development of a specific skill set (i.e., methods of math instruction). Furthermore, it is often the case that a math education course will employ a *practicum* approach to helping students gain "real-world" experience, despite being labeled as service-learning. In a model like this, the focus of the course is on training for a potential career. By using this example, we highlight some of the ways that a critical approach to service-learning can incorporate skill development into a curriculum that causes students to look at the broader questions facing our local communities (including our public school system), and why even those courses that are more focused on practical application are better served examining the cultural relevance and social implications of that application.

Counter-Hegemonic Narrative

In addition to providing students with a skills-based curriculum, a counter-hegemonic narrative in a math education course might take the form of teaching about how sites of education, as well as pedagogy (math pedagogies included), are not netural (Kincheloe 2008). Furthermore, students would be asked to think about what the normative, dominant methods of math education are, and in what ways they might serve to benefit certain students over others (such as through curriculum dicated by common core standards). These methods could be explored explicitly in relation to how low-income students and/or those who attend underresourced schools have been shown to perform more poorly on standardized tests (Good et al. 2003; Guo 1998; Payne and Biddle 1999). Reasons for such disparities would be examined, which then take into consideration the dearth of resources schools in poor communities contend with and how this impacts students' learning, as well as the collective impact of poverty on children's abilities to perform well in school. Students might also be asked to think about how math education pedagogies need to be reformed based on the population of students they are teaching, and how to go about doing so.

Intentional Selection of Service-Learning Sites

As mentioned above, residents in local communities believe that public institutions have responsibility to address the causes and consequences of social inequality as they exist in these communities. Therefore, if we want students to understand what this means, then we must be intentional about having them confront the issues in real time. If we want to teach students about the hidden curriculum in schools (Jay 2003), and its effects on K-12 students of color, for example, then it is appropriate that we select service-learning sites where these realities of our education system might be experienced. It is fine for a practicum model to send postsecondary students into any school where they will have the opportunity to develop teaching skills; however, if we want them to learn what it is like for a teacher to try to educate while confronting a lack of resources and a culture framed by the dominant ideologies that determine the educational trajectory of these students, then we must be intentional about the types of schools with which we partner.

Interrogation of Identity

In the context of a math education course taught from a critical service-learning perspective, the interrogation of one's identity occurs throughout the duration of the course and is integrated with and explored in relation to the rest of the course content and objectives. Students might be asked to consider their own K-12 education experiences broadly, and their math education specifically. They might be prompted to think about the racial and cultural constitution of the schools they attended, to consider the amount of resources in their schools compared to other districts, and to reflect upon how these factors might have shaped their own experiences as a student. Futhermore, they might be asked to explicitly consider how their various identity markers (e.g., race, class, gender) contributed to learning math, and to use their identity as a framework for analyzing learning challenges or successes they experienced during their own math education.

For example, research has shown that female students are less likely to pursue courses and careers in the STEM fields (Jacobs 2005). Given this data, through various exercises and assignments, students would be asked to contemplate how gender impacted their experiences in math courses as they were growing up or how gender contributed to their understanding of their abilities to perform in a subject such as math. They might also be prompted to think about these experiences in relation to their observations in the classrooms where they are serving and with regard for the identities of the K-12 students with whom they are working as part of the service-learning course. Although geared toward supporting students in examining their individual identities, these exercises also help students to situate the factors that inform their individual identities within a larger social context. Accordingly, they are building their critical consciousness by being able to more fully understand the concept of social location broadly and the role social location plays for them as an individual.

THE CHALLENGES OF IMPLEMENTATION AT A PUBLIC RESEARCH UNIVERSITY

The challenges of implementing such a model at a research university are substantial. At institutions where the emphasis for faculty has been placed on conducting and publishing original research, attention to teaching and learning can often take a backseat. The culture of these institutions often places a lower priority on considerations of one's teaching practices. This lack of reflection on teaching practices may also impact efforts to implement a campus-wide approach to service-learning, as some faculty may see this as an encroachment on their academic freedom. It is also the case that some faculty feel like they do not know how to teach outside of their discipline, and believe that discussions about issues such as racism, sexism, and income inequality fall outside their area of disciplinary expertise leading to fear that these conversations may ravel "out of control."

Recent proposed changes to the tenure evaluation process at Purdue University exemplify the blowback that can happen at research universities when attempts to put a greater emphasis on pedagogical innovation are undertaken. In this particular case, recommendations were made to prioritize mentoring of at-risk undergraduates by faculty members, with an emphasis on providing opportunities for undergraduates to engage in research. Whereas some may see a refocus on teaching as a prudent response to the realities of twenty-first-century postsecondary education, some faculty may scoff at the idea that they need to change their approach to teaching (Jaschik 2015). Thus, innovations calling for greater intentionality toward undergraduate development may be met with reservation.

However, if framed within the culture of the research university, we believe a critical approach to service-learning can be more attractive than traditional models. Faculty at research institutions are generally dedicated to the twin educational processes of exploration and discovery, which define the research enterprise regardless of their academic discipline. It is important to incorporate those overarching goals within this strategy of reimagining service-learning as a vehicle for developing students' critical consciousness.

An instructor utilizing this framework might employ a data-driven approach to have students examine the real (vs. perceived) social issues that exist in the diverse communities within which students perform service. That same instructor might consider how the collection and analysis of this data allows for students to engage in informed social critique, particularly regarding public policies relevant to the subject matter of the course. A scaffolded approach to articulating students' social location vis-à-vis various communities may then be coupled with an examination of the historic, economic, and political status of the specific community in which the student works.

In fact, this type of approach is becoming more common within research universities. Faculty at research institutions have increasingly conceptualized their role as engaged instructors over the last 10 years, guiding the incremental learning of students in a structured way that fits with the history of service-learning within higher education (Stanton 2007). Research universities can and should take the lead in creating new models for civic engagement demonstrating the key components of a twenty-first-century education. There are fine examples of research universities creating new centers and research hubs that address other dimensions of civic education or citizenship, including (but not limited to) the work at Tufts University, Tulane University, and Cornell University.

Clearly, there are differences among public and private research institutions, as well as other differences related to the size of the campus. Smaller private colleges can implement campus-wide initiatives around civic engagement based on a shared mission, such as religious ministry. Larger public universities, on the other hand, are more likely to involve campus champions to create model exemplars that can be shared with other departments, schools, and disciplines. The history of developing new frontiers of curriculum development at research universities has tended to favor the simultaneous development of interrelated campus goals. This is true now, as well, since most universities are eager to utilize innovative teaching and learning strategies to increase their students' abilities to solve problems in diverse groups, improve communication skills, and contribute to the public good—regardless of their academic majors. Therefore, despite potential concerns that a model of service-learning as critical consciousness development would be seen as radical in some circles, we contend that such a framework converges with many of the twenty-first-century learning outcomes prominent in higher education today.

CONCLUSION

At the time that it was gaining popularity as a pedagogical model, service-learning challenged the traditional culture of higher education by suggesting that students could learn in valuable and valid ways by leaving campus. In certain circles, service-learning was (and still is) a controversial idea. And so, for practitioners and advocates, simply getting faculty to buy into having their students spend a portion of their course time working in local communities—not as field work, but rather as civic participants—and then to see this as an integral component through which students learn the course material, has been a substantial achievement. But now that service-learning has become more mainstream, the time has come to advance our conceptualization of the purposes of this pedagogical model. It is our contention that we cannot accept neutral and superficial versions of service-learning if we aim it to be an alternative to the "hollow" responses to diversity issues, both on and off campus.

Our neutrality as educators is not neutral: if we are not proponents in the creation of these critical civic engagement courses, our neutrality is a purposeful acceptance to continue and maintain the status quo of inequality and injustice. If we remain passive, we are complicit in the development of apathy toward all groups who are marginalized by the dominant culture. If we do not create civic engagement programs that develop critical self-discovery (Freire 1970), and develop understanding and empathy with and between "in-groups" and "out-groups" (Vaught 2012), we are institutionalizing the cycles of oppression that the mission statements of public universities—laden with social justice rhetoric—are committed to correcting. This framework, with its focus on developing students' habits of mind toward a more critical approach to social analysis through service-learning, allows us to pursue the mandate for diversity learning in a manner that is no longer viewed as hollow.

References

Barrera, D. (2015). Examining our interdependence: Community partners' motivations to participate in academic outreach. *Journal of Higher Education Outreach & Engagement, 19*(4), 85–114.

Barrera, D., Willner, L. N., & Kukahiko, K. (2015). Assessing the development of an emerging critical consciousness through service learning. Unpublished manuscript.

Camacho, M. M. (2004). Power and privilege: Community service learning in Tijuana. *Michigan Journal of Community Service Learning, 10*(3), 31–42.

Carnoy, M. (1989). Education, state, and culture in American society. In H. A. Giroux & P. McLaren (Eds.), *Critical pedagogy, the state and cultural struggle* (pp. 3–23). Albany, NY: State University of New York Press.

U.S. Census Bureau. (2013). *QuickFactsbeta, Los Angeles population (data file)*. Washington, DC: U.S. Census Bureau.

Charleston shooting forces students to look at on-campus racism [Editorial]. (2015). *The Daily Bruin*. http://dailybruin.com/.

Cipolle, S. B. (2010). *Service-learning and social justice: Engaging students in social change*. Lanham, MD: Rowman & Littlefield Publishers, Inc.

Fitch, P., Steinke, P., & Hudson, T. D. (2013). Research and theoretical perspectives on cognitive outcomes of service learning. In P. H. Clayton, R. G. Bringle, & J. A. Hatcher (Eds.), *Research on service learning: Conceptual frameworks and assessment* (Students and faculty, Vol. 2A, pp. 57–83). Sterling, VA: Stylus Publishing.

Freire, P. (1970). *Pedagogy of the oppressed*. New York, NY: Continuum International Publishing Group.

Giroux, H. A. (2011). *On critical pedagogy*. New York, NY: Continuum International Publishing Group.

Good, C., Aronson, J., & Inslicht, M. (2003). Improving adolescents' standardized test performance: An intervention to reduce the effects of stereotype threat. *Applied Developmental Psychology, 24*(6), 645–662.

Gramsci, A. (1995). *Further selections from the prison notebooks*. Minneapolis, MN: University of Minnesota Press.

Guo, G. (1998). The timing of the influences of cumulative poverty on children's cognitive ability and achievement. *Social Forces, 77*(1), 257–287.

Iverson, S. V., & James, J. H. (2013). Self-authoring a civic identity: A qualitative analysis of change-oriented service learning. *Journal of Student Affairs Research and Practice, 50*(1), 88–105.

Jacobs, J. E. (2005). Twenty-five years of research on gender and ethnic differences in math and science career choices: What have we learned? *New Directions for Child and Adolescent Development, 110*, 85–94.

Jaschik, S. (2015). Mentoring as tenure criterion. *Inside Higher Ed*. https://www.insidehighered.com/news/2015/07/20/purdue-moves-make-mentoring-undergraduates-criterion-tenure?utm_medium=social&utm_source=facebook&utm_campaign=IHEbuffer.

Jay, M. (2003). Critical race theory, multicultural education, and the hidden curriculum of hegemony. *Multicultural Perspectives, 5*(4), 3–9.

Jones, S. R., & Hill, K. (2001). Crossing high street: Understanding diversity through community service-learning. *Journal of College Student Development, 42*(3), 204–216.

Kincheloe, J. L. (2008). *Critical pedagogy primer*. New York, NY: Peter Lang.

McLaren, P. (2014). *Life in schools. An introduction to critical pedagogy in the foundations of education* (5th ed.). Reading, MA: Addison Wesley Longman, Inc.

Mitchell, T. D. (2007). Critical service-learning as social justice education: A case study of the Citizen Scholars Program. *Equity & Excellence in Education, 40*(2), 101–112.

Mitchell, T. D. (2008). Traditional vs. critical service-learning: Engaging the literature to differentiate two models. *Michigan Journal of Community Service Learning, 14*(2), 50–65.

Nieto, S. (2000). Foreword. In C. R. O'Grady (Ed.), *Integrating service learning and multicultural education in colleges and universities* (pp. ix–xi). Mahwah, NJ: Lawrence Erlbaum Associates.

Page, S. E. (2007). *The difference: How the power of diversity creates better groups, firms, schools, and societies*. Princeton, NJ: Princeton University Press.

Payne, K. J., & Biddle, B. J. (1999). Poor school funding, child poverty, and mathematics achievement. *Educational Researcher, 28*(6), 4–13.

Peet, M. R. (2006). *We make the road by walking it: Critical consciousness, structuration, and social change.* Unpublished dissertation. University of Michigan.

Rosenberger, C. (2000). Beyond empathy: Developing critical consciousness through service learning. In C. R. O'Grady (Ed.), *Integrating service learning and multicultural education in colleges and universities* (pp. 23–43). Mahwah, NJ: Lawrence Erlbaum Associates.

Smith, D. G. (2009). *Diversity's promise for higher education: Making it work.* Baltimore, MD: The Johns Hopkins University Press.

Stanton, T. K. (2007). *New times demand new scholarship II: Research universities and civic engagement—Opportunities and challenges.* Los Angeles, CA: University of California, Los Angeles and Campus Compact.

Vaught, S. E. (2012). "They might as well be Black": The racialization of Sa'moan high school students. *International Journal of Qualitative Studies in Education,* 25(5), 557–582.

Wang, Y., & Rodgers, R. (2006). Impact of service-learning and social justice education on college students' cognitive development. *NASPA Journal, 43*(2), 316–337.

CHAPTER 12

Student Activism as Civic Engagement: Challenging Institutional Conditions for Civic Leadership at University of Virginia

Walter F. Heinecke, Rose Cole, Ibby Han, and Nqobile Mthethwa

With mounting evidence that American democracy is sliding toward a path of "economic elite domination" and "biased pluralism," and away from "majoritarian electoral democracy" or "majoritarian pluralism" (Gilens and Page 2014, p. 3; see also Barber 1984), definitions of, and approaches to, citizenship and civic engagement in education have been contested (Abowitz and Harnish 2006; Westheimer and Kahne 2004). Since the 1990s, there has been a movement to push back against neoliberalism and its effects by reinvigorating the neglected mission of universities to prepare citizens for democracy and promote civic engagement (Boyte 2015; Kezar et al. 2005). Policy reports such as the *Wingspread Declaration* and *Crucible Moment* are a response to this problem. *Wingspread* called for action on the part of policymakers, university administrators, faculty, and students to reinvigorate and reimagine the public mission of universities (Boyte and Hollander 1999). The authors called for colleges and universities to engage in the "work of citizenship" by "conceiving of institutions of higher learning as vital, living cultures, not simply as an aggregation of discrete units in competition with each other" as many new neoliberal responsibility-centered

© The Editor(s) (if applicable) and The Author(s) 2016   219
K.M. Soria, T.D. Mitchell (eds.), *Civic Engagement and Community Service at Research Universities*,
DOI 10.1057/978-1-137-55312-6_12

budget models promote (p. 9). *The Crucible Moment* calls for higher education to engage in defining the "depth, complexity, and competing versions of what 'civic actually means and entails'" basically calling for clearer definitions of the concept of democracy (The National Task Force on Civic Learning and Democratic Engagement 2012, p. 31). In the intervening years since the *Wingspread Declaration* and *Crucible Moment* report, public universities have responded to the call for civic renewal mostly through expanding service-learning and community engagement programming. The growth of Campus Compact, which now has 1100 institutional members, and the more than 300 institutions who have applied for and received the elective Community Engagement classification from the Carnegie Foundation are evidence of this expansion. However, this activity has only marginally influenced change and "recent reviews of the status of the field have found civic engagement to have made little progress at penetrating the core teaching, learning, and research processes in higher education" (Pollack 2013, p. 228). Some argue that the civic engagement movement itself is marginal, stalled, or adrift (Burkhardt and Joslin 2012; Pollack 2013; Saltmarsh et al. 2009).

THE CHALLENGE OF NEOLIBERALISM

Institutions of higher education in the USA have become increasingly oriented toward their role as players in a neoliberal market economy (Ayers 2005; Bok 2003; Giroux 2002; Slaughter and Rhoades 2004). Reacting to drastic decreases in public funding, institutions increase tuition rates and implement industry-based approaches to cost-cutting (e.g., by hiring more adjunct/contingent faculty, ballooning numbers of administrators, and focusing on students-as-consumers) (Giroux 2014; Levin 2007). A market-based approach to higher education is antithetical to the function of higher education as a public good, much less to supporting education for democracy or democratic citizenship (Barr et al. 2015; Cole and Heinecke 2015; Fallis 2007; Giroux 2002; Kezar 2004; Kezar et al. 2005; Marginson 2012; McDowell 2001; Suspitsyna 2012; Young 1997). This larger reality of higher education in the USA provides critical context for understanding civic engagement on campus (Barber 2012; Burkhardt and Joslin 2012; Kliewer 2013). Kliewer (2013) asserts that the challenge is to "insulate civic engagement from neoliberal ideology" (p. 77). He argues that neoliberalism has had a constraining influence on the civic renewal process in higher education primarily because it "has changed the relationship between the market, civil society and the state" (p. 72) and "the civic engagement field has failed to account for the predominant structures of the paradigm" (p. 73). Kliewer argues that the field of civic engagement in higher education must acknowledge neoliberalism lest it continues to maintain "existing ideological structures that preclude achieving democratic and justice goals—unjust levels of inequality, disengagement, and disempowerment," and, "producing a type of citizen completely defined in relation to a market society, thereby precluding a robust form of democratic engagement in which citizens organize, cooperate, and act outside the bounds of market and economic activity" (p. 73).

STUDENT ACTIVISM

Student activism has a tradition in higher education related to social change and leadership on issues pertinent to society at large and university life (Altbach 1989; Astin 1975; Foster and Long 1970; Kezar 2010; Rhoads 1998). Here, activism "refers to students' efforts to create change on or off campus related to a broad range of social, political, and economic issues often using techniques outside institutional channels such as protests, demonstrations, and rallies" as well as other more subtle forms of activism (Kezar 2010, p. 451). As Ropers-Huilman et al. (2005) explain, "student activism is more than just organizational involvement; instead, it implies involvement in and commitment to social change" (p. 298).

Activism is also regarded as a way in which students learn about "democratic process, citizenship, and leadership" (Kezar 2010, p. 451) and develop skills related to citizenship and civic engagement (Astin 1975; Rhoads 1997, 1998). Student activists practice democracy by assuming citizenship roles through engagement with dissent (Hamrick 1998). However, although many students become involved in activism to learn how to engage in a democracy, they often find themselves shut out from decision-making on campuses (Ropers-Huilman et al. 2005). Ropers-Huilman et al. (2005) also found that student-government could function as a tool of exclusion for some student groups on campus. Levels of student activism are related to the "perceived power of students on campus, the nature of the student body, the background of faculty and staff, the emergence of an informal or formal curriculum around grassroots leadership and activism, and faculty and staff" and whether or not students see and experience the mutual benefits of working together (Kezar 2010, p. 451). Recent trends indicate an increase in student activism in the USA, and it is globally related to student resistance to neoliberal ideology's capture of higher education (Klemenčič 2014).

Specific Institutional Responses: Virginia and Its University

Universities respond to calls for reengaging with their civic missions within the particular cultural contexts of their regions and states (Moglen 2013). The context of citizenship, civic engagement, and activism at the University of Virginia (UVa) is influenced by a national culture of neoliberalism (Kirp 2003; Lightcap 2014) and by state and local political culture of traditionalism and elitism (Tarter 2013). The culture of UVa is a reflection of its history: its founder, Thomas Jefferson, was both a proponent of grassroots democracy and the ideology of the inferiority of non-Whites and women (as well as a slaveholder). This reality has permeated its history: African–American graduate students were not admitted until the 1950s, African–American undergraduates were not admitted in significant numbers until the late 1960s, and women were not admitted as undergraduates until 1970.

In addition, like almost all institutions of higher education in the USA, the University is being urged to counter neoliberal trends in society by lowering tuition, increasing diversity, democratizing its governing process, engaging in service-learning that critically examines root causes of social problems, and pursuing knowledge for the public good from perspectives other than economic and market ideology, "challenging the governing logics of neoliberalism" (Kliewer 2013, p.77), instead of becoming less accountable to public authority and more accountable to private interests like bond ratings and rankings systems. At the same time, UVa is subject to neoliberal forces both externally (e.g., economic and political pressures from legislators to focus on job preparation) and internally (e.g., tacitly accepting the state's underfunding, adopting consumerist mentalities, and "responsibility-centered management," seen by many faculty, staff, and students as common-sense, cost-saving measures [Kliewer 2013]). These contradictions, not directly addressed in the *Wingspread Declaration* or *Crucible Moment*, are problematic for the mission of civic renewal as "neoliberal ideology produces a very specific governing and organizing regime that makes democratic and justice aims difficult to achieve" (Kliewer 2013, p. 74).

Student Activism at UVa

The University of Virginia has a rich history of student activism. The University began admitting African–American graduate students in 1959 and from 1961 to 1980, there were boycotts, marches, and sit-ins led by students who were "fed up with racism" at UVa (Valenzi 2002, p. 28). These actions resulted in many institutional changes, including the establishment of the Office of African–American Affairs (Harold 2014). Students mobilized again in the 1980s, staging an occupation of the Rotunda and demanding that the University divest its holdings from companies in apartheid South Africa (Valenzi 2002).

Students have continued this tradition of protest into the twenty-first century, most notably through the Living Wage campaign, which advocates for fair compensation for the University's low-wage employees. They initiated an occupation of the president's offices in Madison Hall in 2006, resulting in the arrest of 17, as well as a 13-day hunger strike in March 2012.

The University found itself in the national spotlight again in June 2012 when the Board of Visitors forced President Teresa Sullivan to resign, apparently motivated by Sullivan's lack of "strategic dynamism" and resistance to neoliberal change (Lightcap 2014, p. 6; see also Spencer 2012). This crisis in governance sparked a nationwide "groundswell of support" for Sullivan, and the Board of Visitors unanimously reinstated her after two weeks of protests led by students, faculty, and alumni (Spencer 2012, p.1). Students again decried the Board of Visitors during the 2013 academic year, when the Board significantly modified the no-loan policy of the University's flagship financial aid program, AccessUVa (Johnson 2013). A petition circulated by the Restore AccessUVa campaign gained nearly 9000 signatures (Barry 2013).

During the academic year 2014–2015, UVa experienced its most recent tumultuous year of crisis and activism. There was a nationwide search for missing student Hannah Graham during the month of September, ending with a UVa hospital employee on trial for abduction and first-degree murder of the student (Keneally 2015). In November 2014, *Rolling Stone* magazine published a graphic account of an alleged gang rape perpetrated by fraternity brothers 2 years prior and the University's attempt to sweep it under the rug. UVa became "ground zero in the debate over campus sexual assault" (Brown 2014, p.1). Protests against gender-based violence erupted across campus, including a SlutWalk and a faculty-led "Take Back the Party" rally. In response to the article, President Sullivan temporarily suspended the entire Greek system; however, an investigation initiated by *The Washington Post* raised questions about the legitimacy of the claim, leading to *Rolling Stone* retracting the story entirely (Dana 2014). The Columbia School of Journalism later released a comprehensive report on the article's lack of journalistic integrity, describing it as "a story of journalistic failure that was avoidable" (Coronel et al. 2015, p. 1). Still, UVa is one of 55 schools under investigation by the US Department of Education's Office for Civil Rights for possible violations of federal Title IX laws.

The campus was also rocked by Black Lives Matter protests in response to the high-profile cases of police brutality in Ferguson and Staten Island (Robinson 2014). The brutal beating of a Black UVa student, Martese Johnson, by state Alcohol and Beverage Control agents at a local bar, sparked another round of rallies and marches that March (Heskett 2015). In response, the Black Student Alliance developed a 26-page proposal titled "Towards a Better University," outlining issues of racial inequality on Grounds (the term used for "campus" at UVa) and what the administration should do to rectify them (Black Student Alliance at UVA 2015). Other students marched in protest and disrupted a meeting of law enforcement officers.

Lastly, there was student outrage just a week after the incident of police brutality when the Board of Visitors voted to implement an 11 % tuition increase for incoming students in a plan called "Affordable Excellence" that was not released to the public until their vote (Anderson 2015a, b). Over 200 students participated in a rally and sit-in at the Board of Visitors' meeting, showing their dissent.

Citizenship and Civic Engagement at UVa

Citizenship and civic engagement are a central part of the University's mission and an important part of its brand (Lampkin 2000). There are references to this aspect of the University's mission peppered throughout its public documents, web pages, and administrators' speeches. The University has implemented several programs related to civic engagement through such efforts as the Jefferson Public Citizens program and the Meriwether Lewis Institute for Citizen Leadership. In addition, the University has been touted in some scholarly works as exemplary when it comes to citizen leadership, education for civic responsibility, and student self-governance (Eramo 2010; Sawicki 2009; Thornton and Jaeger 2006).

However, these resources provide a limited perspective on the University's approach to civic education. While the University administration, both in written documents (e.g., Strategic Plan) and presentations, often refers to the ideals of Jeffersonian democracy and the civic purpose of the university, it should be acknowledged that "[a]n expression of democratic purpose may not necessarily result in a more democratic curriculum. Mission statements often represent ideals and aspirations" (Youngberg 2008, p. 8). Indeed, there are indications that the meaning of citizen-leaders is unclear at the University (Sawicki 2009), and the focus of civic engagement programs and initiatives rarely embrace social activism and resistance movements as indicative of developing civic leaders. The present study adds the voice and perspective of student activists traditionally marginalized in the university student-governance culture.

METHODS

The conceptual framework for the study drew on several components. First, we were guided by definitions of citizens and citizenship as defined by Westheimer and Kahne (2004) and Abowitz and Harnish (2006). They provide three citizen/citizenship typologies that have some overlap: Personally Responsible/Civic Republican, Participatory/Liberal; and Justice-Oriented/Critical. We were particularly interested in how mainstream Personally Responsible/Civic Republican and Participatory/ Liberal forms might contrast with the latter definition, Justice-Oriented/Critical, in the context of crises related to gender and race. Second, we employed theoretical concepts from political cultural analysis (Elazar 1984; Marshall et al. 1989; Tarter 2013) and organizational cultural analysis (Colby et al. 2003; Schein 2009, 2010; Tierney 2008) to examine how larger political and historical forces shape the organizational culture at UVa as it relates to its efforts to promote education for democracy and civic engagement in the midst of student activism. Lastly, we employed aspects of Kezar's (2010) methodological approach to "examine the strategies, obstacles, and ways students navigated power conditions" related to organizational change and civic engagement on campus (p. 452). This study is part of a larger research project examining civic renewal and student activism at multiple sites. For this chapter, we focused on interviews conducted with ten student activists who held various positions such as presidents and past presidents of student cultural organizations, leaders of social change-oriented contracted independent organizations (CIO) organizations (such as Living Wage,

Socio-Economic Diversity), and unaffiliated activists (such as informal student and community groups not recognized by the University pushing for reform in governance, financial aid, and tuition). We chose these participants because previous research on civic engagement and leadership conducted at UVa (Eramo 2010; Sawicki 2009; Thornton and Jaeger 2006) utilized participants from mainstream student-government organizations and administrators from the University. We purposefully chose participants to gain insights on the meaning of civic engagement in higher education from the perspective of underrepresented students who are student activists. All ten activists interviewed were women of color, majoring in a variety of subjects including social sciences, the sciences, and humanities. All of the students had been involved in activism for several years. We also collected a sample of over 100 media reports about crises and activism at UVa over the past 3 years, as well as scholarly articles and dissertations written about the University. Lastly, the data also includes the University's own reports and statements related to citizenship, democracy, and civic engagement. These documents were treated as an additional data source to compare the University-sanctioned perspective of activism alongside student perspectives and were analyzed in the same manner as the interview data, using analytic induction (Erickson 1986). Analytic assertions were developed from multiple readings of the data corpus and then tested for accuracy through a review of the data for confirmation or disconfirmation.

Results

Our findings reflect a clash between different forms of civic leadership promoted by the institution and engaged by activist students. The University promotes student participation in a depoliticized, non-activist conception of democracy and citizenship, despite embracing a Jeffersonian framework (that originally included a populist, anti-institutional, and activist form of democracy). Student activists engage in civic leadership that reflects a justice-oriented citizenship (Westheimer and Kahne 2004) or critical citizenship (Abowitz and Harnish 2006) via a resistance-/social change-oriented frame. The democratic ethos of the institutional culture marginalizes student activists who exercise resistance capital (Yosso 2005) and utilize different strategies to demonstrate civic leadership. Specifically, the analyses conducted for this study revealed the following themes:

1. The University of Virginia's culture and civic ethos reflects an elitist democratic and neoliberal culture that frames civic participation and citizenship in a depoliticized and non-activist manner.
2. This culture of democratic elitism is mirrored in the student body generally and is replicated in the culture and system of student self-governance.
3. Student activists, attempting to exercise civic leadership through a critical/justice-oriented citizenship frame, experienced conflict with the institutional civic culture resulting in being marginalized, isolated, and co-opted by formal student groups with ties to University administration.

Elitist Democratic Culture: Traditions, Student Self-Governance, and Leadership

The activists interviewed were aware of, and engaged with, concepts like neoliberalism, elitism, hierarchy, and competition for prestige. Students offered sentiments such as, "elitism is definitely embedded in our culture" (activist involved in local community), and "the culture that you do see, the one that is most in-your-face, is definitely the preppy elitism of UVa" (activist working on income inequality) that demonstrated their engagement with these concepts. This environment, from the activists' perspectives, cultivated a focus on individual advancement and a civically disengaged, apathetic student body. It spurred these activists into action to counter the University culture of elitist democracy and apathy in ways that reflect resistance capital (Yosso 2005).

The students we interviewed described a school culture in which there was intense competition among students for prestige related to student-career advancement and leading to social stratification at UVa. One student activist, a woman of color focused on the institutional support of students from low socioeconomic backgrounds, echoes what most interviewed students identified as an institutional culture dominated by the Greek system: "in your first year, if you don't see, if you don't have other options [than the Greek system], you're very limited in what you can do ... and you definitely have to more actively seek out different cultures [to achieve social standing]." A student deeply involved with organizing for justice and equity for students from low-income backgrounds further explains:

[There are] things that are super competitive to get into, because they're looking for a certain type of UVa student. Typically it follows White, upper-class, middle-class values … So, being able to speak in a certain manner, compose yourself in a certain manner, dress in a certain manner, are the things that these clubs look for in addition to the mainstream values that they think UVa encapsulates.

The culture of traditionalism, prestige, and elitism leads some students to feel marginalized and apathetic, but it also energizes a minority of students to find alternative means to enact a counter narrative of engagement and change. Another activist (involved in planning key events related to racial issues on campus), describes a "system that's already given [students] all these definitions. Here's who you are, here's your identity … it's this identity being handed to you, being this mold where it's like 'here, fit into this.'" She illustrates how strong the traditional culture of the University is felt by many students, activists, and non-activists alike. This system, she explains, relies on "labels" related to traditions that lead, in her opinion, to "alienation":

They give us honor, you have self-governance which is generally about leadership, so what does leadership mean to you … this is who you are, but we never really get the chance to define what those things are as students for ourselves … you should be able to define what honor is to you.

Activists described this climate as conservative, quiet, apathetic, and "neo-liberalized," with most students not being engaged or concerned with social issues of marginalized peoples. "There's not that many student activists," explains a former president of a cultural student union. She suggests that activism is "taboo" at UVa. Another student activist involved in a cultural organization described the relationship between neoliberalism, elitism, and student engagement:

But also it seems the majority of my peers have adopted a kind of…I guess it is slightly neoliberal…where everything's fine, let's make money, let's have fun, nothing gets their gears grinding, it seems…that the University does or that's just happening in the world. … There's a lot of students that we've already lost in the fight. I think it's part of that elitism, there's nothing really grinds your gears cause it's not directly affecting you.

An activist involved in campaigns for climate change and fair wages credits her developing understanding of neoliberal culture as key to her engagement: "I got involved [with activism] because I started to understand the neoliberal culture, I had some classes that made me think we need critical self-reflection." As described by our participants, the university civic culture influences the general student culture within which students make meaning of civic engagement and social activism within a frame of competition, status, and elitism—symptoms of neoliberalism and barriers to a civic ethos. This culture of elitism pervades the system of student self-governance, leadership programming, and student leadership development.

The Culture of Democratic Elitism and Student Self-Governance

The culture of elitism shapes student self-governance and the culture of student engagement. The University promotes its leadership programming as related to Jefferson's beliefs about university education producing "educated, civic-minded leaders who could guide the democracy into a bright future" (University of Virginia Office of the Dean of Students 2015). However, according to activist students interviewed, the culture at UVa constructs a hierarchy of students and student groups. At the top of the hierarchy are official student organizations known as Agency Groups, which act on behalf of the University and provide specific University services. The student leaders of Agency Groups assume responsibilities delegated from the governing board and the administration (e.g., University Programs Council, University Judiciary Committee [UJC], Honor Committee) and "Special Status Groups" that act as agents for the University for certain functions delegated to them by the administration (e.g., Class Councils, Student Council ["StudCo"], School Councils, University Guides). Many of the leadership positions are elected from the general student body, but most of the associated positions are appointed by the student-government leadership.

Below the Agency Groups are the Contracted Independent Organizations (CIOs) which constitute most of the student organizations (approximately 700) at UVa. These groups are independent of the University, except that they receive funds from StudCo. CIOs range from cultural groups to hobby and recreational groups. The CIOs most pertinent to this study are the cultural groups such as the Black Student Alliance, The Latino Student Alliance, and the Asian Student Alliance as well as some activist organizations such as United for Undergraduate Socio-Economic Diversity (UFUSED) and Living Wage Campaign. The latter two organizations tend to challenge the University administration in ways that other CIOs do not.

Outside of the formal Agency Groups and CIO structure are a group of informal and independent student groups that tend to be more progressive and assertive, such as UVa Students United, Climate Action, and the Alliance for Social Change. One of our student participants (active with community activist groups unaffiliated with the University) described the structure and hierarchy this way:

> (T)here's definitely a hierarchy. There are organizations like Honor and JeffSoc and U-Guides, top-tier leadership things that you can get involved in without knowing what they really do. More of the resources, funding, gets funneled into them, versus minority organizations struggle to get funding. ... And so it seems to me that organizations that really [advocate] for substantial consciousness and for substantial change actually don't get much of the funding, and to me, that seems very deliberate. The more that the University can give those resources to organizations that don't really have some kind of conscious motive, that means they're placing a hierarchy, in that status. ... And it just kind of goes down from there. Black students are at the bottom, Latino students are at the bottom. There's definitely a hierarchy. And like I said earlier, it's a result of the culture that exists there.

The elitist structure of student organizations also has substantive effects on the ability to influence. "I think the StudCo groups definitely have the ear of the University," while it is difficult for informal groups to get a meeting, "because those students are supposed to be representative of the student body, they get more time with the administrators ... that's part of the power [of being involved with formal organizations]—the University's interested in what you're doing," one activist told us. Another participant (an activist who participates in organizations unaffiliated with the University) further characterized more formal student organizations—"these groups at the top, StudCo, whatever"—as functioning as "mouthpieces of the administration" and "replicating the same power dynamics among the student body." She also, as all of our participants did, links concerns about organizing with an understanding of the culture explaining that "people are attracted to prestigious organizations, more well-funded organization" as showing how "that hierarchy is replicated among students." She expresses concern for her peers and society: "we're gonna go out in the world, become policymakers, teachers, doctors, and replicate that same structure within society! And that's why activism and consciousness-raising is super important." Resistance to this culture of elitism coupled with a desire to engage a critical discourse of citizenship shaped student activists' reactions to crises related to race and gender during the 2014–2015 academic year.

Responding to Crisis

The University's depoliticized approach to civic engagement became transparent during the crises of 2014–2015 when student activists responded with actions representative of a social justice and critical discourse conception of citizenship. Some of the activists we interviewed attributed the crises themselves to the way in which the traditional civic culture "kept the lid on" gender and racial conflict related to the University's history.

The student activists' ability to respond effectively to the events, policies, and culture undergirding the crises brought into stark relief the civic ethos of the institution; it revealed a culture that often remains hidden. The activists told us that this culture illuminated problems associated with low levels of activism and student engagement including inter- and intragroup cooperation, identity politics, the "siloing" of and coalition building among activist groups, co-optation of CIOs, and a student culture of apathy, racial insensitivity, and sexism.

Student activists felt there were different levels of engagement with the sexual assault and the race crises that plagued UVa in 2014–2015. They perceived greater student engagement around the sexual assault issue because it affected more White women. They also felt that the type of activism the sexual assault crisis elicited was one where mainstream organizations responded to work with the administration to protect the reputation of the institution rather than to protest university culture and policy. They characterized the response by many student organizations to the *Rolling Stone* article as "prolific and rapid" but also as "more damage control than anything else," reflecting a disposition among many students toward institutional loyalty rather than critical change.

The campus culture, according to the interviewed activists, contributed to identity politics that hampered student activists' ability to join together on various issues during the crises. As one activist put it, "in the Alliance thing, you just saw different kinds of feminism. What gets people involved in certain issues is basically their identities, and if you have a school of limited identities then you're gonna have a school of limited issues."

Different approaches to civic engagement were also held in different esteem at UVa, according to the activists. Direct action was described as "taboo," and it was clear that the mainstream student civic culture, as well as the administration, promoted prolonged dialogue over direct political action and protest. While all of the student activist leaders we interviewed had been involved with events that provided space for dialogue, they were frustrated that many of these initiatives felt superficial and symbolic. For example, the administrative response to one student group's efforts to spotlight issues of racial profiling and overpolicing through Black Lives Matter protests and direct action was a request to produce a report for the administration about racial inequality. This was the fourth report requested and provided in 20 years, and many of those involved felt these reports have not been accompanied by any substantive change. A student leader of a minority CIO provided this example:

> we raise the roof, and then things calm down again and new leaders come in. And then they learn all about it, and then they raise the roof, and then things calm down. The same thing happening over and over again. So ... we have the same issues that we've been having for the last 10 years. What I've been advocating for the past year, the first ... president advocated during her term. So I don't see any change.

Some activists felt that groups were co-opted into a civic culture that continually transforms student protest and resistance from action-oriented to discussion-oriented, precluding substantive action or change. Activists saw this as a deliberate strategy and, as a result, the same issues had been talked over for years with no change or substantive action, thus benefiting UVa's administration. One CIO activist, who was outspoken about socioeconomic diversity, explained how this created divisions among students hoping to effect change on Grounds:

> There's such a struggle over "okay, should we escalate this and do a direct action or should we start slow and start with dialogue?" And I think that something that's a core part of the University community is this idea of dialogue, and how talking things out will just solve the issues, these deep-seated issues that have been going on for centuries at this University. The types of issues that come with being historically an institution for White, affluent, males. And as time has progressed, we've had women at this University, Black students at this University, Latino students at this University, low-income students at this University, and it has interrupted the core, founding values of this University. So some student groups will go straight to dialogue, and get co-sponsored by Sustained Dialogue to host a dialogue about issues like

sexual assault or issues like, let's brainstorm policies that need to be created to make this a more inclusive space for Black bodies. And then let's compile our notes from this dialogue and give it to administrators. There's this idea of appealing to the administrators, of appealing to the people who are in power, the people who ultimately have the leverage to make decisions that will impact all of our lives. So the way to appeal to them isn't through rallies, it isn't through protest, it's through dialogue. ... or that's the assumption that many students have here. That's what makes the dialogue tactic appealing for a majority of students. Because it's more comfortable and they think that administrators will listen if you speak. ... But some students think also that being a part of these traditional organizations they'll be more listened to, that they'll have the power from the administration, when in reality they end up being the administration's mouthpiece and doing and thinking and saying the things the administration wants them to do, think, and say.

The frustration exhibited by the student activists responding to crises of race and gender reflects a conflict between the institutional civic culture with certain enlightenment dispositions toward citizenship and students who are working from discourses of critical citizenship.

DISCUSSION

When investigating the progress of the civic engagement movement, it is important to understand the institution's cultural context and how it relates to dimensions of civic responsibility (Thornton and Jaeger 2006). Examining the democratic spirit and culture of civic engagement at the University of Virginia within a context of crisis and student activism illuminated the specific types of civic leadership reflected in the institutional culture and how that culture marginalizes student leaders who operate from a discourse of critical and justice-oriented citizenship. Questions of civic identity are illuminated in these interactions highlighting who is welcomed and who is not welcomed into the University's civic space (Abowitz and Harnish 2006). Varied definitions of key concepts revolving around democracy and citizenship have significant implications and raise political issues for civic renewal efforts (Westheimer and Kahne 2004). The University's ascription to "civic republican" and "political liberal" frameworks of citizenship conflicts with the citizenship orientations of the activists we interviewed, students from underrepresented groups (women of color and students from low-socioeconomic backgrounds) who, representing marginalized voices of minorities, women, and low-income students (all only recently admitted to

UVa), operate from a "critical discourse" or reconstructionist definition of citizenship that "raise issues of membership, identity, and engagement in creative, productive ways" (Abowitz and Harnish 2006, p. 666). Activist versions of citizenship break with liberalism and elitist forms of democracy in that they focus less on individual rights and freedom and more on collective or communal aspects of civic engagement.

CONCLUSION

The National Task Force on Civic Learning and Democratic Engagement stated that "[d]emocracy is the defining characteristic of our country" and asked that Universities "model institutional citizenship by employing democratic processes and practices" (p. 69). One of the most significant challenges in this effort is the development of political skills relating to dealing with difference. If activists and dissenters are marginalized in the assumed safety of the democratic culture that the higher education environment aims to provide, what does that say about the ability of American public research universities to prepare students for active and engaged participation in a diverse democracy? Universities must reexamine their civic cultures in this era when many administrators, faculty, and students have been captured by neoliberal ideologies and elite discourses.

University leaders should take into account changing and multiple definitions of democracy and citizenship if they are to successfully lead the way to civic renewal in higher education. Calls for civic renewal should be seen as calls for cultural renewal and institutional analysis because they force administrators to examine their operational definition of democracy and citizenship and the root conflicts between neoliberalism and democracy. Our results indicate that leaders of institutions committed to civic renewal will have to take a deep and hard look at their institutional cultures and time-honored traditions and move beyond the impression-management strategies of survival and competition. This will require different attitudes toward critique, dissent, and the politics of difference often found in the organizational cultures of research universities. Leaders should seek out and encourage divergent voices in the effort to engage in civic renewal. Starting with an examination of the culture of democracy and civic spirit on the institution is essential as this factor influences how universities define civic engagement strategies such as service-learning, extra- and co-curricular programming, and curricular approaches to civic renewal. The stakes are high: "When students perceive their institution as preaching one thing and living another, they are likely to become cynical" (Colby et al. 2003, p. 93). Without attention, universities run the risk of creating apathy and cynicism rather than inspiring engagement among students who are cognizant of the difference between university definitions of democracy and citizenship as they are actually practiced.

REFERENCES

Abowitz, K. K., & Harnish, J. (2006). Contemporary discourses of citizenship. *Review of Educational Research, 76*(4), 653–690.

Altbach, P. G. (Ed.). (1989). *Student political activism: An international reference handbook.* New York, NY: Greenwood Publishing Group.

Anderson, N. (2015a). U-Va. will raise tuition 11 percent next fall, one of highest increases in the nation. *The Washington Post.* http://www.washingtonpost.com/news/grade-point/wp/2015/03/24/u-va-will-raise-tuition-11-percent-next-fall-one-of-highest-increases-in-the-nation/.

Anderson, N. (2015b). Medical executive quits U-Va. governing board, blasts administration on way out. *The Washington Post.* http://www.washingtonpost.com/news/grade-point/wp/2015/04/13/medical-executive-quits-u-va-governing-board-blasts-administration-on-way-out/.

Astin, A. W. (1975). *The power of protest: A national study of student and faculty disruptions with implications for the future.* San Francisco, CA: Jossey-Bass.

Ayers, D. (2005). Neo-liberal ideology in community college mission statements: A critical discourse analysis. *The Review of Higher Education, 28*(4), 527–49.

Barber, B. R. (2012). Can we teach civic education and service-learning in a world of privatization, inequality, and interdependence? *Journal of College and Character, 13*(1), 1940–1639. doi:10.1515/jcc-2012-1869.

Barber, B. R. (1984). *Strong democracy: Participatory politics for a new age.* Berkeley, CA: University of California Press.

Barr, D., Boulay, B., Selman, R., McCormick, R., Lowenstein, E., Gamse, B., et al. (2015). A randomized controlled trial of professional development for interdisciplinary civic education: Impacts on humanities teachers and their students. *Teachers College Record, 117*(2).

Barry, M. N. (2013). Keep UVA affordable and reinstate no loan policy now! http://petitions.moveon.org/sign/keep-uva-affordable-and.

Black Student Alliance at UVA. (2015, April). Towards a better university. http://www.bsaatuva.com/towards-a-better-university.html.

Bok, D. (2003). *Universities in the marketplace: The commercialization of higher education.* Princeton, NJ: Princeton University Press.

Boyte, H. C. (2015). *Democracy's education: Public work, citizenship, & the future of colleges and universities.* Nashville, TN: Vanderbilt University Press.

Boyte, H., & Hollander, E. (1999). *Wingspread declaration on renewing the civic mission of the American research university.* Providence, RI: Campus Compact.

Brown, W. H. (2014, November 23). Dishonor code: Rape, reputation and repercussion at U.Va. https://quiteirregular.wordpress.com/2014/11/23/dishonor-code-rape-reputation-and-repercussion-at-u-va/.

Burkhardt, J. C., & Joslin, J. (2012). If this is a movement, why don't we feel anything moving? *Michigan Journal of Community Service Learning, 18*(2), 72–75.

Colby, A., Ehrlich, T., Beaumont, E., & Stephens, J. (2003). *Educating citizens: Preparing America's undergraduates for lives of moral and civic responsibility.* San Francisco, CA: John Wiley & Sons.

Cole, R. M., & Heinecke, W. F. (2015). The civic classroom in higher education: Contested terrain. *Citizenship Teaching & Learning, 10*(2), 185–201.

Coronel, S., Coll, S., & Kravitz, D. (2015, April 5). *Rolling Stone's* investigation: "A failure that was avoidable." *Columbia Journalism Review.* http://www.cjr.org/investigation/rolling_stone_investigation.php.

Dana, W. (2014, December 5). A note to our readers. *Rolling Stone.* http://www.rollingstone.com/culture/news/a-note-to-our-readers-20141205.

Elazar, D. J. (1984). *American federalism: A view from the states.* New York, NY: Harper & Row.

Eramo, N. P. (2010). *Under construction: A case study of student self-governance at the (Unpublished doctoral dissertation).* University of Virginia, Charlottesville, VA.

Erickson, F. (1986). Qualitative methods in research on teaching. In M. C. Wittrock (Ed.), *Handbook of research on teaching* (3rd ed., pp. 119–161). New York, NY: MacMillan Press.

Fallis, G. (2007). *Multiversities, ideas and democracy.* Toronto, ON: University of Toronto Press.

Foster, J., & Long, D. (1970). *Protest! Student activism in America.* New York, NY: Morrow.

Gilens, M., & Page, B. I. (2014). Testing theories of American politics: Elites, interest groups, and average citizens. *Perspectives on Politics, 12*(3), 564–581.

Giroux, H. (2002). Neo-liberalism, corporate culture, and the promise of higher education: The University as a democratic public sphere. *Harvard Educational Review, 72*(4), 425–464.

Giroux, H. (2014). *Neo-liberalism's war on higher education.* Chicago, IL: Haymarket Books.

Hamrick, F. A. (1998). Democratic citizenship and student activism. *Journal of College Student Development, 39*(5), 449–460.

Harold, C. (2014, February 10). The creation of OAAA. http://blackfireuva.com/2014/02/10/the-creation-of-oaaa/.

Heskett, C. (2015, March 18). University student, honor committee member Martese Johnson arrested. *The Cavalier Daily.* http://www.cavalierdaily.com/article/2015/03/university-student-honor-committee-member-martese-johnson-arrested.

Johnson, J. (2013, September 22). Students protest changes to U-Va. financial aid program. *The Washington Post.* http://www.washingtonpost.com/local/education/students-protest-changes-to-u-va-financial-aid-program/2013/09/22/35efef64-22ed-11e3-a358-1144dee636dd_story.html.

Keneally, M. (2015, February 10). Hannah Graham: A look back at UVA student's disappearance. *ABC News.* http://abcnews.go.com/US/back-uva-student-hannah-grahams-disappearance/story?id=28857580.

Kezar, A. (2010). Faculty and staff partnering with student activists: Unexplored terrains of interaction and development. *Journal of College Student Development, 51*(5), 451–480.

Kezar, A. J., Chambers, A. C., & Burkhardt, J. (Eds.). (2005). *Higher education for the public good: Emerging voices from a national movement.* San Francisco, CA: Jossey-Bass.

Kezar, A. (2004). Obtaining integrity? Reviewing and examining the charter between higher education and society. *The Review of Higher Education, 27*(4), 429–459.

Kirp, D. L. (2003). *Shakespeare, Einstein, and the bottom line: The marketing of higher education.* Cambridge, MA: Harvard University Press.

Kliewer, B. W. (2013). Why the civic engagement movement cannot achieve democratic and justice aims. *Michigan Journal of Community Service Learning, 19*(2), 72–79.

Klemenčič, M. (2014). Student power in a global perspective and contemporary trends in Student organising. *Studies in Higher Education, 39*(3), 396–411.

Lampkin, P. M. (2000). The student experience at the University of Virginia. http://vpsa.virginia.edu/sites/vpsa.virginia.edu/files/2020StudentExperience.pdf.

Levin, J. (2007). Neo-liberal policies and community college faculty work. In J. Smart (Ed.), *Higher education handbook of theory and research* (Vol. XXII, pp. 451–96). New York, NY: Springer.

Lightcap, T. (2014). Academic governance and democratic processes: The entrepreneurial model and its discontents. *New Political Science, 36*(4), 474–488.

Marginson, S. (2012). The "public" contributions of universities in an increasingly global world. In B. Pusser, K. Kempner, S. Marginson, & I. Ordorika (Eds.), *Universities and the public sphere: Knowledge creation and state building in the era of globalization* (pp. 7–25). London, UK: Routledge.

Marshall, C., Mitchell, D. E., & Wirt, F. M. (1989). *Culture and education policy in the American states.* New York, NY: Falmer Press.

McDowell, G. R. (2001). Land-grant universities and extension into the 21st century: Renegotiating or abandoning a social contract. Ames, IA: Iowa State University Press.

Moglen, S. (2013). Sharing knowledge, practicing democracy. In D. Allen & R. Reich (Eds.), *Education, justice, and democracy* (pp. 267–284). Chicago, IL: University of Chicago Press.

Pollack, S. S. (2013). Critical civic literacy. *The Journal of General Education,* *62*(4), 223–237.

Rhoads, R. A. (1997). Interpreting identity politics: The educational challenge of contemporary student activism. *Journal of College Student Development, 38*(5), 508–519.

Rhoads, R. A. (1998). *Freedom's web: Student activism in an age of cultural diversity.* Baltimore, MD: Johns Hopkins University Press.

Robinson, O. (2014, December 4). "We can't breathe": Students, community members stage protest against race-based brutality. *The Cavalier Daily.* http://www.cavalierdaily.com/article/2014/12/uva-students-community-members-stage-protest-against-race-based-police-brutality.

Ropers-Huilman, B., Carwile, L., & Barnett, K. (2005). Student activists' characterizations of administrators in higher education: Perceptions of power in the system. *The Review of Higher Education, 28*(3), 295–312.

Saltmarsh, J., Hartley, M., & Clayton, P. (2009). Democratic Engagement White Paper. Boston, MA: New England Resource Center for Higher Education, Retrieved from http://repository.upenn.edu/gse_pubs/274

Sawicki, A. (2009). *Developing citizen leaders at the University of Virginia.* Unpublished Master's thesis. University of Virginia, Charlottesville, VA.

Schein, E. H. (2009). The corporate culture survival guide, 2nd Ed. San Francisco, CA: Jossey-Bass.

Schein, E. H. (2010). Organizational culture and leadership, 4th Ed. San Francisco, CA: Jossey-Bass.

Slaughter, S., & Rhoades, G. (2004). *Academic capitalism and the new economy: Markets, state and higher education.* Baltimore, MD: The Johns Hopkins University Press.

Spencer, H. (2012, June 25). Sullivan oustermath: A timeline of UVA in tumult. *The Hook.* http://www.readthehook.com/104355/ouster-aftermath-timeline-uva-tumult.

Suspitsyna, T. (2012). Higher education for economic advancement and engaged citizenship: An analysis of the U.S. Department of Education discourse. *The Journal of Higher Education, 83*(1), 49–72.

Tarter, B. (2013). *The grandees of government: The origins and persistence of undemocratic politics in Virginia.* Charlottesville, VA: University of Virginia Press.

The National Task Force on Civic Learning and Democratic Engagement. (2012). *A crucible moment: College learning and democracy's future.* Washington, DC: Association of American Colleges and Universities.

Thornton, C. H., & Jaeger, A. J. (2006). Institutional culture and civic responsibility: An ethnographic study. *Journal of College Student Development, 47*(1), 52–68.

Tierney, W. G. (2008). *The impact of culture on organizational decision-making: Theory and practice in higher education* (1st ed.). Sterling, VA: Stylus Publications.

University of Virginia Office of the Dean of Students. (2015). Leadership development. http://www.virginia.edu/deanofstudents/programsandservices/leadership.html.

Valenzi, K. D. (2002). Protest! A history of student unrest at Virginia. *UVA Alumni News.* http://archives.uvamagazine.org/atf/cf/%7B8A7B03C1-B900-49F1-B435-B2B4777BFF0E%7D/%20%20%20Protest%2026-31.pdf.

Westheimer, J., & Kahne, J. (2004). What kind of citizen? The politics of educating for democracy. *American Educational Research Journal, 41*(2), 237–269.

Yosso, T. J. (2005). Whose culture has capital? A critical race theory discussion of community cultural wealth. *Race Ethnicity and Education, 8*(1), 69–91.

Young, R. (1997). *No neutral ground: Standing by the values we prize in higher education.* San Francisco, CA: Jossey-Bass.

Youngberg, L. (2008). *The democratic purpose of postsecondary education: Comparing public, private nonprofit, and private for-profit mission statements for expression of democratic social purpose.* Unpublished doctoral dissertation. Utah State University, Logan, UT.

CHAPTER 13

Seeking Social Justice: Undergraduates' Engagement in Social Change and Social Justice at American Research Universities

Tania D. Mitchell and Krista M. Soria

Developing students' social justice commitments becomes a more urgent task of service-learning and community engagement as institutions of higher education are challenged to prepare students for our increasingly diverse democracy—developing what Musil (2003) terms "generative citizens." People who "understand the residual legacies of inequality" have a "sophisticated knowledge of the levers that can make systems more equitable," and "seek the well being of the whole" as they come to value community as "an interdependent resource filled with possibilities" (para. 19). Service-learning and community engagement were often assumed to be practices inherently connected to concerns of social justice (Kendall 1990; Warren 1998). While some scholars have called this assumption into question (Robinson 2000), others have suggested that scholars and practitioners be more intentional in their practice to demonstrate a commitment to social justice and develop these commitments in students (Maybach 1996; Mitchell 2008; Rosenberger 2000). Hurtado (2007) suggested that a priority of higher education should be "encouraging students to develop a sense of social justice and to become responsible citizens" (p. 191). Is service-learning the practice that can produce those developments?

© The Editor(s) (if applicable) and The Author(s) 2016   241
K.M. Soria, T.D. Mitchell (eds.), *Civic Engagement and Community Service at Research Universities*,
DOI 10.1057/978-1-137-55312-6_13

Prior research suggests that service-learning can be a pedagogical tool that develops students' commitments to social justice (Einfeld and Collins 2008; Mitchell 2014; Moely et al. 2002a). Mitchell's (2014) qualitative study demonstrated that service-learning experiences that encouraged reflection on experience, identity, in dialogue with others, and with focus on structural conditions that undergird social concerns supported students in sensemaking that yields commitments to justice. Similarly, Einfeld and Collins (2008) research with nine students in prolonged service placements (300 h or more for a year) concluded that "effective" training and reflection was essential to lead students to social justice commitments (p. 104). They discovered that while "each participant acknowledged and witnessed inequality ... some participants developed a social justice paradigm and others adopted a charity paradigm" (p. 104). The Civic Attitudes and Skills Questionnaire (CASQ) developed by Moely and colleagues is one of the few quantitative instruments specifically designed for service-learning experiences. It includes an eight-item scale on social justice attitudes that asks items such as: "It is important that equal opportunity be available to all people"; "In order for problems to be solved, we need to change public policy"; and, "People are poor because they choose to be poor" (Moely et al. 2002b, p. 19). In their study, service-learning students increased their awareness of social justice issues and, compared to their nonservice-learning counterparts, their social justice attitudes as well (Moely et al. 2002b). Importantly, none of these studies explores the quality of the engagement experience beyond number of hours served and generalizing the issues central to the community work (e.g., poverty, education). And, only Mitchell (2014) interrogated whether students in these experiences see their service to the community as opportunities to learn about social justice or as action in service of social justice.

Perhaps because of the challenge to operationalize a commitment to (not to mention a definition of) social justice, or due to the prioritizing of academic and civic outcomes in service-learning research, there are few empirical studies exploring connections between service-learning and social justice. This chapter contributes to empirical work on community engagement more broadly but also adds to the literature on social justice and service-learning. This study explores how students classify their community engagement experiences and the outcomes developed in the different types of experiences.

PURPOSE OF THE CHAPTER

Given the lack of data related to the proportion of undergraduates who participate in social justice-oriented service, the first goal of this chapter was to analyze data to discover how undergraduates characterized the nature of their community-based service activities at large public research universities. Students were asked to classify their service within categories including charity, public or collective action, social change, empowering others, social action, participatory democracy, and social justice.

In addition to a lack of data regarding the proportion of undergraduates who may participate in social justice-oriented service, there is also a lack of quantitative research about the outcomes of students' participation in social justice; therefore, the second purpose was to discover whether students' participation in social justice community-based activities was positively associated with their engagement in social perspective-taking, reflecting on social problems, and implementing social change both inside and outside of their collegiate classrooms.

The two guiding research questions for this chapter are: (1) What proportion of undergraduate students characterize their community-based service work as social justice above and beyond other types of service? And (2) Is students' engagement in social justice-oriented community activities associated with social change outcomes above and beyond other types of service and controlling for input and environmental variables? These social change outcomes—social perspective-taking inside and outside of classes, reflecting on social problems inside and outside of classes, and implementing social change inside and outside of classes—reflect the aims of generative citizenship (Musil 2003) and may help practitioners understand what types of service experiences (or whether students' characterizations of those experiences) matter in developing students with the knowledge and skills to be engaged and responsible citizens in a diverse democracy.

The conceptual framework for this study draws from Astin's (1993) input-environment-output model, which hypothesizes that the background characteristics of undergraduate students (inputs) and relevant aspects of the higher education experience (environment) influence outcomes. Our statistical approach reflected this model in that controls for inputs (e.g., sex, racial/ethnic identity), and additional higher education experiences (e.g., students' academic majors and academic levels) were included as separate blocks in models predicting students' outcomes. With this approach, we isolated these variables' contributions from the focal independent variables—students' participation in social justice-oriented service and other types of service. Following this model, we utilized hierarchical linear regression models in our analysis to discover the amount of variance explained by students' participation in community-based activities (including those characterized as social justice) above and beyond the variance explained by input and environmental variables. Hierarchical multiple regression analyses are commonly used by researchers seeking to examine the variance-specific measures explained above and beyond the variance accounted for by control measures (Petrocelli 2003).

METHODS

SERU Instrument

The Student Experience in the Research University (SERU) survey is administered annually within a consortium of large public research universities that are members of the Association of American Universities (Center for the Studies of Higher Education 2010). In spring 2014, the SERU survey was administered to eligible undergraduate students enrolled at seven institutions. The Institutional Review Boards at each of the respective institutions provided full approval to administer the survey. From the overall survey respondents, we obtained a small subpopulation of students who were randomly assigned to complete a survey module that included items related to students' participation in community engagement activities.

The SERU survey contains over 600 items. The purpose of the instrument is to gather data on students' satisfaction, academic engagement, use of time, perceptions of campus climate, research experiences, leadership, developmental outcomes, and civic/community engagement, among other areas (Douglass et al. 2012; Soria 2012, 2015; Soria et al. 2013; Soria, Nobbe et al. 2013; Soria et al. 2015; Soria and Stebleton 2012, 2013; Soria and Thomas-Card 2014; Soria and Troisi 2014). Researchers have provided evidence for the internal consistency of students' responses over several administrations of the survey; for example, Chatman (2011) noted that reliability estimates of seven primary factors (ranging from $\alpha = 0.72$ to $\alpha = 0.92$) developed from core survey items remained consistent over 3 years of survey administration.

Participants

We obtained survey responses from 3093 undergraduate students enrolled at seven large public research universities. Female students comprised the majority of the sample (67.5 % compared to 32.5 % male). In addition, 6.82 % were Hispanic, 0.34 % American Indian, 9.02 % Asian, 3.09 % Black, 7.92 % international, 2.84 % multiracial, and 69.74 % White. Within the sample, 23.24 % were the first in their families to attend higher education, 4.40 % identified as low-income, 14.50 % as working-class, 44.90 % as middle-class, 33.20 % as upper-middle or professional-middle, and 2.9 % wealthy.

Dependent Measures

We utilized 20 survey items to measure students' engagement in social change inside and outside of the classroom. The items asked students to rate the frequency with which they engaged in 10 activities in the classroom and 10 activities outside of the classroom on a scale from one (never) to six (very often). The 10 activities included the following: acknowledge personal differences, appreciate the world from someone else's perspective, interact with someone with views that are different from their own, discuss and navigate controversial issues, define an issue or challenge and identify possible solutions, implement a solution to an issue or challenge, reflect upon the solution of an issue or challenge, reflect on community or social issues as a shared responsibility, reflect on their personal responsibility for community or social issues, and act on community or social issues. We collapsed those variables into six factors, which we describe below.

Independent Measures

Block One

We utilized several measures of students' precollege demographics in our analysis that were either indicated on the SERU or provided by institutional research offices at the respective institutions. Institutions provided students' sex (coded female = 1, male = 0) and race or ethnicity (dummy-coded with White students as the common referent). We also used students' first-generation status and defined students as first-generation if they were the first in their families to pursue a bachelor degree (1 = first-generation, 0 = non-first-generation). Students also provided information regarding their social class, and we retained the variable as a continuous variable (suggesting that a higher number means a higher self-identified social class). Prior studies have provided evidence for the validity of students' self-reported social class using the same measures utilized in this analysis (Soria and Barratt 2012).

Block Two
In the second block, we entered variables associated with undergraduates' experiences in higher education, including their academic level (as defined by the number of credits earned, e.g., freshman = 1, sophomore = 2, etc.) and academic major (coded into primary groups with the common referent including undeclared majors).

Block Three
The measure included in the third block asked students to indicate the best characterization of the nature of their community-focused experiences during the academic year. Students were asked to only select one item from the list, and, in order from the greatest proportion selected to the least proportion selection, 51.7 % selected charity (providing help to individuals), 15.7 % empowering others, 9.1 % societal change (changing societal conditions or views), 8.6 % public or collective action, 6.4 % other, 3.9 % social justice, 3.1 % social action (rally, sit in), and 1.6 % participatory democracy (changing laws). For the purposes of data analyses, we dummy-coded the different categories with charity work serving as the common referent variable for each of the other categories.

Data Analyses

We first utilized a factor analysis for the purpose of data reduction— to explain a larger set of measured variables with a smaller set of latent constructs. To develop the dependent measures used in this study, we conducted a factor analysis on 20 items with oblique rotation (promax). Rather than relying upon Kaiser's eigenvalue rule (which can overestimate the number of factors), the scree plot test (which can suffer from subjectivity and variability), or Bartlett's test (which is sensitive to sample size), we utilized Velicer's (1976) minimum average partial (MAP) method to estimate the factors (Courtney 2013). We utilized the procedures outlined by Courtney (2013) to analyze the data using SPSS R-Menu v2.0 (Basto and Pereira 2012). Velicer's MAP values indicated a distinct sixth step minimum squared average partial correlation suggesting six factors.

The six factors we consequently retained were (1) social perspective-taking *in class*, (2) social perspective-taking *outside of class*, (3) engagement in social change *in class*, (4) engagement in social change *outside of class*, (5) reflecting on social problems *in class*, and (6) reflecting on social problems *outside of class*. The three items comprising students' social perspective-taking (in and outside of class) include the frequency with which they acknowledge personal differences, appreciate the world from someone else's perspective, and interact with someone with views that are different from their own. The five items comprising students' reflection on social problems (inside and outside of class) include the frequency with which they discuss and navigate controversial issues, define an issue or challenge and identify possible solutions, reflect upon the solution of an issue or challenge, reflect on community or social issues as a shared responsibility, and reflect on their personal responsibility for community or social issues. Finally, the two items comprising engagement in social change (inside and outside of class) were the frequency with which students implement a solution to an issue or challenge and act on community or social issues. We computed the six-factor scores using the regression method and saved them as standardized scores with a mean of zero and a standard deviation of one. Each of these factors had good reliability ($\alpha > 0.85$).

After conducting the factor analysis, we conducted hierarchical least squares regression analyses. As noted earlier, theoretical frameworks about undergraduates' development suggest students' demographic characteristics, and environmental contexts might covary with collegiate experiences, thereby potentially confounding the effects of those collegiate experiences (Astin 1993; Pascarella and Terenzini 2005). To that end, we entered data into these three blocks to assess the variance-specific collegiate experience items explained above and beyond the variance accounted for by control measures (Petrocelli 2003): (1) pre-college characteristics; (2) collegiate experiences; and (3) community-based service experiences.

LIMITATIONS

This study is limited in generalizability due to the voluntary participation of not only the universities choosing to be a part of the consortium but also students within these large research universities. It may therefore be difficult to extrapolate the findings to students at other types of institutions. Additionally, it is difficult to ascertain how students distinguished their participation in social justice community-based activities over other categories of service. The measure itself is limited in that some of the categories may not be conceived as necessarily mutually exclusive from each other; for instance, social justice work may involve working for social change or in the pursuit of social action and, thus, students may not have been able to distinguish these categories given their mutual commonalities.

RESULTS

We will present the results for our six models first by classroom-based activities and next by outside-of-classroom activities for students' engagement in social perspective-taking, reflecting on social problems, and taking action to promote social change. For our first model, the results suggest that students' community-based activities accounted for unique variance in students' engagement in social perspective-taking in class beyond the variance explained by the two previously-entered blocks ($R = 0.272$, $R^2 = 0.074$, $p < 0.001$, R^2 $change = 0.006$, $p < 0.001$). The results suggest that the community-focused activities significantly and positively associated with students' social perspective-taking in class included experiences characterized as empowering others ($\beta = 0.076$, $p < 0.001$) and engaging in social change ($\beta = 0.035$, $p < 0.001$).

Additional variables entered into the first and second blocks were significantly associated with students' social perspective-taking in class. Females were significantly more likely to engage in social perspective-taking in class compared to males. International students were significantly less likely to engage in social perspective-taking in classes. Students enrolled in arts and humanities majors, social sciences majors, and education majors were significantly more likely to engage in perspective-taking in class while students enrolled in general sciences and STEM academic majors were significantly less likely to engage in social perspective-taking in classes. Students' academic level was also significantly and positively associated with this outcome.

For our second model, the results suggest that students' community-based activities accounted for unique variance in students' reflection on social problems in class beyond the variance explained by the two previously entered blocks ($R = 0.253$, $R^2 = 0.064$, $p < 0.001$, R^2 $change = 0.007$, $p < 0.001$). The results suggest that the community-focused activities significantly and positively associated with students' reflections on social problems in classes included experiences characterized as empowering others ($\beta = 0.072$, $p < 0.001$), collective action ($\beta = 0.044$, $p < 0.01$), and engaging in social change ($\beta = 0.043$, $p < 0.05$).

Additional variables entered into the first and second blocks were significantly associated with students' reflecting upon social problems in class. Females were significantly more likely to reflect upon social problems in classrooms compared to males, although international students were significantly less likely to reflect upon social problems in classes compared to their peers. Students enrolled in arts and humanities majors, social sciences majors, health majors, and education majors were significantly more likely to reflect upon social problems in classes. Students enrolled in general sciences and STEM academic majors were significantly less likely to reflect upon social problems in classes. Students' academic level was also significantly and positively associated with this outcome.

For our third model, the results suggest that students' community-based activities accounted for unique variance in students' social action in class beyond the variance explained by the two previously entered blocks ($R = 0.200$, $R^2 = 0.040$, $p < 0.001$, R^2 $change = 0.007$, $p < 0.001$). The results suggest that the community-focused activities significantly and positively associated with students' social action in class included experiences characterized as empowering others ($\beta = 0.071$, $p < 0.001$), collective action ($\beta = 0.054$, $p < 0.01$), and participatory democracy ($\beta = 0.036$, $p < 0.05$).

Additional variables entered into the first and second blocks were significantly associated with students' social action within academic classes. Asian students were significantly more likely to engage in social action over their peers. Students enrolled in education majors and health majors were significantly more likely to engage in social action within classes. Students enrolled in general sciences and STEM academic majors were significantly less likely to reflect upon social problems in classes. Students' academic level was also significantly and positively associated with this outcome.

For our fourth model, the results suggest that students' community-based activities accounted for unique variance in students' engagement in social perspective-taking outside of class beyond the variance explained by the two previously entered blocks ($R = 0.220$, $R^2 = 0.048$, $p < 0.001$, R^2 $change = 0.005$, $p < 0.001$). The results suggest that the community-focused activities significantly and positively associated with students' social perspective-taking outside class included experiences characterized as empowering others ($\beta = 0.062$, $p < 0.001$) and social justice ($\beta = 0.056$, $p < 0.001$).

Additional variables entered into the first and second blocks were significantly associated with students' social perspective-taking outside of class. Females were significantly more likely to engage in social perspective-taking outside of class compared to males. International students were significantly less likely to engage in social perspective-taking outside of classes. Students enrolled in social sciences majors and education majors were significantly more likely to engage in perspective-taking outside of class.

For our fifth model, the results suggest that students' community-based activities accounted for unique variance in students' reflection on social problems outside of beyond the variance explained by the two previously entered blocks ($R = 0.210$, $R^2 = 0.044$, $p < 0.001$, R^2 $change = 0.012$, $p < 0.001$). The results suggest that the community-focused activities significantly and positively associated with students' reflection on social problems included experiences characterized as empowering others ($\beta = 0.086$, $p < 0.001$), collective action ($\beta = 0.044$, $p < 0.05$), social change ($\beta = 0.071$, $p < 0.001$), and social justice ($\beta = 0.057$, $p < 0.001$).

Additional variables entered into the first and second blocks were significantly associated with students' reflecting upon social problems outside of class. Females were significantly more likely to reflect upon social problems outside of class compared to males. International students and Black students were significantly less likely to reflect upon social problems outside of classes. Students enrolled in arts and humanities majors, social sciences majors, and education majors were significantly more likely to reflect upon social problems outside of classes. Students' academic level was also significantly and positively associated with this outcome.

For our sixth model, the results suggest that students' community-based activities accounted for unique variance in students' social action outside of class beyond the variance explained by the two previously-entered blocks ($R = 0.168$, $R^2 = 0.028$, $p < 0.001$, R^2 $change = 0.009$, $p < 0.001$). The results suggest that the community-focused activities significantly and positively associated with students' social action outside of class included experiences characterized as empowering others ($\beta = 0.079$, $p < 0.001$), collective action ($\beta = 0.036$, $p < 0.05$), social change ($\beta = 0.060$, $p < 0.05$), and social justice ($\beta = 0.032$, $p < 0.05$).

Additional variables entered into the first and second blocks were significantly associated with students' social action outside of class. Female students were significantly more likely to engage in social action over their peers. International students and Black students were significantly less likely than their peers to engage in social action. Students enrolled in social sciences majors were significantly more likely to engage in social action outside of classes. Students' academic level was also significantly and positively associated with this outcome.

DISCUSSION

The results of this study suggest that different types of community-focused service work may yield ubiquitous outcomes. Across the board, students who worked in community-focused service that they characterized as empowering others were significantly more likely than their peers to report engagement in all six social change outcomes both inside and outside of the classroom. Students who also participated in social change and social justice work were most likely to engage in perspective-taking inside and outside of their classes (respectively). Students who participated in social change and collective action were most likely to have spent time reflecting on social problems inside and outside of classes and also to participate in social action inside and outside of classes. Participatory democracy-type activities were associated with students' in-class social change action.

Participating in social justice community-based work was associated with perspective-taking, reflection, and action outside of classes only. In fact, other than community-focused experiences empowering others, social justice activities were the only one significantly and positively associated with all social change outcomes outside of the classroom. These results may suggest that students who engaged in social justice community-based work may be more likely than their peers to enact social change in their communities as opposed to on their own campuses in classroom-based contexts. Since students who saw their work as social justice had positive associations with social change outcomes *outside of class*, it may be important to understand how students come to be engaged in this social justice work and how to bring those kinds of connections and opportunities into the curricular experience so that students can experience this social change outcomes in their classroom experiences as well.

IMPLICATIONS

While the data demonstrate that community engagement activities are positively associated with a number of outcomes considered essential to preparing students for active engagement in a diverse democracy, it also suggests that students' conceptions of their activity matter. The effects observed lead us to understand that the frameworks we provide students for their community engagement work may have different impacts both inside and outside the classroom. However, we do not know what activities students were participating in or what it was about those activities that led them to characterize their community-based work differently. How are these different activities distinguished in the minds of students?

It is important to acknowledge that the majority (51.7 %) of students in our sample classified their community engagement as charity and less than 4 % identified their community work as social justice. This finding reflects Joseph Kahne's assertion that we "pay least attention" to community engagement efforts aimed toward social justice (Tugend 2010, para. 13). And, yet, these different frameworks do appear to matter. The significant relationships between the various social change outcomes and the different community engagement frameworks indicate that practitioners should be attentive to providing different opportunities for engagement for students that utilize varied approaches for responding to social concerns. Even more importantly, we recommend that practitioners be clear with students in explaining what these different approaches are (i.e., how charity differs from participatory democracy) so that students are able to understand and appropriately classify their work. Similarly, we recommend that researchers reevaluate the scale to consider if the different classifications of engagement are appropriate and distinct enough to be a more reliable measure. For example, the category of "empowering others" feels more a condition or result of engagement as opposed to a category or type. The hope might be that social change, social justice, participatory democracy, or, potentially, even charitable acts would allow others to feel empowered; so while it makes sense that 15.7 % of respondents characterized their community work as empowering others, there is little clarity as to what that means in terms of community engaged practice.

CONCLUSION

As evidenced by students' characterizations of their community engagement practice, it is clear that the connections between service-learning and social justice once assumed (Kendall 1990; Warren 1998) can no longer be. The data presented show that few students see their community-focused-service work as social justice, and when students do characterize their work as social justice, those efforts are most positively associated with social change outcomes *outside of class*. So, what does that mean for the possibility of service-learning and community engagement to develop generative citizens? It seems that community engagement experiences must be explicit in their intention toward social justice in order to provide the opportunities for students to develop social change outcomes (both inside and outside the classroom) that best prepare them to be active and engaged participants in our increasingly diverse democracy.

REFERENCES

Astin, A. W. (1993). *What matters in college: Four critical years revisited.* San Francisco, CA: Jossey-Bass.

Basto, M., & Pereira, J. M. (2012). An SPSS R-Menu for ordinal factor analysis. *Journal of Statistical Software, 46*(4), 1–29.

Center for the Studies of Higher Education, University of California Berkeley. (2010). SERU-AAU consortium. http://cshe.berkeley.edu/research/seru/consortium.htm.

Chatman, S. (2011). *Factor structure and reliability of the 2011 SERU/UCUES questionnaire core: SERU project technical report.* Berkeley, CA: Center for Studies of Higher Education, University of California.

Courtney, M. G. R. (2013). Determining the number of factors to retain in EFA: Using the SPSS R-menu v2.0 to make more judicious estimates. *Practical Assessment, Research, & Evaluation, 18*(8), 1–14.

Douglass, J. A., Thomson, G., & Zhao, C.-M. (2012). The learning outcomes race: The value of self-reported gains in large research universities. *Higher Education, 64,* 317–355.

Einfeld, A., & Collins, D. (2008). The relationships between service-learning, social justice, multicultural competence, and civic engagement. *Journal of College Student Development, 49*(2), 95–109.

Hurtado, S. (2007). Linking diversity with the educational and civic missions of higher education. *The Review of Higher Education, 30*(2), 185–196. doi:10.1353/rhe.2006.0070.

Kendall, J. C. (1990). Combining service and learning: An introduction. In J. C. Kendall (Ed.), *Combining service and learning: A resource book for community and public service* (pp. 1–33). Raleigh, NC: National Society for Internships and Experiential Education.

Maybach, C. W. (1996). Investigating urban community needs: Service learning from a social justice perspective. *Education and Urban Society, 28*(2), 224–236. doi:10.1177/0013124596028002007.

Mitchell, T. D. (2008). Traditional vs. critical service-learning: Engaging the literature to differentiate two models. *Michigan Journal of Community Service Learning, 14*(2), 50–65.

Mitchell, T. D. (2014). How service-learning enacts social justice sensemaking. *Journal of Critical Thought and Praxis, 2*(2), Article 6. http://lib.dr.iastate.edu/jctp/vol2/iss2/6.

Moely, B. E., McFarland, M., Miron, D., Mercer, S., & Ilustre, V. (2002a). Changes in college students' attitudes and intentions for civic involvement as a function of service-learning experiences. *Michigan Journal of Community Service Learning, 9*(1), 18–26.

Moely, B. E., Mercer, S. H., Ilustre, V., Miron, D., & McFarland, M. (2002b). Psychometric properties and correlates of the Civic Attitudes and Skills Questionnaire (CASQ): A measure of students' attitudes related to service-learning. *Michigan Journal of Community Service Learning, 8*(2), 15–26.

Musil, C. M. (2003). Educating for citizenship. *Peer Review, 5*(3). https://www.aacu.org/publications-research/periodicals/educating-citizenship.

Pascarella, E. T., & Terenzini, P. T. (2005). *How college affects students: Vol. 2. A third decade of research.* San Francisco, CA: Jossey-Bass.

Petrocelli, J. V. (2003). Hierarchical multiple regression in counseling research: Common problems and possible remedies. *Measurement and Evaluation in Counseling and Development, 36*, 9–22.

Robinson, T. (2000). Service learning as justice advocacy: Can political scientists do politics? *PS: Political Science and Politics, 33*(3), 605–612.

Rosenberger, C. (2000). Beyond empathy: Developing critical consciousness through service learning. In C. R. O'Grady (Ed.), *Integrating service learning and multicultural education in colleges and universities* (pp. 23–43). Mahwah, NJ: Lawrence Erlbaum Associates.

Soria, K. M. (2012). Creating a successful transition for working-class first-year students. *The Journal of College Orientation and Transition, 20*(1), 44–55.

Soria, K. M. (2015). Institutional and instructional techniques to promote undergraduates' intercultural development: Evidence from a multi-institutional student survey. In R. D. Williams & A. Lee (Eds.), *Internationalizing undergraduate education: Critical collaborations across the curriculum* (pp. 47–62). Rotterdam: Sense Publishers.

Soria, K. M., & Barratt, W. (2012). *Examining class in the classroom: Utilizing social class data in institutional and academic research.* New Orleans, LA: Association for Institutional Research Forum.

Soria, K. M., Fink, A., Lepkowski, C. C., & Snyder, L. (2013). Undergraduate student leadership and social change. *Journal of College and Character, 14*(3), 241–252.

Soria, K. M., Nobbe, J., & Fink, A. (2013). Examining the intersections between undergraduates' engagement in community service and development of socially responsible leadership. *Journal of Leadership Education, 12*(1), 117–140.

Soria, K. M., Snyder, S., & Reinhard, A. (2015). Strengthening college students' capacity for integrative leadership by building a foundation for civic engagement and multicultural competence. *Journal of Leadership Education, 14*(1), 55–71.

Soria, K. M., & Stebleton, M. J. (2012). First-generation students' academic engagement and retention. *Teaching in Higher Education, 17*(6), 1–13.

Soria, K. M., & Stebleton, M. J. (2013). Social capital, academic engagement, and sense of belonging among working-class college students. *College Student Affairs Journal, 31*(2), 139–153.

Soria, K. M., & Thomas-Card, T. (2014). Relationships between motivations for community service participation and desire to continue service following college. *Michigan Journal of Community Service Learning, 20*(2), 53–64.

Soria, K. M., & Troisi, J. N. (2014). Internationalization at home alternatives to study abroad: Implications for students' development of global, international, and intercultural competencies. *Journal of Studies in International Education, 18*(3), 260–279.

Soria, K. M., Troisi, J. N., & Stebleton, M. J. (2012). Reaching out, connecting within: Community service and sense of belonging among college students. *Higher Education in Review, 9*, 65–85.

Tugend, A. (2010). The benefits of volunteerism, if the service is real. *New York Times.* http://www.nytimes.com/2010/07/31/your-money/31shortcuts.html?_r=0.

Velicer, W. F. (1976). Determining the number of components from the matrix of partial correlations. *Psychometrika, 41*, 321–327.

Warren, K. (1998). Educating students for social justice in service learning. *The Journal of Experiential Education, 21*(3), 134–139.

CHAPTER 14

Revisiting the Civic Mission of the American Public Research University

Tania D. Mitchell

Recently, the *East Bay Express* published a profile on the University of California at Berkeley's American Cultures Engaged Scholarship (ACES) program titled "Tumbling the Ivory Tower" (Burke 2015). The title suggests, and the ACES program in its implementation aims to "[break] down the ivory tower by bringing the university's brain power to issues in the communities that surround it, and learning directly from those communities in the process" (para. 10). It is the story of a public research university implementing its civic mission. And, simultaneously, it is a story of a public research university struggling to implement its civic mission. The ACES program, once robustly supported by a gift from the Evelyn and Walter Haas, Jr. Fund, has run out of funding and is seeking to be considered an institutional priority of the university (with the institutionalized funds such prioritizing would warrant).

Boyte and Hollander (1999) warned that universities "have often drifted away from their civic mission" (p. 7). In response to the *Wingspread Declaration* and with the support of organizations like Campus Compact and grants from the, now defunded, Learn and Serve America program of the Corporation of National and Community Service, institutions of higher education energetically responded to the call for civic renewal. Service-learning and community engagement are now "more fully integrated"

© The Editor(s) (if applicable) and The Author(s) 2016
K.M. Soria, T.D. Mitchell (eds.), *Civic Engagement and Community Service at Research Universities*,
DOI 10.1057/978-1-137-55312-6_14

in the curricular and co-curricular practices of the university so that it is a "regular feature of educational life" (Lounsbury and Pollack 2001, pp. 332–333). Recent findings from national surveys confirm this institutionalization. More than 70 % of undergraduate seniors reported volunteering in the local community either occasionally or frequently (Franke et al. 2010), and 62 % of seniors and 52 % of first-year students reported taking at least one class that included service-learning (National Survey of Student Engagement 2014). In this text, Williams, Soria, and Erickson reported that 66.2 % of undergraduate students participated in community service during the 2013 academic year. And yet The National Task Force on Civic Learning and Democratic Engagement (2012) laments that the influence of community engagement in our institutions is "partial rather than pervasive" (p. 8). The U.S. Department of Education (2012) goes further, challenging postsecondary institutions "to both expand and transform their approach to civic learning and democratic engagement, rather than engage in tinkering at the margins" (p. 13).

This challenge is not merely a question of quantity. Several chapters in this text affirm that public research universities are creating experiences and opportunities that, as Boyte and Hollander (1999) encouraged, allow "students, faculty, staff, [and] administrators to use their many talents for the greater good"(p. 8). The challenge of transformation issued by the Department of Education is the one we must tackle.

The chapters in this volume point toward the important developmental opportunities afforded by community engaged practice. The frameworks, research, and examples offered highlight student involvement in the community and the impacts and implications of that engagement. The research reported in this text provides new insights into the ways research universities create and constrain civic leadership development, and presents new models for assessment and practice that may do more to deepen civic learning and the civic capacities of today's undergraduate students.

What, then, would it mean to transform practice?

One challenge of scholarship on service-learning and community engagement is its limited insight into the programmatic realities of engaged practice (Howe and Fosnacht 2015). The community engagement experiences of students are rarely interrogated to help scholars and practitioners understand the specifics that yield democratic outcomes. It is not enough that students are connected to opportunities to serve the community. How they are connected, what constitutes engagement, and the meaning students make from that experience must also matter if research universities are to succeed in their civic mission.

As public research universities consider their civic missions and the programmatic interventions used to realize them, more must be done to document, report, and investigate the quality of engagement experiences and the results of different types of engagement. Research by Mitchell and Soria (this volume) and Howe and Fosnacht (2015) suggests that different types of civic learning experiences may better support students' development for democratic engagement. To suggest that community engagement experiences operating from a charity framework may yield different outcomes than a social change framework are likely not surprising. Morton (1995) asked service-learning scholars and practitioners to be attentive to these different approaches long ago. But, we still have limited insight into what a social-change-focused community-engaged practice looks like, or how students experience and make meaning of that different framework in understanding their responsibility to civil society.

The challenge issued by the U.S. Department of Education (2012) is largely focused on students. What are the civic opportunities provided for students? How do we ensure that students do not "graduate with less civic literacy and engagement than when they arrived" (p. 13)? The work of public research universities to prepare students for active and informed engagement in our diverse democracy is an integral part of this work. It is a mistake though, as much research on service-learning and community engagement has led us, to operate as though the civic mission of public research universities rests solely in the developmental outcomes of students.

Another critical aspect of the civic mission of public research universities is to serve the public—the communities, cities, states—where we are located. Transforming engagement in service of our civic mission changes "being present" in the community to ensuring that our presence strengthens the communities where we engage. If we fail to do that, Simpson (2015) warns, we take several risks:

> It potentially furthers the idea of democratic work as charity, repositions educators and students as the primary beneficiaries of civic or social justice service-learning work, locates relationships with community organizations as secondary to pedagogical and curricular objectives, and rearticulates and normalizes problematic power relationships. (p. 105)

Realizing the civic mission demands that public research universities take active steps to counter these risks. In their book, *Deepening Community Engagement*, Hoy and Johnson (2013) argue that engagement must be "more pervasive, deep, and integrated with the core of the institution" (p. xviii) in order to truly be transformed. Thinking about what it would mean to create community engagement experiences that are more pervasive, deep, and integrated, Mitchell (2013) imagined the impact would be widespread, and

> transformative for students who, through linking critical inquiry and community engagement, are gaining the knowledge, skills, and values to … create more equitable systems for the future public good. They are also transformative for communities where, through partnerships with higher education institutions, innovative practices create new opportunities to address critical community concerns. Higher education institutions are also transformed as community engagement changes the ways faculty members teach and research, the ways students learn and develop, and the ways lines between campus and community are blurred and reconfigured. (p. 263)

To expand on these ideas, I argue that pervasiveness means that all members of the campus community (i.e., students, faculty, staff, administrators) recognize and understand their connection to the civic mission, and that they feel able and fortunate to do work that connects to that mission. Depth emphasizes engaged work that moves beyond charitable gestures to focused partnerships that seek to understand the multiple dimensions of community concerns while investing time, resources, and effort into work that aims to effectively and meaningfully respond to those concerns in ways that strengthen communities. Integration requires an understanding of public research universities as institutions that not only *serve* the community, but *are part of* the community. From this place of integration, public research universities cannot shirk responsibility for "the wellbeing of the whole" (Musil 2003, para. 19). Research universities are successful when the communities where they reside share in that success.

A student engaged in the ACES program at Berkeley considers this type of pervasive, deep, integration "radical academic work" (Burke 2015, para. 54). The student, Austin Pritzkat, a fifth-year political science major, first got involved in the ACES program through a class in his first year at the university. He has been involved in the program ever since. He credits the program with helping him to understand his social location and his ability to effect change in the community. "ACES," from his perspective, "doesn't work to completely dismantle, but at least erode, the wall that gets created between this ivory tower—the university—and the community" (Burke 2015, para. 54).

Erosion is often viewed negatively as a process that symbols weakening, but the erosion that Pritzkat hints at is a sign of strength—a positive transformation that "though incomplete ... represent[s] substantial progress toward a more inclusive and a more just system of higher education" (Boyte and Hollander 1999, p. 8). Public research universities are poised to significantly influence and shape the future of our democracy. To realize the civic mission of higher education "requires intense and self-conscious attention" (Boyte and Hollander 1999, p. 9). The intention and investment with which higher education institutions approach engaged work matters in the experiences and lives of the people working in—and impacted by—these efforts. More work is required to realize the civic mission of public research universities, but this mission justifies the prioritization of such investments; deserves advancement in research and policy agendas; and demands intentional collaboration, reflection, and action to strengthen our communities for a more inclusive and just world.

REFERENCES

Boyte, H., & Hollander, E. (1999). *Wingspread declaration on renewing the civic mission of the American research university.* Providence, RI: Campus Compact.

Burke, S. (2015, September 23). Tumbling the ivory tower. *East Bay Express.* http://m.eastbayexpress.com/oakland/tumbling-the-ivory-tower/Content?oid=4508733&showFullText=true.

Franke, R., Ruiz, S., Sharkness, J., DeAngelo, L., & Pryor, J. (2010). *Findings from the 2009 administration of the College Senior Survey (CSS): National aggregates.* Los Angeles, CA: Higher Education Research Institute Graduate School of Education & Information Studies, University of California, Los Angeles.

Howe, E., & Fosnacht, K. (2015, March). *Promoting democratic engagement during college: Looking beyond service-learning.* Paper presented at the annual meeting of the National Association of Student Personnel Administrators. New Orleans, LA.

Hoy, A., & Johnson, M. (Eds.). (2013). *Deepening community engagement in higher education: Forging new pathways.* New York, NY: Palgrave Macmillan.

Lounsbury, M., & Pollack, S. (2001). Institutionalizing civic engagement: Shifting logics and the cultural repackaging of service-learning in U.S. higher education. *Organization, 8*(2), 319–339.

Mitchell, T. D. (2013). Critical service-learning as a philosophy for deepening community engagement. In A. Hoy & M. Johnson (Eds.), *Deepening community engagement in higher education: Forging new pathways* (pp. 263–269). New York, NY: Palgrave Macmillan.

Morton, K. (1995). The irony of service: Charity, project and social change in service-learning. *Michigan Journal of Community Service Learning, 2*(1), 19–32.

Musil, C. M. (2003). Educating for citizenship. *Peer Review, 5*(3). https://www.aacu.org/publications-research/periodicals/educating-citizenship.

National Survey of Student Engagement. (2014). *Bringing the institution into focus—Annual results 2014.* Bloomington, IN: Indiana University Center for Postsecondary Research.

Simpson, J. S. (2015). *Longing for justice: Higher education and democracy's agenda.* Toronto, ON: University of Toronto Press.

The National Task Force on Civic Learning and Democratic Engagement. (2012). *A crucible moment: College learning and democracy's future.* Washington, DC: Association of American Colleges and Universities.

U.S. Department of Education. (2012). *Advancing civic learning and engagement in democracy: A road map and call to action.* Washington, D.C.: Office of the Under Secretary and Office of Postsecondary Education, U.S. Department of Education.

INDEX

© The Editor(s) (if applicable) and The Author(s) 2016
K.M. Soria, T.D. Mitchell (eds.), *Civic Engagement
and Community Service at Research Universities,*
DOI 10.1057/978-1-137-55312-6